Every Reason to Fail

*The Unlikely Story of Miss Montana
and the D-Day Squadron*

Bryan Douglass

outskirts
press

To all veterans, smokejumpers, and first responders. This was for you.

Table of Contents

Appendices

Beauty, science, freedom, and adventure. Aviation
combines all these elements that I love.
                                    – Charles Lindbergh

Acknowledgments

MY WIFE, DAWN, deserves the most thanks for relentlessly encouraging me in the writing of my first book, not to mention allowing me to spend most of a year on the restoration and the trip to Europe. Thank you, Harry Haines. You were the first person to tell me I must write this book. Many thanks go to my voluntary reviewers: Eric Zipkin, Art Dykstra, Kim Maynard, Al Charters, Randy Schonemann, Crystal Schonemann, Eric Komberec, Eric Ristau, and Dawn Douglass. It's a better book because of your comments and corrections. My copy editor, Susan Ray, taught me some things I didn't know and corrected my errors. Thanks to those who generously gave me photographs to be included in the book: Rich Cooper, Eric Komberec, Tom Bauer (Missoulian), Keith Wolferman, Chris Rose (AOPA), Amy Myers, Natalie Abrams, Keely Flatow, Al Charters, Shawn Modula, Greg Jones, Shanna Mae Swanson, Bryan M, Mecky Creus (Sound Off Films), Carsten Koenig (Airbase Fassberg), Kevin Danz (IFlyBigSky), and Chris McGowan. Finally, this story would not have been possible without all the people who made it happen: volunteers, jumpers, crew, supporters, and donors. I hope it meant as much to you as it did to me.

For more information such as daily reports prepared by Benjamin Smith, travel maps, color photos, videos, the 1954 accident report, and links to a multitude of media covering the story, go to the website at Everyreasontofail.com.

Introduction

I WROTE THIS story because a few of you told me I must. There are two parts to that: that it must be written and that I ought to be the one to write it. You get to decide if either is true. That I ought to write it makes a bit of sense because I was in the story from the beginning—at least the most recent one. That it must be written at all becomes clearer every day. As the events of 2018 and 2019 fade into history, many of you continue to tell us how much it all meant to you. In that respect I hope this story brings you along, makes you feel like you were there, and that maybe you find your connection with us, our history, and with this remarkable airplane. I hope you will find the inspiration to try something worthwhile that seems impossible. Mostly, I hope you enjoy the story, because we sure did.

Fair warning, though. This is my first book, and only time will tell if it will be my last. You will have a say in that, whether you think it's worth recommending to your friends or giving to others. In one sense, I don't much care whether you like it or not because I don't pretend to be a real author, or expect to earn a living as a writer. This story just demanded to be told. In another sense, I very much hope you like it, and if my telling of it makes you feel like you were there, then I will have done my duty. Sometimes the best you can hope is to do your duty.

There are many details in this story: dates, times, people,

numbers, airplanes, places, and events. They are as accurate as possible based on my recollection, the collective memory of The Crew, our notes, photographs, and interviews with others who were there. Any mistakes in recounting the details are entirely mine. I've also tried to credit everyone who helped make this story happen. If I neglected someone, I am sorry.

This story is about much more than an airplane, but in it you will experience the world of aviation…and aviators. Like any people with a common passion, we have our own jargon. I could have avoided aviation jargon but chose not to because it was used during the actual doing of things and it seemed inauthentic to change it. I do, however, try to make sure you don't get lost when the story involves IFR, VFR, and TFR.

There is one thing about aviators that is consistent in my experience. We have a reputation for being stoic, tough, emotionless, fearless, and intently focused on our jobs. This is true of most of us. Yet we do have emotions like normal people. If you catch us just right, which usually requires a tale involving great danger or courage (and aircraft), tragic death (by aircraft), or beautiful women or little children (with or without aircraft), we will cry like babies and not care if anyone sees us do it. The hard part is knowing when it will happen and what will be the right tale.

Last, there were some funny and salacious things as well as some drama and conflict that actually happened but are not in this book. As the saying goes, What happens in Iceland stays in Iceland. Pilots are typically an irreverent lot, prone to all sorts of unruly behavior, profanity, and activities not fit to talk about in church. This may come from the early days of aviation when your odds of returning from a flight were truly about fifty percent; early pilots were not living for the future. Even so, pilots are also mostly an honorable bunch. If we say we'll do something, we will strive to do it. And I committed from the beginning that this book would be suitable for all audiences and not a tell-all, so you don't get to know everything. Sorry.

1

The Beginning

IF THIS AIRPLANE could talk, the stories she could tell. In her seventy-five years she has seen work and service, tragedy, and glory. She worked at blue-collar jobs, like cargo and transport. She served the country that created her by carrying smokejumpers into harm's way. She transported athletes to ball games and GIs home for Christmas leave. She worked hard for fifty-four years and 25,000 flight hours. Then the people who had flown her and loved her brought her home to Montana.

She sat idle for eighteen years, admired by visitors as she collected dust in a museum hangar. We like to think she was patiently waiting to be resurrected for new flights, new glory, and making new history. While so many of her kind sat rotting in weed patches around the world, this plane was destined for a return to greatness.

This is the story of N24320, a Douglas C-47 with a long and unique history. In the end, hers is far more than the story of an airplane. Like many famous airplanes, she has touched people and places that will forever be bound to the old girl. And out of a chance encounter between pilots in a small-town Georgia café, she was restored to flight, made new history, and is informing a new generation of all that she and her kind accomplished.

All good stories have a good ending. The best stories have a good beginning and middle as well. This is one of those. In fact, this story has four beginnings, lots of middle, and two near endings. The final ending is not yet written. We will do our part to make sure we don't live to see it.

The first beginning was when N24320 was born as a C-47 on May 4, 1944, at the Douglas factory in Long Beach, California. She was given Douglas serial number 20197, accepted by the U.S. Army Air Force, and assigned Army serial number 43-15731. She was one of over 10,000 C-47s built for U.S. operations during World War II. Douglas Aircraft Company first built the DC-3 in the 1930s, and it became a revolutionary design in the booming commercial airline race. "DC" stands for Douglas Commercial, and the DC-3 was third in a long line of "Douglas Commercials" that ended with the DC-10.

However, the DC-3 is the greatest of the Douglas Commercial line, having actively served from the 1930s to the present. The DC-3 is widely considered the most successful airplane design in history. Whether or not it was the best, its efficiency, versatility, brawn, reliability, and long history of active use firmly establishes it among the best.

DC-3 and C-47 are used interchangeably in this story. Technically the C-47 is a DC-3 modified with different engines, a cargo door, reinforced cabin floor, glider-tow capability, and other enhancements for military service. Nicknames for the DC-3/C-47 include Skytrain, Gooney Bird, Dakota/Dak (British and French), Doug, Dumbo, and Skytrooper. There were many variants produced for different military branches and missions. General Eisenhower credited the bulldozer, the jeep, the half-ton truck, and the C-47 for helping win World War II. There have been many books written on this incredible machine, so that is all you get here.

We don't know what N24320 did for her first two years, which probably means she didn't do much. She was built too late in the war to be needed overseas, so she never served the military in Europe or the Pacific. She could have ended her days rotting in a boneyard or remote foreign field as so many did—except for a man from Missoula, Montana, named Bob Johnson.

2

The Second Beginning

HER SECOND BEGINNING was in 1946, when the man from Montana purchased N24320 from military surplus for $15,000 and flew her home to Missoula. Bob Johnson was an early pioneer in aviation, particularly in the challenges of mountain aviation, and he wrote the life path for N24320. Bob eventually bought three C-47s, but N24320 was the first.

Bob Johnson is virtually unknown outside of Montana, but in Missoula he is still a legend. He dropped out of high school at fifteen in 1908 and never returned. After several years working odd jobs and a brief stint in the Army at the end of World War I, Bob opened a gas station and battery shop in 1921. A few years later, after dabbling in bootlegging and making moonshine during prohibition, the aviation bug bit him. This was a remarkable thing in the 1920s because there were few airplanes, Missoula had no airport, and money was scarce. It all came together in the winter of 1926, when Bob sold his gas station, cashed in his life insurance policy, and added his life savings and moonshine profits to finance flight instruction in Spokane.[1]

Bob returned to Missoula in March 1927 in the OX-5 Swallow that he had assembled and learned to fly. In September of that year, Bob competed in an air race from Long Island, New York, to Spokane, Washington, placing tenth out of a field of twenty-seven in his division.[1] Today it's hard to imagine someone with six months of experience flying a primitive and unreliable airplane in a cross-country air race. However, there were no high-time pilots or reliable airplanes, so they didn't know any better. Most importantly, it tells you something about young Bob Johnson.

Returning to Missoula after the air race, Bob continued flight instruction, scenic flights, and anything else to make a living in the air. He formed Johnson Flying Service in December 1928 and for almost fifty years would scratch a living from aviation. In the early years, he flew Travel Airs, then Ford Trimotors, and his work included commercial flights, air mail, backcountry resupply, spraying forests for insect pests, charter flights, and ultimately smokejumping.[1] Yet his line of work came with a cost.

Bob's older brother, Dick, also a World War I Army veteran, followed Bob into aviation in 1927 at the age of forty. Bob eventually hired Dick, with whom he had always been close, first as a mechanic, then soon gave him all the flying he could handle. Dick was the daredevil of the pair, constantly taking unnecessary risks and wrecking more than one of Bob's airplanes. In 1938 Dick survived the crash of Bob's first Ford Trimotor at the Big Prairie airstrip in the backcountry of Montana. N435H was Bob's favorite Trimotor, and he never forgave Dick for its loss.

In March 1945, Dick was flying a Travel Air for the United States Forest Service and state of Wyoming, counting elk in the high country near Jackson Hole. There were two other men on board when a snow squall caught them, and the plane went down in thick timber. The crash killed Dick Johnson and another man. The third man nearly froze to death before help arrived, but he survived. Bob Johnson and Jack Hughes arrived the next morning in two more Travel Airs to help in the search, but it was too late. Two days later Bob flew Dick's body home to Missoula. The loss of his brother hit Bob hard, causing him to contemplate his own future and the future of his flying business.

In the wake of the tragic loss of Bob's brother, pilot Orman

Lavoie persuaded Bob that the future was in C-47s, which were plentiful and cheap after the war. It surely must have been a big decision, but also perhaps therapeutic for Bob to think about expanding into the modern planes. So it was that Bob purchased N24320 from the U.S. Army in 1946. This was the second beginning for N24320; it was also a new start for Bob Johnson and Johnson Flying Service.

While we know the main events of her time with JFS, we don't know—and will probably never know—all the individual stories of her life of service in the Mountain West. Many of the stories that mechanics, pilots, smokejumpers, and passengers had to tell have been lost to history. A few anecdotes are recorded in the Museum of Mountain Flying, or occasionally told by aging visitors to the museum. These visitors always look up at her with bright eyes and knowing smiles, and they say she always treated them well.

We know that she had 25,000 hours of flying time and that she fought fires, had close calls, and landed overloaded in too-short, rough mountain strips. Some very famous mountain pilots flew her. She also met with tragedy on at least two occasions. When you look at her, you can see her life story written on her skin—there are dents behind the cockpit from ice coming off the propellers as she descended out of cold clouds over Montana, and many dents behind the door from more static-line jumps than can be counted. If only she could talk indeed.

3

Mann Gulch

BETWEEN 1946 AND 1949 Bob Johnson used N24320 primarily as a smokejumping and backcountry cargo plane. These were the early days of the USFS and smokejumping, long before the Wilderness Act closed many backcountry runways to aircraft. It was the heyday of backcountry flying. The first sentence of Norman Maclean's authoritative book *Young Men and Fire* reads, "In 1949 the smokejumpers were not far from their origins as parachute jumpers turned stunt performers dropping from the wings of planes at county fairs just for the hell of it plus a few dollars, less hospital expenses."[2]

The Forest Service had first considered using aircraft in 1917. They officially started using them to spot wildfires in 1925 and to drop supplies in 1929. The first actual jump by two smokejumpers onto a fire was on July 12, 1940. One of those pioneering jumpers was Earl Cooley.

The summer of 1949 was unusually hot in Montana. By August, conditions were extreme. At about four o'clock on the afternoon of August 4, a thunderstorm passed north of Helena, Montana, over some of the most rugged and remote terrain in the area. On August 4 conditions were ideal for lightning-caused fires to start but not to spread. By the morning of August 5, the lightning had triggered many new fires, one of which was in Mann Gulch. By then,

6

conditions for fires to spread had become ideal, with winds picking up dramatically and the temperature nearing 100 degrees. In fact, the Forest Service had rated fire danger on August 4 at sixteen out of 100; on August 5, the fire danger rated seventy-four out of 100. When asked to explain what the seventy-four meant, the local ranger said it meant the fire danger was "explosive."[2]

By the early afternoon of August 5, the Forest Service was looking for men to fight dozens of new fires. This meant searching the bars for able-bodied men willing to work on fires accessible from the ground. But the remote fire in Mann Gulch was a job for the elite smokejumpers from Missoula.

The Forest Service ranger in Helena called Missoula at 1:50 p.m. to request smokejumpers. At two thirty p.m., N24320 took off from Missoula with pilot Ken Huber, copilot Frank Small, spotter Earl Cooley, foreman Wag Dodge, and fifteen smokejumpers. The flight from Missoula to Helena was extremely rough, a sure symptom of the high winds they would soon face on the ground. Some of the men got sick. Merle Stratton threw up in his helmet and begged off from the jump. He quit smokejumping upon returning to Missoula.[2]

As Earl Cooley helped young Eldon Diettert with his gear on the way to the fire, Diettert mentioned he had been called away from his nineteenth birthday party. On any given day the jumpers were selected from a rotation. All of the jumpers were on the plane that day by the luck of the draw.[2]

As they approached the fire, Cooley lay on the floor of the plane on the left side of the open door; foreman Wag Dodge lay on his belly on the right side of the door. This way, they could both see the ground below. These were two of the most experienced smokejumpers in the Forest Service. Cooley's job was to see the fire's location, terrain, and winds and to communicate with the pilot via headphones to direct the drops. The foreman's job was to concur with the spotter, then lead the first jump out the door. After several passes over the fire, Cooley and Dodge agreed on a plan and communicated it to pilot Ken Huber.[2]

Dodge led the first group of four to jump, followed by successive passes putting out four, four, and three jumpers respectively, followed by their gear. In the meantime, a fire observer (and former smoke-jumper) on the ground had hiked into the gulch from the bottom, putting sixteen men on the fire by approximately 4:10 p.m. It was nearly five p.m. by the time they had retrieved their gear and started to approach the fire. By 5:56 p.m., eleven would be dead; two more would die in the hospital the next day.[2]

The phenomenon that occurred that day became known as a "blowup" but was poorly understood at the time. It was a mystery how a small, well-behaved fire of fifty acres could suddenly turn into a firestorm that exploded into three thousand acres in a few hours with an intensity that destroyed everything in its path. The men who jumped out of N24320 that day experienced it, but only three lived to tell about it.[2]

The entire story is told in superb detail in *Young Men and Fire* by Norman Maclean. The short version is that the conditions were extremely dry, the terrain was steep and formed a funnel, the winds suddenly picked up, and at that time nobody knew how to predict or survive a blowup. Two men, Robert Sallee and Walter Rumsey, would outrun the fire as it sped toward the ridge top, taking cover on the other side of the ridge in a pile of rocks. When he saw he could not outrun the fire, Wag Dodge intuitively started an escape fire, then ran into the burned area and took cover. These three were the only survivors. The others either couldn't outrun the fire or didn't believe Dodge when he ordered them to join him in the area burned by his escape fire. It was the first known use of an escape fire to create a survivable space ahead of a blowup. The technique is still taught to firefighters today.[2]

The loss of thirteen firefighters at Mann Gulch in 1949 remains the seventh deadliest wildland firefighter incident in U.S. history; it was the fifth deadliest at that time.[3] Of the sixteen men on the ground that day in Mann Gulch, twelve were military veterans, many of them having fought in World War II. They ranged from eighteen to thirty-three years old. The thirteen victims ranged in age from nineteen to twenty-eight. Ironically, the youngest and the oldest smokejumpers survived.[2]

Once you know the Mann Gulch story, you can never again pass through the door of N24320 without seeing Cooley and Dodge lying by the door, looking out over the fire that would soon claim thirteen lives. This was the first time that N24320 crossed paths with death, but it wouldn't be the last.

4

The First Near Ending &
Third Beginning, 1954

AT 8:38 P.M. on December 22, 1954, N24320 took off from Newark, New Jersey, with five crew members and twenty-three passengers on a charter for the Army. All twenty-three passengers were active-duty GIs headed home for Christmas leave. They planned stops at Allegheny County Airport near Pittsburgh, Pennsylvania; Colorado Springs, Colorado; Monterey, California; and Tacoma, Washington. They were destined for Fort Carson, Colorado; Fort Ord, California; and Fort Lewis, Washington. Just before eleven p.m., the plane ran out of gas just short of the Allegheny County Airport and ditched in the dark in the Monongahela River. Nine passengers and Captain Harold Poe drowned in the icy waters.

The official Civil Aeronautics Board accident report released in April 1955 said the accident had a clear cause: "The Board determines that the probable cause of this accident was fuel exhaustion brought about by inadequate flight planning. Contributing factors were inadequate crew supervision and training."

The simple explanation is that the crew didn't take on enough fuel to make it from Newark to Allegheny, and when it became apparent that they wouldn't make it, they were unable to divert to another airport where they could safely land. They left Newark with

225 gallons on board and estimated the flight time to be one hour and forty minutes. They estimated they had two hours and forty minutes of fuel on board. Three hours and thirty-nine minutes after takeoff, they radioed that they were out of gas but within sight of Allegheny County Airport. Two things about the flight are amazing: how wrong was their estimated flight time and how they were able to nurse three hours and thirty-nine minutes of flight from 225 gallons. It was only barely not enough.

Eyewitnesses, including survivors, told the *Pittsburgh Press* that Captain Poe did a masterful job of ditching the airplane at night. All crew and passengers survived the ditching without injury, which left the airplane floating about thirty-five feet from the west shore. Those who could swim made the frigid trip to shore where witnesses aided them. As the airplane sank, the current carried the plane 450 feet downstream, where it came to rest about seventy-five feet from shore. Those who could not swim and who were not rescued by locals, drowned. Witnesses reported that Captain Poe and others made several trips to and from the sinking airplane to rescue GIs, but on his last attempt, Captain Poe succumbed to the cold and drowned.[4]

The accident report doesn't describe the damage to the airplane, but photographs show N24320 being hoisted from the river with damage to the number one (left) engine, left wingtip, and left aileron. There was surely much more. Johnson repaired N24320, and they flew her home, where she worked for Johnson for another twenty years. It's remarkable that they chose to repair her when surplus C-47s were readily available for a reasonable price. It was Johnson's decision to keep N24320 flying instead of sending her to the scrap heap. It was the first near ending and the third beginning.

According to historical records, JFS owned N24320 until 1977, when the registration transferred to Evergreen International. In 1979 Basler Flight Service of Oshkosh, Wisconsin, bought the plane. In 1985 McNeely Air Charter in West Memphis, Arkansas, became the new owner.[5] That was where she resided until Dick Komberec found her in 2000.

N24320 being lifted from Monongahela River, 1954

5

The Second Near Ending

DICK KOMBEREC WAS born and raised in Drummond, Montana, and learned to fly in a Piper J3 Cub when he was sixteen. Dick spent two years in the Army after high school, then went to work for JFS after being discharged. He worked for JFS from 1968 to 1975 and flew N24320 extensively, probably several hundred hours. N24320 was an old friend to Dick Komberec.[6]

During Dick's years at JFS, Bob Johnson owned and operated over a hundred airplanes. He owned many Cessnas: 150s, 172s, 180s, 182s, 185s, and a 411. He operated ten to twelve helicopters, several Travel Airs, several Twin Beeches, one DC-2, three DC-3s, one DC-4, one B-26, six TBMs, three P2Vs, and one Aztec. He also leased a B-17. JFS hired approximately a hundred seasonal pilots every year, of which about thirty were full-time and worked—or tried to—year-round. Dick was one of the permanent pilots, and he got plenty of flight time. He says it was because he didn't spend all his time in the bar, so he was ready to fly when opportunities arose. He estimates he flew about 1,200 hours per year when he worked for JFS, an impressive tally.[6]

Dick says that N24320 was the first DC-3 in the country used for smokejumping, still in its infancy in the late 1940s. Before that time smokejumpers commuted to work on fires in Ford Trimotors, Travel Airs, and some smaller planes. The best they could do with those planes was to put four or five jumpers and minimal gear on a fire. The introduction of the DC-3 was a game changer due to its much larger capacity, speed, and short-field capability. When N24320 came along, it was able to put a dozen jumpers or more on a fire, plus lots of gear. Dick says the DC-3, more importantly *this* DC-3, made smokejumping into what it is today. N24320 brought a quantum leap in capability that made smokejumping more effective and useful.[6]

One of the early Johnson pilots was Orman Lavoie, the man who had persuaded Bob to buy N24320. Nicknamed "Frenchy" because of his last name, Orman pioneered both smokejumping and cargo operations in the new DC-3. The DC-3/C-47 had been incredibly effective during the war, but its capabilities in the rugged Rocky Mountains were unproven. Orman demonstrated, virtually single-handedly, what they could do. There were many small airstrips in the northern Rocky Mountains; most of them were built not in the best place available, but in the only place available. They were often short and crooked, with dangerous approaches, on moderate slopes, and always at high altitude. These strips had iconic names such as Moose Creek, Johnson Creek, Schafer Meadows, Spotted Bear, and Big Prairie. Many remain today and are still used by the Forest Service and others. In those days they served as the primary means to supply remote ranger stations in the backcountry.[6]

The DC-3/C-47 is a large, powerful airplane. It is almost sixty-four feet long with a ninety-five-foot wingspan. Its two engines provide 1,200 horsepower each, and the plane was designed to carry twenty-eighty paratroopers or passengers. Most DC-3s/C-47s weigh about 17,000 pounds empty and are limited to about 25,000 pounds maximum takeoff weight.

Conventional wisdom questioned whether a DC-3 could make it into or out of these airstrips. Orman Lavoie proved that it could. He had flown small Stinsons to these strips and developed the technique to do it in a DC-3. He proved to many doubters that if you could get a Stinson into a remote airstrip, you could do it in a DC-3. At least he could. He then taught his technique to other Johnson pilots, some of whom also became legends. They included Jack Hughes, Kenny Roth, Bob Sanderson, Penn Stohr, Warren Ellison, and Swede Nelson. All these men spent many hours in the front seats of N24320.

Any pilot will tell you that after a certain number of hours in any plane you form a relationship. It might be a good one or a bad one, but a relationship it is. Most pilots can tell you without hesitation every plane with which they have formed such a relationship. They are a little like old girlfriends. You may not have loved them all, but you never forget them.

N24320 was one of Dick Komberec's old girlfriends, and one of the good ones. Dick flew her many hours between 1968 and 1975, firefighting, smokejumping, hauling cargo, and spraying for insects. Sadly, when JFS was sold in 1975, Dick was the pilot who flew all three of the "Dougs" to their new homes, including N24320. But just because they were gone didn't mean they were forgotten.[6]

After leaving JFS, Dick went to work for Western Airlines and, when Delta bought Western, went on to an even longer career and retirement at Delta. During his career he would periodically see N24320 on the ramp at Chicago or Milwaukee. It was good to see his old friend alive and well. In 2000 when Dick was landing a Delta flight at Memphis, he spied a row of DC-3s on the ramp across the river in West Memphis, Arkansas, and resolved to get a closer look.[6]

In those days DC-3s were everywhere. The thousands that were available after the war had dispersed to the four corners of the earth, finding new life in all kinds of pursuits. Nearly everything that could be done from the air was done in a DC-3. Even so, by the 1960s more modern planes were being built so more and more DC-3s were parked, often for good. If a DC-3 was severely damaged, it was often replaced with a newer design.

The next time Dick returned to Memphis, he rented a car and drove to West Memphis, Arkansas. Dick says he had a feeling he was going to find N24320 in that row of DC-3s he had spotted from the air. It had been nearly twenty-five years since Dick last flew her.[6]

He recognized the old girl by the number on her tail, but she didn't look good. It didn't look like she had been used in a while, and she was in a state of disrepair. Dick returned to Missoula on a mission to bring her home. He raised $125,000 from seven Missoula donors to buy her from McNeely Charter Service. McNeely installed low-time engines and propellers on her, completed other updates, and then two pilots from McNeely flew her to Missoula on a ferry permit. Dick Komberec and Rick Nash rode along. Dick says they flew over Mann Gulch on the way to Missoula because it seemed like the right thing to do.[6]

That was how N24320 returned home in October 2001 and ended up in a hangar at the Museum of Mountain Flying at the Missoula International Airport. Rick Nash donated $1 million to build the hangar that would house N24320. The intent was to get her flying, but it was not to be…yet. She became the centerpiece of the museum and arguably the most famous airplane in Montana.

However, the best they could do was conduct minimal maintenance and pull her out of the hangar every year or three, pre-oil the engines, and fire them up. It was mostly an act of nostalgia for former JFS pilots and mechanics. At best, it was a well-intended effort to keep the old girl on life support. It looked like she might end her days collecting dust in the museum dreaming of former glory. It was the second near ending.

6

The Fourth Beginning

EIGHTEEN YEARS LATER, the fourth beginning of N24320 started by complete coincidence in a small café in a small Georgia town. Dick's son Eric had just bought a 1944 V77 Stinson Reliant and invited me to help him fly it home to Montana. We picked up the plane on March 19, 2018 and planned to leave the next day. Poor weather prevented our departure on March 20, so the seller of the plane took us to dinner at the Grits Café in Forsyth, Georgia. We were enjoying dinner when a distinguished woman entered and waved to our host.

She soon came over, and we were introduced to Connie Bowlin. Connie is famous in the aviation community and a prominent figure in the warbird world. Connie knew our host and that Eric was buying the antique Stinson. During that brief conversation Eric told Connie about the Museum of Mountain Flying in Missoula and how it held historic planes, including a DC-3. Connie asked if we had heard of the group of DC-3s flying to Normandy in 2019 for the 75th anniversary of D-Day. Neither of us had, so she told us more.

She explained that twenty or thirty American DC-3s were planning to fly to England in June 2019 to reenact and commemorate the 75th anniversary of the D-Day invasion of France. Other DC-3s were coming from elsewhere in the world and, on the anniversary of D-Day, all the planes would fly in formation across the English Channel and

drop paratroopers in replica World War II uniforms and round parachutes onto original D-Day drop zones in Normandy, France. After
the events in England and France, the planes would fly to Germany to
commemorate the 70th anniversary of the Berlin Airlift.

Eric looked at me and said, "We have one of those; we should
go with them." We didn't know it at the time, but it was the fourth
beginning.

Some journeys start with great anticipation, planning, and ex-
pectation. Others start with a bang, like war or a romance. Unlike
these, the fourth beginning of N24320 started completely out of
the blue, unexpectedly, and gradually. None of the characters in the
story had any idea what was about to consume them for the next
fifteen months, or the challenges, experiences, anguish, and rewards
it would bring.

The Stinson Reliant is not a fast airplane. It cruises at around
110 knots, and the headwinds we faced the first day had our groundspeed as low as seventy or eighty knots. As a result, we stayed low,
usually 500 to 1,000 feet above the ground. Eric was used to flying low and slow in helicopters, but this was a new experience for
me. For someone like me accustomed to flying high and fast, it was
wonderful.

We took off from Upson County Airport south of Atlanta,
picked our way across western Georgia, through Mississippi, and
refueled at Jackson, Tennessee. We pressed on across Missouri and
refueled again at Clinton, Missouri, south of Kansas City. Our final
leg for the day was to Beatrice, Nebraska, where we spent the night.

The next day took us from Nebraska to fuel stops at Hot
Springs, South Dakota, and Billings, Montana; we arrived in Polson,
Montana, just before dark. The second day we had favorable tailwinds, seeing ground speeds up to 130 knots. We still flew low to get
the best tailwinds. When you fly 500 feet above the ground, you see
things you miss from higher altitudes.

In the early days of aviation, there were no modern navigational aids, so pilots would navigate using road maps, a compass, and

"dead reckoning." Sometimes they would fly low enough to read the name of a town on a water tower to determine their location. This trip was like that. There were even times we could read the names on small-town water towers. It was a lovely trip, unhurried, learning a new plane, seeing new country from a new perspective. More than once we would look down and see a farmer or rancher standing in his field, eyes shaded against the sun, looking up to see a low-flying, unusual-sounding plane. Sometimes we'd get a big wave as we passed overhead, as if he knew this was something special and to wish us well.

It was about eighteen flight hours from Georgia to Montana. We didn't spend the entire time talking about the D-Day Squadron. We discussed it from time to time, and both of us pondered what challenges it would involve—whether it was even possible. For me, the idea of flying a seventy-five-year-old C-47 across the United States and the North Atlantic to take part in historic World War II anniversaries had a huge appeal. It did for Eric too, but for different reasons.

After landing in Montana, we both went back to our lives. If I had been alone when I heard about the D-Day Squadron, I probably would have said, "That sounds amazing. I hope they have a great time and I can't wait to see it on the news." Eric saw it as a mandatory job for N24320, a calling she was destined to answer. And he was right.

Over the next few weeks, we both talked about it with various people, still not sure if it was possible. We knew it would take money that we didn't have, but we didn't know how much. We were completely in the dark about the task that lay before us—the complete restoration of a seventy-five-year-old airplane. But the momentum and interest soon started to build.

Some were understandably concerned about the safety of a historic airplane on such a bold undertaking. They opposed the mission because they saw the preservation of the airplane as the highest priority. However, we believed that if we did it right, we had a very good chance of giving her—and the museum—new life when she got back home.

We viewed the dissenters as handwringers, which wasn't fair but it made us feel better about our dream. We knew that the best way to preserve an airplane is to keep it flying. To us, the benefits clearly outweighed the risks. As we started to assemble the team and consider our assets and resources, we became more confident we could do it.

To be sure, there was youthful exuberance involved in our desire to complete the mission. Most pilots dream of being Lindbergh flying solo across the Atlantic, or Chuck Yeager breaking the sound barrier for the first time. Think Walter Mitty; that's as far as it goes for most of us, but it definitely goes that far. Very few of us ever get the chance to do something remotely close to what Lindbergh and Yeager and Earhart and other famous aviation pioneers accomplished. There just aren't many new challenges to which normal pilots can aspire. But this smelled like a real challenge. If we succeeded, it would be something we could be proud of and might just change our lives.

Things happened quickly after word got out. We had a meeting with the board of the Museum of Mountain Flying in early April. By that time, I had made contact with Eric Zipkin, the leader of the D-Day Squadron in Connecticut. The D-Day Squadron was the organization that would plan, lead, and represent the airplanes from the United States. Eric provided us with a tentative schedule, an estimate of the costs we could expect to incur getting to and from England, and other helpful information. We started to think about a prospective flight crew, the required schedule to get everything done, and how we would raise money.

The first members of our committee included Eric and Tia Komberec, me, Mike and Kathryn Anderson, Dick and Barbara Komberec, and Kathy Ogren. Randy and Crystal Schonemann joined us in April or May. The museum board was a separate body with oversight of our committee, although Dick and Kathy were in both groups from the start.

Our team was taking shape and more key members would soon join, but an important task remained.

7

The Right Name

WHEN WE FIRST learned of the D-day Squadron and the mission to fly to Normandy, N24320 did not have a name. She had always been the "Mann Gulch" plane—and she always would be. She was affectionately known as "three two nothing" by some who had flown her or jumped out her door. Other airplanes in the D-day Squadron had famous and iconic names: *Placid Lassie, "That's All, Brother," Liberty, Betsy's Biscuit Bomber, D-Day Doll, Spirit of Benovia, Flabob Express, Clipper Tabitha May, Miss Virginia, Virginia Ann, Hapenstance,* and *Rendezvous With Destiny.* Some sported the same battle-tested names from the war or even D-Day. We knew that if N24320 was going to make the journey in such company, she should have such a name. The name had to represent all of Montana, not just Missoula or the museum, and somehow had to be historically appropriate. It had to be just right.

Soon after returning from Georgia and thinking that the project might just be feasible, Eric sent me a remarkable photograph. It was a black-and-white image of the nose art on a B-25 bomber from World War II. The name painted on the plane was eyecatching— *Miss Montana.* More remarkable was the fact that Eric's grandfather, Malcolm Enman, had flown this very plane in battle in the Pacific before returning home to live out his life in Drummond, Montana. We had the perfect name. N24320 would be christened the new *Miss*

Montana. If we succeeded in our mission, she would be recognized around the world and proudly represent the entire state of Montana.

Mike and Kathryn Anderson worked with VictoryGirl.com to develop the new nose art. Mike and Kathryn originated the great idea to add the outline of the state because it is unique and instantly recognizable. The name and font were copied exactly from Malcolm Enman's B-25 bomber, and the girl was changed to a saucy World War II Vargas girl in a red dress. Perhaps most elegant of all, she carried something in her hand: USFS smokejumper wings. She would always carry a tribute to the Mann Gulch victims and all smoke-jumpers who had jumped out her door.

The new identity was accepted with enthusiasm and was a big hit on all the hats, T-shirts, and stickers we soon sold. The old JFS hands nodded approvingly, if grudgingly, at the new identity. The Komberec family had a legacy to honor Captain Enman, and the state of Montana had a new ambassador. It was a name that had been battle-tested by a decorated Montana aviator and was now poised to make new history if we could accomplish the 2019 mission to England, France, and Germany. It felt right to all of us and, in a very short time, it seemed like it had always been her name.

As soon as the new name was chosen it became obvious that we would name our project "Miss Montana to Normandy." It was an inspiring—and aspiring—name that was to become famous throughout Montana and the world, motivate all of us to put in untold hours of work, lose time at our day jobs, and capture the imagination of the thousands who eventually followed our progress.

Captain Enman's B-25 (photo by Eric Komberec)

8

Starting Point

WHEN WE BEGAN the restoration of *Miss Montana*, in one sense we didn't have that far to go. After all, the plane had flown to Missoula from Arkansas in 2001, and the engines had been started every few years and minimally maintained. Our Pratt & Whitney engines and Hamilton props had few hours on them, and the airframe appeared to be solid. In reality, we had a huge job ahead of us. We just didn't know it yet. To accomplish the mission of flying to Europe and back safely, the airplane would need to be restored from front to back, top to bottom. It would be a massive undertaking.

The team decided early that we would do it right. Our long-term mission was more than a round-trip flight to Europe for the 75th anniversary of D-Day. It was to bring her home from that mission and continue to fly and promote the history of the C-47, mountain flying, smokejumping, and to honor veterans and first responders of all kinds. We imagined the plane as the centerpiece of the museum, promoting the museum mission for years to come.

My early cost estimate was $250,000, including engine and prop overhaul, complete airframe inspection and repairs, and rebuilding the cockpit and instrument panel. It also included the costs to get to Europe and back. We were concerned that we wouldn't be able to raise that amount. It turned out that the cost estimate was off by 100 percent. It also turned out that it didn't matter much because of the generosity and enthusiasm of our supporters.

Looking objectively at the project in April of 2018, we had no crew, no money, no volunteers, no plan, no schedule, no labor, and no publicity. However, we had a historic airplane, a hangar to work in, an inspiring mission, a passionate committee, and far too much confidence. More than one person who toured the plane in late 2018 has told us they thought we were crazy to think we could pull it off.

We eventually completed the following tasks to restore the plane, the vast majority between December 2018 and May 2019:

- IRAN (inspect and repair as necessary) both Pratt & Whitney engines
- Overhaul all engine components – starters, fuel pumps, hydraulic pumps, generators, ignition boosters
- Clean, strip, and paint engine mounts
- Clean entire firewall forward
- Remove, clean, and reinstall engine oil tanks
- Clean and repair cowl-flap actuation system
- Overhaul propellers
- Repair exhaust pipes
- Inspect entire airframe for corrosion and repair, as necessary
- Install new fabric on the left elevator
- Completely strip the cockpit and repaint
- Remove, refinish, reinstall pilot seats with new upholstery
- Remove old round instruments and rebuild them
- Add modern GPS, communication radios, and navigation radios
- Install four Garmin G5 instruments
- Install Dynon D3 battery backup instrument
- Install new emergency locator transmitter
- Install ADS-B transponder (new generation transponder for reporting our location)
- Install red LED panel lights
- Replace old antennas with new

- Remove the archaic vacuum system that drove legacy instruments
- Remove old communication and radio equipment
- Remove unnecessary wiring
- Remove old plastic cargo-area liner
- Install new insulation throughout cockpit and cargo area
- Install new faux leather interior liner
- Purchase and install paratrooper seats
- Remove cargo floor, strip and coat with nonskid coating
- Remove and install new custom wood floors in the cockpit, forward cabin, and rear cabin
- Install new ultrabright LED landing lights
- Rebuild the tail-wheel strut
- Weigh the finished plane
- Replace pitot tubes
- Install modern intercom with rear receptacles
- Install jump light with remote switch (so jumpmaster in the back can communicate with flight crew)
- Replace hydraulic, fuel, and oil hoses
- Install new aluminum blast tubing
- Add a USB charging station
- Remove cargo area aluminum kick panel, clean, prime, replace
- Remove, clean, replace cargo area windows
- Clean out grime and accumulated debris under cargo floor
- Construct from scratch and install a new anchor-line cable
- Rebuild/replace landing gear actuators
- Replace one brake expander tube
- Overhaul flap-position indicator
- Overhaul hydraulic system
- Remove, clean, inspect all four fuel tanks – replace one, patch another
- Overhaul and reinstall fuel level senders in the four tanks
- Patch holes in the airplane skin

The list seems impossible today. In fact, it nearly was. It's hard to say for certain why we succeeded. Part of it was the help from "saviors" who stepped in at exactly the right times. The biggest factor was that though we often doubted, we never quit. There were many times when it seemed we could not succeed. Whenever we felt that way, we thought of the volunteers who had put their hearts and souls into it, the generous donors, and the jumpers who were preparing to jump over Normandy at their own expense. We just couldn't quit without giving it our best shot.

The good news was we had a little over a year to pull it off. The bad news was that we only had a little over a year to pull it off.

9

AOPA Fly-In

THE PACE OF the restoration was slow between March and June of 2018. We did virtually no work on the plane herself. We talked about it often and assembled our committee. Then an opportunity arose that would give us a huge boost. The Airplane Owners and Pilots Association held one of their four regional fly-ins at Missoula in June 2018. The AOPA regional fly-ins had been held since 2014 and were an unqualified success. The concept was to organize gatherings like the world's largest fly-in held at Oshkosh, Wisconsin every year, but make them smaller, of shorter duration, and spread about the country so people could come who might not make it to Oshkosh.

Local pilots and aviation buffs in Missoula had been trying to get AOPA to bring one of their fly-ins to Missoula for two years. It was an uphill battle, because Missoula is surrounded by a large area with few people and fewer airplanes and pilots. Still, the Missoula folks persevered and eventually succeeded in getting the June 2018 fly-in scheduled for Missoula. It turned out that people from across the country needed an excuse to come to Montana and, despite one day of atrocious weather, more people would attend the Missoula gathering than most of the previous fly-ins.

It wasn't clear from the start how we could parlay the AOPA event into something to help our project. Eric Komberec began communicating with AOPA early on about some kind of involvement. Certainly, the Museum of Mountain Flying was a big tourist attraction to the fly-in attendees, and AOPA promoted it as such. Even so, the *Miss Montana* project was mostly unknown at the time, and, even to those who knew about it, it was still a starry-eyed goal with little chance of success. People were watching to see if we had the ability, persistence, labor, and luck to pull it off. In retrospect, most people who heard about it thought we were nuts. We know that because they have told us; in truth, they were closer to being right than we were.

Eric Komberec tried to get AOPA to let us promote *Miss Montana*, but he wasn't getting much of a response. Then Eric found out that AOPA needed help parking cars, so he offered to staff the parking with museum volunteers for two dollars per vehicle. AOPA agreed, and that got us in the door.

AOPA had planned for some time to feature a beautifully restored Beech Staggerwing as the centerpiece of the event. The Staggerwing was to be flown from its home in California to Missoula. However, three weeks before the Missoula event, the Staggerwing crashed in New Mexico, killing the owner and destroying the airplane. AOPA scrambled to find a replacement, which they discovered just across the airport in the Museum of Mountain Flying. Eric was already working with AOPA on the parking, so it was easy to tell them about our C-47 and the Normandy mission. They jumped at the chance to have such an iconic airplane at show center. They had already heard of the D-Day Squadron and the mission to Europe, so it was a perfect fit for the show.

By that time, we had designed, produced, and installed the new *Miss Montana* nose art on the left side of the nose. It was still a closely held secret, so we covered it with black plastic until the unveiling. We decided to use the AOPA event to unveil the nose art and to announce our goal to make her airworthy and take her to Normandy. It was a pretty heady time. We had done exactly nothing to get the airplane ready to fly, had raised no money, and had no real idea how we were going to do almost anything. But our fundraising was about to get a substantial boost.

Shortly before the AOPA event, a long-time patron made an unsolicited $100,000 donation to the museum. He was unaware at the time of the *Miss Montana* project. We contacted him, told him about the project, and he agreed we could use his donation for that purpose. That single donation put us in the ball game. We originally thought our budget would be $250,000, so we were nearly halfway to our goal. More than that, it told prospective donors we could raise money and might persuade them to contribute. That is exactly what happened.

On the day before the AOPA event started, on June 14, 2018, we hooked up the tug to *Miss Montana*, top-secret nose art securely covered, and towed her across the airport to the center of the show. This large vintage airplane made a dramatic and imposing center-piece for the entire event, chin held high and shoulders square. We are still learning how the AOPA event helped us get started, but at the time we knew we had an opportunity to get national press and a huge boost in local awareness.

In preparation for the event, we began to think about how to best articulate our mission. At a committee meeting a week or two before the event, we decided the best way to describe it was we wanted to "take old history and go make new history." It was a fitting descrip-tion of our goal.

AOPA asked us to speak at the Friday evening dinner, when the airplane and mission would be introduced and the nose art unveiled. I volunteered and began preparing a speech. Barbara Komberec, Eric's mother, wanted to speak about her father's legacy and his part in the new identity. Over a few days we fashioned a tag-team speech. AOPA told us we could have five or ten minutes, but we took close to twenty. Nobody seemed to mind, and the entire crowd cheered when the nose art was revealed by pulling an orange-and-white parachute canopy off the nose.

That evening, two other donors committed $25,000 each,

bringing us to a total of $150,000, plus what we raised from cash donations and selling merchandise. It was an incredible start to fundraising and the first inkling we had that this mission would be bigger than any of us could imagine and would touch so many people in different ways. As we found out later, it was also when many of our future volunteers became aware of the project and determined to help.

The next weekly AOPA newscast highlighted the successful Missoula fly-in as well as the unveiling of the *Miss Montana* nose art and the ambitious project before us. It was the first of many national stories.

Prepared to unveil the nose art, AOPA event (author photo)

10

The Women

IT'S NO SECRET that men have dominated aviation, like many early industrial revolution professions, from the beginning. There are many reasons, most of which are irrelevant at this date so far removed from the Wright Brothers and the Kill Devil Hills. The most recent statistics indicate that female pilots make up seven percent of all pilots today.[7]

About 1,100 women flew noncombat missions in World War II as Women Airforce Service Pilots. While they contributed immeasurably to the war effort, they were considered civilians and not granted military benefits or funerals. In order to apply, they had to earn a private pilot license at their own expense and pay their own way to Texas for WASP training. Thirty-eight WASPs would die during the war. None of the WASPs went on to military aviation careers because it wasn't allowed until several decades later. The WASPs were disbanded in late 1944 but were retroactively—and belatedly—granted veteran status in 1977.[8]

There was a noticeable increase in female pilots during the loud feminist glory years between 1960 and 1980, but there has not been much change since. Compare this to the number of women today as physicians and surgeons (31.8 percent), police and sheriff officers (15 percent), boat captains (8.2 percent), air traffic controllers (26 percent), and aerospace engineers (9.2 percent). Almost no women worked in these professions in 1960.[9]

In the group of fifteen airplanes that eventually made up the D-Day Squadron there were exactly *three* women who served as pilots or mechanics. Crystal Schonemann was a mechanic on our crew; the other two women were pilots of other planes. Each plane had multiple pilots and mechanics who were meaningfully affiliated for the duration of the mission. There were at least a hundred total crew members for the D-Day Squadron. Less than three percent of those crew members were women.

The conundrum is that it doesn't take superior strength or mechanical ability to fly an airplane. Unless you're flying a Ford Trimotor *and* having to work on it yourself, there is no inherent advantage for males in the profession. In fact, considering the many traits at which women typically excel, the numbers ought to be much more even.

One explanation is that men are simply perceived by many to make better pilots, and this discourages women from entering aviation. Statistically this is just not true. Another credible theory is that the training environment—mostly male instructors teaching in ways that work best for male students—discourages females from completing flight training. There may also be the complicated gender relationship between male instructors and female students that puts some women off, discouraging them from completing training. Based on personal experience, the women who do pursue aviation seem to be very competent and determined.

The real reason for a discussion of women is to point out that through no real fault or intent of our own, the *Miss Montana* crew, volunteers, and jumpers were made up of an unusually large number of women. We are immensely proud of that fact.

These are the women of *Miss Montana*:

- Crystal Schonemann was on The Crew that made the entire trip to Europe and back as an apprentice mechanic and all-around good hand. She was one of those three women

D-Day Squadron crew members. She worked her butt off on the restoration and was an important contributor for the entire project.

- On June 5, 2019, 200 paratroopers in authentic World War II uniforms jumped out of D-Day Squadron airplanes under round canopies. Exactly *seven* of them were women. Four of them jumped out the door on *Miss Montana*. One of them, Kim Maynard, was the very first woman smokejumper in Montana.
- Approximately one third of all the volunteers that made the *Miss Montana* story happen, showing up and putting in long hours doing inglorious work, were women, and hardly a one had ever laid a hand on an airplane before.
- On Friday, January 18, 2019, before our engines or propellers returned from overhaul, approximately twenty women showed up for a Rosie the Riveter workday. The ages ranged from eleven to over seventy. This was not the only day these women worked on the plane. We were amazed by how much work they got done. They cleaned, polished, riveted, attached stuff, and eagerly did whatever we needed. Some of us expected it to be primarily a social occasion and photo opportunity. We should have known better because, by the end of the war, sixty-five percent of U.S. aviation workers were women.[10] These airplanes were originally built by women.

It's a little hard to say why we had so many women involved. It's possible that Montanans still have a bit of the frontier ethic in that *what you do* means more than *who you are*. In fact, pioneer women worked alongside their husbands at farming, cutting wood, and defending the family. They also did their traditional female jobs. Montana is not far removed from frontier roots. It's also plausible that we badly needed the help and women stepped up, so we put them to work. Every single woman volunteer contributed significantly to the effort with a positive attitude, good humor, and reliability.

No matter the reason, as an organization we are very proud of our women volunteers and we owe them a huge debt of gratitude. They seemed to have fun as well.

The other two women D-Day Squadron pilots were Kathy Royer, a pilot for *Placid Lassie*, and Kathryn Burnham, a pilot for *Hap-enstance* (N341A). Kathy Royer is an Airbus captain from Florida as well as an experienced private and tailwheel pilot. Kathryn Burnham is an experienced British DC-3 captain and airline pilot who came to train in Missoula in preparation for the D-Day Squadron mission. She had been flying DC-3s for decades elsewhere in the world but due to regulatory nonsense, her type certificate was not valid in the U.S. Thus, she came to Missoula to train with Frank Moss and complete her check ride with Bob Steenbock. We enjoyed her company and sharp British humor while she was in Missoula and count her as another new friend.

Rosie the Riveter Party, January 18, 2018 (author photo)

(L-R) Leah Rediske, Dawn Douglass, Erika Simmerman
(photo by Tom Bauer, Missoulian)

Crystal Schonemann (photo by Keith Wolferman)

Six of the seven women jumpers on June 5: (L-R) Sarah Van Holm, Baylee Brush, Annette Dusseau, Sarah M, Kim Maynard, Amanda Holt (photo by Chris Rose, AOPA)

11

Oshkosh 2018

AIRVENTURE, MORE COMMONLY known as Oshkosh, is the world's largest fly-in held every year at the end of July. The magic happens at Wittman Regional Airport in Oshkosh, Wisconsin. Hundreds of thousands of people pour through the gates in a week, and tens of thousands of planes come and go. For that week every year, Wittman Airport is the busiest airport in the world. As we started work on *Miss Montana*, we learned that there would be several D-Day Squadron planes at Oshkosh, including *Placid Lassie*, "*That's All, Brother*," and *Virginia Ann*—along with their crews. While none of us could spend the entire week, we resolved to go for a few days to meet some of the other crews, potential sponsors, and Eric Zipkin, the leader of our D-Day Squadron.

Mark Bretz, local business owner, pilot, and supporter, offered to fly a few of us to Oshkosh in his Pilatus PC12, which was a big help. We could get there and back faster and make better use of our time. The airshow runs from Sunday to Sunday, although many people and airplanes arrive earlier. However, the opening Sunday is by far the busiest arrival day of the week.

In 2018, a severe thunderstorm had passed through Saturday evening and Sunday morning, causing many arriving airplanes to land a short distance away from Oshkosh to await better weather. When the weather cleared around noon on Sunday, they all headed

40

for Oshkosh at once.

The arrival corridor on a typical opening Sunday is extremely hectic. That day, however, was a perfect storm that resulted in unprecedented congestion. Some planes spent hours in a holding pattern before being told they could not land. It was a tribute to the dedication of the FAA controllers as well as the pilots that there were no accidents. Fortunately for us, as a turbine aircraft we had a different arrival procedure than the thousands of small aircraft backed up southwest of the field. We had to hold for only a few minutes before being cleared to land.

On the plane were Mark Bretz, Eric and Tia Komberec, Mike Anderson, and me. It was the first time at Oshkosh for Eric, Tia, and Mike. We stayed for only three days but made the best of it. We attended the Warbird dinner on Sunday night and had the opportunity to see Connie Bowlin again—and thank/blame her for what she had started. We met with Phillips 66 and asked them to sponsor our project. And we finally got to meet Eric Zipkin in person and talk about the developing plans for 2019.

Eric Zipkin invited us to attend the public unveiling of *"That's All, Brother,"* which had just finished a complete and authentic restoration. It was a magnificent event, with GI reenactors, two beautiful C-47s, 1940s music, Tuskegee Airmen Charles McGee and George Hardy, and the last remaining Pathfinder pilot, David Hamilton. We spent some time with the Tuskegee Airmen and David Hamilton and gave *Miss Montana* T-shirts to all three. As we looked upon the work of art that was *"That's All, Brother,"* we started to get some idea of what we were up against back in the hangar in Missoula.

12

Two Tragedies

ON JULY 21, 2018, two days before the start of Oshkosh 2018, a C-47 named *Bluebonnet Belle* crashed on takeoff in Texas. The plane was one of several C-47s owned and operated by the Commemorative Air Force. There were thirteen people on board; six were seriously injured and the remaining seven were either un-injured or sustained minor injuries. The plane had barely lifted off when it stalled, caught a wing and crashed and burned. *Bluebonnet Belle* was one of the Commemorative Air Force C-47s that was plan-ning to join the D-Day Squadron.

The accident was the topic of discussion at Oshkosh among the D-Day Squadron and, because the entire event had been captured on video, there was much speculation as to the cause. For us, it was a wake-up call that even the most experienced operators can make mistakes. We hadn't even learned to fly ours yet.

On January 21, 2019, a DC-3 owned and operated by Preferred Airparts, one of the top suppliers of DC-3 parts, crashed on takeoff in Ohio, killing pilot Brian Stoltzfus and copilot Curtis Wilkerson. Once again, they were some of the most experienced DC-3 people in the world. Furthermore, the Preferred Airparts plane had been converted to turbine engines, which are much more reliable than the radial engines on most DC-3s. I had been working with Preferred Airparts for many months by that time, buying all sorts of parts, including our paratrooper seats.

The DC-3 community is not large. Brian Stoltzfus was the nephew of Karl Stoltzfus, who owns and operates Dynamic Aviation as well as *Miss Virginia*, a beautiful DC-3 in the D-Day Squadron. Karl is the consummate gentleman, and we were privileged to meet him in Europe. The Stoltzfus family has owned and operated DC-3s for decades. Everyone in the DC-3 community knows and respects the Stoltzfus family.

We didn't spend a lot of time talking about these tragedies, but it definitely hit close to home; many people heard about "the DC-3 crash in Ohio" and asked us about it. The media asked about it. The standard—and correct—answer was that we don't speculate about accident causes; we wait until the investigators investigate and attempt to determine the cause. Then we learn from it.

The follow-up answer was that tragedies do happen, even to the most experienced aviators, and we ignore that fact at our peril. However, flying is still remarkably safe when done right, and if we dwelt on tragedies like these we would never get off the ground. Nevertheless, it was a reminder to us that this was no game we were playing. This was serious business, and the mission we were contemplating would involve much greater risk than the conditions under which these accidents happened.

13

Restoration Begins

Those who could give, gave. Those who could work, worked.
Those who could clean, cleaned. Those who could fly, flew.
— Mark Bretz

AFTER THE JUNE AOPA fly-in and unveiling of the nose art, actual work on the airplane was still slow to start. Soon after the fly-in, we removed the engines and propellers and sent them off for overhaul. The engines went to Anderson Aeromotive in Grangeville, Idaho. We sent the propellers to Northwest Propeller Service in Puyallup, Washington. We removed the plastic material that covered the inside of the cargo area to reveal the underlying insulation and metal framework. A few volunteers started showing up in August and tackling tasks that obviously needed to be done, but it wasn't until October or November that we accumulated enough volunteers to really get to work.

In late 2018, we removed all the instruments from the cockpit, stripped the metal surfaces, and prepared them for paint. The heavy-duty cargo floor panels were removed, stripped, and coated with a sturdy nonskid coating. The structure and moving parts beneath the floor were inspected for corrosion or other problems. The area under the floor had a large amount of what became known, among other impolite names, as "gunk." The consensus was that it was a hardened mixture of oil, hydraulic fluid, dirt, chicken manure, vomit, and other unknown substances. Regardless, it all had to be removed using putty knives, scrapers, and rags. All the internal and external metal parts were inspected for corrosion. A small amount was found and repaired.

One of the more difficult tasks was the fuel tanks. The airplane has four fuel tanks of approximately 200 gallons each. They are suspended in the belly between the engines. When we removed the tanks, we found crud, rust, dirt, and corrosion. We removed the multiple access hatches on each tank to reach the interior. Then we removed the sumps and inspected the rubber baffle in each tank, which keeps the fuel from sloshing too much.

Almost everything was corroded, bolts were rusted, and some of the covers were leaking. All the covers had to be removed, cleaned of very stubborn old sealant, corrosion sanded down where possible, and the covers repaired and reinstalled with new gaskets and sealant.

One of the worst corroded parts was the sump, the lowest point in the tank where the drain valve is located. All four of our sumps were too badly corroded to reuse. We looked for replacements and could not find any for less than $1,000 each. This is a piece of aluminum about six inches wide and eight inches long. Eric contacted a relative who was a master machinist, and he was able to duplicate the part, make completely new ones out of solid aluminum, and anodize them for us to reinstall. They were works of art.

One tank was so corroded that we bought a replacement tank instead of repairing all the corrosion. When the replacement tank arrived, it was in fairly good shape but had a dozen mummified lizards inside. A fabrication expert at Northstar welded a huge aluminum patch on another tank to replace a corroded skin. Some of the corrosion that we found on the fuel tanks (and elsewhere) may have dated back to the plunge in the Monongahela in 1954. The fuel tanks were one of the last things we finished before the first engine start.

Perry Francis was one of the earliest volunteers, and he started rebuilding the cowlings, which took months. However, when they were done, they worked—and continue to work—flawlessly. Some of the other firewall-forward parts were disassembled, cleaned, inspected, and repaired as necessary.

For the most part, this period consisted of taking the airplane apart and figuring out what needed to be repaired or replaced. We also started figuring out where to buy DC-3 parts. There aren't many places to buy such things, but we quickly became familiar with every business trading in DC-3 parts and were able to find most of the things we needed. Fortunately, many parts were also standard aviation hardware available from many sources or even from two great shops on the Missoula airport: Neptune Aviation and Minuteman Aviation.

During this period, a handful of volunteers would show up around ten a.m. on weekdays and work until about four p.m.; more would come on weekends. The museum was normally open to the public from May to September. There were two reasons for this. The flow of visitors slows down after Labor Day—some days nobody comes in. More importantly, the museum had no functioning heat and had not had for many years.

Soon after the AOPA event, there was foolish talk of having her ready to fly by the end of February. This wasn't truly a goal because we didn't have a plan to make it happen. In fact, we never had a comprehensive plan. The difference between a goal and a wish is that a goal is accompanied by a plan and resources to make it happen. This was a wish.

By the end of November, we still didn't have the engines or propellers back and we still had no heat in the museum. The latter would turn out to be a big problem because the winter of 2018-19 was the coldest since 1936. We had record snow amounts and record cold temperatures. For several days in late February we had to shovel four-foot snowdrifts to clear a path to get in the museum. In December and January, the temperature *inside* the museum was 20 to 30 degrees Fahrenheit.

We set up propane burners inside and around the plane, or

radiant heaters next to where volunteers worked. All the volunteers dressed warmly, as if they were snowmobiling or shoveling snow. It was one more obstacle that we didn't need, but it did show us which volunteers were committed. For the most part, everybody soldiered on and tried to stay warm by constantly moving, but it was tiring to be cold all the time. We probably could not have continued under those conditions for the rest of the winter, at least not at the pace needed to get the job done.

Starting in December, Dick Komberec and Kathy Ogren did heroic work to remove the inoperative ground-source heating equipment supplying the in-floor radiant heat and install a modern natural-gas boiler. Kathy Ogren donated the funds and Dick ramrodded the installation using local contractors. With the extreme cold and snow causing problems all over town, we had trouble getting contractors to do the work, it had problems once it was installed, and it didn't get warm in the hangar until late January. That was also about the time the engines and propellers returned and Jeff Whitesell joined the team. Although we were obviously far behind, things started looking up.

As soon as Jeff Whitesell joined us, he started dividing the firewall-forward work down into manageable tasks. He would see something that needed to be done, assign someone to the task, and move on to the next one. Much of it he would do himself. Unfortunately, he was still working two jobs and could be in Missoula only a week or ten days per month. However, when he was in Missoula, he worked long hours and accomplished much. One of the biggest problems Jeff discovered was how we sent the engines to Anderson Aeromotive for overhaul.

There are several accessories on the engines that are normally either removed by the engine owner before sending for overhaul or removed during overhaul. Anderson overhauls only the engine and a few components but does not work on fuel pumps, feathering pumps, hydraulic pumps, starters, or generators. We left most of those components on the engines when we sent them off to Anderson—where they promptly removed them all and set them aside. When the engines were returned all shiny and new, those components were missing.

Jeff Whitesell quickly figured out what had happened, and we had Anderson ship us the parts. At that point, Jeff demanded that we overhaul all the accessories. We immediately scrambled to send the accessories to various shops for overhaul. Of course, no single shop works on all the accessories and hardly any shop works on more than one or two. And all these shops were also working on parts from the other D-Day Squadron planes. This process continued almost until our first engine start in April. We could have saved much time if we had sent the components for overhaul when we sent the engines and props.

Even after the engines were running, we were buying spares of these same engine components for our "flyaway kit." The flyaway kit is a large pile of parts and tools required to keep the airplane running properly and that you take with you when you travel (hence, "flyaway"). It includes oil, hydraulic fluid, spare parts, and tools. We had almost nothing for our flyaway kit when we started, and it was one of the last things we finished in the days before leaving for Europe.

During this entire process we continued to raise money. It was remarkable how well our community and state supported us. A list of our major donors is included in the appendix, but many thousands of people donated. We got a letter with $200 from a widow in Glendive, Montana, thanking us for what we were doing and wishing her veteran husband were still alive to see it. All the stories like this would take a week to tell. But one of the best indications of our support was when we needed to buy the paratrooper seats.

When the restoration started, the airplane had no seats in the cabin. It had been a cargo plane when it came home, and there were no provisions for seating. Some of the D-Day Squadron planes had nice airline-type interiors and some, like *Placid Lassie*, had spartan interiors but had added airline seats for passengers. Many DC-3s just sit the paratroopers on the floor. We had nothing, but we wanted to add paratrooper seats like the C-47s had during the war. After a search of the usual sources for parts, we learned they are hard to find and expensive. We finally found a full set at Preferred Airparts for $15,000.

We didn't have any funds in our budget for such a big expense, so we put out the word to our jumpers, donors, and supporters. Anyone could sponsor a seat for $800. We asked that each sponsor name an honoree— such as jumpers who would jump over Normandy, relatives who were veterans, or former Johnson pilots. We sold the sponsorships in about four days and were able to purchase the seats. The list of those honored by sponsors is listed in the appendix. A plaque was mounted behind each seat with the name and affiliation of each honoree.

The Core Four under newly installed engine in March.
(L-R) Randy, Crystal, Bryan, Eric (photo by Eric Komberec)

14

The Crew

EVERY GOOD STORY requires the development of characters. The characters in this story were already well developed—all I must do is introduce them. There are other characters in this story you will meet such as volunteers and supporters, but you must first meet The Crew. I'm telling the story, but it was The Crew that created much of it.

The Crew includes the pilots and mechanics who served aboard the plane during all or part of the journey between May 19 and June 24, 2019. These are the people who shared the incredible experiences leading up to and during that period and are most responsible for all that happened. They all worked tirelessly on the airplane for most of a year and completed the necessary training to earn a spot on The Crew. There are ten of them, including Skip Alderson, The Ancient One. They aren't perfect, and I rib them occasionally for what you should consider minor human flaws. I'll also rib myself because it's only fair. But make no mistake, I love every one like a brother and would do it all over again with any or all of them. We didn't share a foxhole, but the feeling is the same.

There was talk early on of having up to a dozen crews of two pilots each for the entire mission. This was clearly not practical, but none of us had ever done this before. There were several reasons it couldn't work that way. There were few DC-3 type-rated pilots available, especially those who would be willing and able to pay for their own travel and take weeks off work. Most of the pilots who were qualified, available, and interested were already committed to other airplanes in the D-Day Squadron. We also couldn't promise anybody that we would even make it.

For all these reasons we had to build our crew starting with most-ly local pilots who believed that we would succeed, were willing to prepare and train, and were willing and able to crew the airplane for all or most of the mission. The way it worked out was nearly ideal. These are the people you'll enjoy getting to know.

Eric Komberec – Pilot in Command

Eric has been a friend for over ten years, and I've known his fa-ther, Dick, for over thirty years. It's a flying family. Like many of us blessed with good parents, you can't know the son without knowing the father. Dick learned to fly as a teen and hasn't stopped. A career that included flying cool planes in cool places for Johnson Flying Service was followed by a career with Western Airlines and Delta, flying arguably less cool airplanes in more ordinary places because he had bills to pay. Dick has forgotten more about airplanes and helicopters than most of us will ever know. Dick is also a serious rancher, heavy equipment operator, and miner. That is the soil that Eric sprouted from.

Eric probably started putting his hands on the controls of air-planes and helicopters before he learned to walk. He is now in his thirties and has many thousands of flight hours, spread equally be-tween helicopters and planes. He is also a very good flight instructor, as I can attest from personal experience. Eric is the epitome of a professional pilot. His current job is flying BAE 146 planes modified and operated by Neptune Aviation as air tankers; he drops red fire retardant on wildland fires from a huge, serious four-engine jet and loves doing it. He's spent his life flying and is as instinctive at the controls as anyone I've known. He's also a committed father and husband, which is more important than any of the flying stuff.

Nobody would disagree that Eric is the idea man in our group. He is a visionary. Like most visionaries, he is full of ideas; some of them are even brilliant. And, like most visionaries, he needs somebody around to point out the ones that aren't. For that he has the rest of us and his wife Tia. *Miss Montana* would not have made it to Normandy without Eric's skills, hard work, and vision. It's a privilege to know him and fly with him.

Eric is probably the most stoic among us, with Randy a close second. It takes a lot to get a reaction out of him, which can be a good thing unless you are trying to get him to change his mind about something. The most important things for Eric are flying safely, flying cool airplanes, and having fun, not necessarily in that order.

It's not possible to describe Eric without including his wife, Tia. Both are extremely savvy with social media, hardworking, and passionate about *Miss Montana* and aviation. Tia contributed immeasurably—and mostly in the background—by handling shirt and hat orders and sales, planning banquets and fundraisers, running our social-media presence, and securing support from donors (including Phillips 66). They come as a pair, and it's clear Eric couldn't succeed without Tia—it sure wouldn't be as pretty. Their two adorable girls, Taylor and Avian, were a hit at many events, leading the crowd in the Pledge of Allegiance in strong, clear voices.

Randy Schonemann – Mechanic and Pilot

Randy is a native Arizonan who moved to Montana ten years ago. He's a very thoughtful, skilled mechanic and a darn good pilot. He hears things when the airplane is running that nobody else hears, and notices problems before anyone else does. It's a skill we are all trying to learn from him. He's as good a pilot as any of us and better in many ways because of his knowledge of the whole machine.

Randy has worked at Neptune Aviation since moving to Missoula, and his early time there included time working on the P2V air tanker fleet. The P2Vs were retired a few years ago, but they had radial engines and were the same vintage as N24320, so Randy's (and Neptune's) knowledge and experience with radial engines was essential. He didn't have any experience with DC-3s when he started this project...but he does now. He's a quick study.

Randy has a quirky, irreverent sense of humor that catches you off guard, which is usually a sign of high intelligence. He is much smarter than he looks. There is no question that Randy—and his wife, Crystal, because they come as a pair—were two of the "saviors" of the project. He and Crystal dedicated most weekends, many evenings, and their entire Christmas vacation to working on the airplane. Apparently, they enjoyed it. Neptune also gave him two months off starting in early May to finish getting the plane flying and to make the entire trip. Simply put, but for Randy and Crystal we would not have succeeded. We also wouldn't have had as much fun.

Crystal Schonemann – Mechanic and Den Mother

Crystal is also from Arizona, and she improved both the appearance and the class of the entire crew. She's persistently happy, encouraging, and pleasant to be around—yet blunt when necessary. She was the self-described "Den Mother" of The Crew and without a doubt kept the entire event much more civilized than it might have otherwise been. On the other hand, she shares Randy's irreverent sense of humor and nobody must watch their language around her.

She is a tough woman, willing and eager to climb on top of a Pratt & Whitney engine and get her hands dirty and bloody. She's strong enough to pull in parachute deployment bags (D-bags) after a jump and brave enough to ride along with a bunch of crazy aviators across the North Atlantic. In short, she was a perfect addition to The Crew and an essential part of our success. Besides all that, she's just fun to have around, which might be the first and most critical requirement for a good crew member.

Crystal was the official timekeeper, noting in her log the time on every flight when we started engines, began to taxi, took off, landed, and parked. She was usually the first one out the door to install gust locks on the wings and tail, chock tires, and install the landing gear pins.

Randy and Crystal are both emergency medical technicians, which did not go unnoticed by the older members of The Crew. However, Randy made it clear from the beginning that regardless of the medical need, Crystal would not be doing mouth-to-mouth resuscitation on any of The Crew except him. Crystal spent countless hours working on the plane during the restoration and the trip to Europe. As a result, she knows it well; she is actively working on her airplane mechanic certification.

Randy and Crystal are embarrassingly fond of each other despite having been married seventeen years. Maybe most remarkably, they got along without apparent incident for the entire restoration of the airplane and the five weeks we spent together on the road. That just seems impossible.

Randy and Crystal served a critical role during the jump operations. They strapped on parachutes when the jump door was open (in case they fell out), coordinated communications between the jumpmaster and cockpit, and stood by to help if a jumper got into trouble getting out of the plane. After each jump, they retrieved the D-bags.

Bryan Douglass – Copilot

I'm probably the anomaly of The Crew. I came to aviation late in life, although the seeds were planted when I was young. My uncle was a pilot in the Air Force unit that flew Air Force One in the 1960s and 70s, and his adventures around the world are vivid memories. My first airplane flight was in a Cessna 152 to earn a Boy Scout merit badge when I was about age twelve. My high-school friend and college roommate, Doug Shane, became an aerospace engineer and went on to an exceptional career as an engineer and test pilot with Burt Rutan, Scaled Composites, and beyond. Scaled Composites is the company that built and flew the Voyager nonstop around the world without refueling in 1986. They also built and flew Space Ship

One that won the coveted X-Prize for pioneering new ways of getting to space.

My connection to aviation and DC-3s started at four or five years old in the early 1960s. My mother would take my dad to Municipal Airport in downtown Kansas City for business trips. After saying goodbye, we would climb the stairs to a viewing lobby that looked out onto the ramp. I distinctly remember watching Dad walk across the ramp below and climb into a majestic tailwheel airplane, a TWA DC-3. It was my first memory of being fascinated with aviation. It was a fantastic notion that he could get on that plane and in only a few hours be in New Mexico, a mystical place available to me only in books.

My pilot license came when I was forty-eight. The itch was finally scratched, and I was hooked. Soon, I had built an RV-10 kit airplane, giving us a plane that we have flown around the country in the years since. When this project started, I was a private pilot with an instrument rating. If I had any hope of joining the trip and being the least bit useful, I would need several more ratings or endorsements: tailwheel, multi-engine, commercial, and DC-3 Second in Command (SIC) type rating.

Upon mentioning that to Doug Shane at the beginning of the project, his response was, "What's the problem? You have a goal and a deadline, now go do it." Thanks to his encouragement, all four were eventually in hand, with the SIC type rating finished two days before we left for Normandy. With my experience and training, I had no illusions of qualifying as a Pilot in Command (PIC) right away, but achieving the necessary training to go along as SIC was well worth it.

My day job is engineering, so I have experience in organization and planning. That may be why someone gave me the title early on of Vice Project Chair and Logistics Director. This was the most challenging project of my life. The organization and planning were nearly nonexistent; reacting to crises was the norm. Delays were common. Logistics mostly consisted of trying to get the rest of our committee to sit down and actually plan ahead, plus finding and buying lots of stuff. However, it was also a good lesson for me in that the only thing that ultimately matters is the end goal. The perfect need not be the enemy of the good.

I also got to do a fair bit of work on the restoration. Building a kit airplane made me moderately competent with metal work, instrument wiring and installation, and miscellaneous other things. Radial engines were completely new, but Randy and Jeff were great teachers. It was tremendously rewarding to be a part of this entire project from the beginning to the successful end.

After we returned from Europe, somebody designated Eric, Randy, Crystal, and me the "core four" because we made the entire trip from our departure from Missoula on May 19 to our return on June 24. While it's true, it should not diminish the importance of, nor the contributions from, the other crew members and volunteers. Still, the four of us were thrilled to be there for the whole ride and each of us is eternally grateful for the opportunity.

Jeff Whitesell – Pilot in Command

Jeff Whitesell was a late addition to the project, joining us at the end of January 2019, but the timing of his arrival was crucial. Jeff had flown an entire career with Delta, officially retiring at sixty-five shortly before leaving on the trip to Normandy. His passion had long been old airplanes with radial engines. He had owned several, including a Martin 404 airliner that he operated for many years until September 11, 2001, when insurance premiums went through the roof.

Jeff grew up with a father who owned and operated these airplanes and he brings a lifetime of knowledge, not only of the machine but how to operate it. He is a certified flight instructor and has a second job flying float planes for Kenmore Air out of Seattle. Like Dick, he's forgotten more about these old planes than most of us will ever know.

Jeff was clearly another savior of the project. He came along when our engines had just returned from overhaul, but we were far behind schedule in getting the engines and propellers installed and all the other tasks completed. We didn't know how far behind we were. He took responsibility for the "firewall forward" part of the airplane, which means all the parts and pieces included on and related to the engines and propellers. He also worked on many other jobs and was a resource of not only knowledge and experience but spare parts and tools that he had accumulated over his many years.

In his own words, Jeff was a "grouchy old airline pilot" facing mandatory retirement and not liking what he saw. He had pulled old airplanes out of the weeds around the world to get them flying and wasn't intimidated by our project. I'm still not sure I believe him, but he claims *Miss Montana* spoke to him the first time he saw her. It had been quite a few years since Jeff had flown a DC-3, but Nico Von Pronay, The Ancient One, and Jeff were the only ones among us with actual DC-3 experience. Jeff was the obvious choice to make the first flight in *Miss Montana* on May 12.

Jeff came to us by chance. Late in 2018 during a regular D-Day Squadron conference call, Eric Zipkin mentioned that he had been contacted by several pilots and mechanics interested in getting involved in the project but without a connection to a specific plane. Eric asked if any of us wanted those names. By then it was obvious that we were short of experience in our prospective crew and needed all the mechanical help we could get, so I requested them.

I didn't know any of the names, so I forwarded them to Dick Komberec. Jeff Whitesell was one of them. It turns out that Dick and Jeff worked together at Delta, so Dick contacted Jeff at once. Jeff came to see the project in late January. Soon thereafter he became immersed in the project. It was all pretty amazing.

Art Dykstra – Pilot in Command

Art is a local Missoula pilot in his fifties, born and raised in Montana, who has made his living flying but successfully avoided going to the dark side and flying for the airlines. Every person who has trained with him will tell you that he is an excellent and instinctive instructor—he just has the personal and technical touch that the job requires.

He worked his way up from backcountry pilot to instructor to corporate pilot to Forest Service smokejumper pilot to helicopter pilot…and has never been out of work. To do that in a place like Missoula takes a lot of hard work, skill, and dedication.

Art can fly about anything…and has. He's flown Cessnas of all types, Twin Otters, Learjets, Falcons, Pilatus PC-12s, and recently started flying helicopters. Suffice it to say Art is the envy of every pilot in Missoula who dreams of flying for a living.

I've flown with Art and watched him fly a lot now. He is incredibly professional in the cockpit and flies the DC-3 extremely well. His background in mountain flying and dropping smokejumpers made him a perfect fit for this mission, and he flew as PIC for all the jump missions in Europe.

Art is fun to travel with, a source of knowledge and experience, and a valued member of The Crew. One of the biggest considerations for Art being a key member of The Crew was that he was a local guy and very much wanted to obtain his DC-3 PIC type rating and continue to fly *Miss Montana* after the Europe trip. He had also been a dedicated board member of the Museum of Mountain Flying for many years and a lifetime member. He had paid his dues in many ways, concrete and intangible.

Art also had an early connection to the DC-3. He was a young married guy living in California. He was unhappy with his job and looking for something more meaningful. He was on the beach at Catalina Island one day, when a large, unusual sounding airplane flew over him coming in to land. It was a DC-3, and its sound, shape, and mystique drew his interest. He decided then and there that he wanted to learn to fly and that someday he wanted to fly *that* airplane, even though he didn't know what it was. The DC-3 launched him on the career he loves, and through this project he was able to fulfill one of his dreams. It's remarkable how many of us had prior connections to the DC-3.

One example of how Art is motivated and driven is that he was the first among us to obtain his SIC type rating. He did it on his own in late 2018 with the great folks with *Flabob Express* in California. He also was the most intentional and serious about going on to obtain his PIC type rating, which he did in the Western DC-3 along with Eric and Nico. He did a ton of work on the cockpit overhaul and instrument panel as well as the engine installation/troubleshooting and fuel tanks.

Nico Von Pronay – Pilot in Command

Nico is a charming guy in his early forties who has accomplished incredible things in aviation and in life. He was born in Germany but emigrated to the U.S. to attend college in Southern California. He eventually learned to fly in the U.S. and now lives in Anchorage, Alaska. Rated in airplanes as well as helicopters, he is a certified instructor and currently flies international cargo in 747s for a major cargo carrier. He also owns a DC-3 that he pulled out of the weeds in Florida, got running, and flew all the way to Alaska.

He became involved with our project in December 2018 when we found out about him through mutual acquaintances. We invited Nico to the ground school and were at once impressed by his knowledge, wisdom, and experience with the DC-3—not to mention what a hoot he was to have around. He could have taught the ground school.

Those are the factual things about Nico. The most important thing about Nico is that he is the most positive, upbeat, and fun person you'll ever meet. It is obvious to anybody that he enjoys every second he's around *Miss Montana*. He is always smiling and laughing. It didn't matter what was happening or the challenges we faced, Nico was always upbeat. It was contagious—and frequently needed.

You couldn't fly as copilot with Nico for more than about twenty minutes before he would turn and look at you, or punch you on the shoulder and proclaim, "This is so freakin' awesome!" It happened dozens of times, and we never tired of it.

This trip may have meant more to Nico than anyone else on The Crew. He got to do something very special on the eleventh anniversary of his naturalization as a U.S. citizen ("This is so freakin' awesome!"). Then he got to fly *Miss Montana* all over Germany and circle at low altitude over his hometown ("This is so freakin' awesome!"). He was on the front page of many German newspapers after our welcome in Erfurt (that *was* freakin' awesome). He was truly the native son done well.

Without question, all of us were happy to have him and we were a better crew when he was along. He's also a pretty darn good stick, and he landed and took off very competently in the most challenging conditions we faced. We should all aspire to be as good as he is, in more ways than one.

Giuseppe Caltabiano – Copilot

Giuseppe is a native-born Sicilian who has become a U.S. citizen, a successful businessman, and passionate aviator with a remarkable record to his name. Giuseppe, or "Gman," as he will tell you to call him, has flown a lot of aircraft, most notably a Cirrus, a Pilatus PC-12, and a Citation Mustang. He and two others successfully circumnavigated the globe—pole to pole—in a Pilatus PC-12 in 2017. He obtained his SIC type rating in the DC-3 a few days before we departed for Europe.

Miss Montana was the only D-Day Squadron airplane with two "enemy" pilots on the crew. Both Nico and Giuseppe had "defected" to the United States, were welcome additions to The Crew, and made substantial contributions to our success.

During our ground school, Gman told us that his grandparents would take him to the beaches of Sicily and explain how the Americans had pushed the war effort over the top and secured victory. They told him, "You are alive because of Americans." Gman is a naturalized U.S. citizen and is shameless in his devotion to his adopted country.

Due to his personal and business commitments, Gman couldn't make the entire trip, but he joined us June 2 in England and flew as SIC on several legs before he had to leave from Germany June 10. He continues to be involved in *Miss Montana*, and it's a good thing he is.

Mark Bretz – Copilot

Mark is a successful Montana businessman who was a big and early supporter of the *Miss Montana* project. He believed in us before we believed in ourselves. He's an accomplished pilot who worked his way up from small single-engine Cessnas to twins, then turboprops and jets, and now helicopters. He's a very good pilot who loves flying and is fun to have on The Crew. He joined us at Wiesbaden and remained with us until Fassberg. He bunked like the rest of us on the seats in flight and in the barracks at Fassberg. Never one to complain, he brought maturity and experience. He has his DC-3 SIC type rating and continues to fly right seat when able. Mark is extraordinarily generous, helping all kinds of people in need, and he doesn't much care if anybody knows about it.

Skip Alderson – Pilot in Command Emeritus

Ivan "Skip" Alderson, affectionately known as The Ancient One (because it will irritate him and it's true), is the oldest member of The Crew and the only person on The Crew with actual time in N24320 before 2019. Skip flew for JFS in the 1960s and 70s and has hundreds of hours in the left seat of N24320. Even though he wasn't current and didn't spend any time flying, he is an honorary member of The Crew for good reason.

Skip grew up in Oregon, soloed at sixteen, and earned his private license at seventeen. He joined the Civil Air Patrol and enlisted in the Air Force at nineteen, serving from 1962 to 1964. Skip had read two books as a young boy that he remembered vividly: *Glacier Pilots* about Bob Reeve and his pioneering Alaska bush flying, and *Tall Timber Pilots* about Johnson Flying Service. He dreamed of joining one of those great legends and eventually did. At the end of 1964, he made his way to Missoula and got a job as night watchman for Johnson Flying Service.

Skip earned his ratings and flew various planes at JFS until he eventually became a PIC in the DC-3, the Lockheed Electra, and others. Skip says it was the only place in the world, maybe in history, where a guy could start as night watchman and work his way to air-line captain in six years.

Skip was flying the Lockheed Electra for JFS in the summer of 1975, when Jack Hughes asked him to fly N24320 on a "bug-spray-ing mission." The catch was that the mission was in Africa. Skip was enjoying the Electra but did as he was told and saddled up to take N24320 across the North Atlantic.

The story of that trip deserves a book by itself. Skip and his new crew followed a route to Scotland similar to the route we flew in 2019. Coincidentally, they lost an oil cooler on the number two en-gine in Saskatoon (just like we did in Germany). In northern Canada they lost their magnetic compass one night in instrument conditions. The only other navigation instrument they had was an automatic direction finder. The ADF was reliable when there were airports or navigation aids around to direct you, but in northern Canada there were few. The magnetic compass was essential for this reason.

Skip finally picked up a weak ADF signal at a still-unknown air-port. They diverted to the airport, descended in the dark, found the airport, and flew down the runway with their landing lights on. They were able to read the number on the runway, which is the magnetic heading of that runway. They were able to calibrate their directional gyro using this information and make their way to Iqaluit.

They flew from Saskatoon, Canada, to Prestwick, Scotland, with stops in Iqaluit, Sonderstrom, and Reykjavik, just as we did, but with only one rest. After twenty-eight flight hours they finally rested overnight in Reykjavik before their last leg to Scotland. Maybe *Miss Montana* flew so well in 2019 because she already knew the way.

There are rumors that the *actual* mission to Africa was something secret on behalf of the U.S. government, but we've yet to get the whole story out of Skip.

While he couldn't make the crossings in 2019, he met us in Europe and hung out with The Crew for two weeks, regaling visitors with stories about flying "the old girl" in the "good old days." Skip knows a great deal about the airplane and was helpful on many levels. One of his most annoying roles was to occasionally remind the pilots flying that the props were not synchronized, which results in an unpleasant thrumming that is felt and heard in the back of the plane.

15

Volunteers

THIS PROJECT WOULD have failed without our army of volunteers. Period. Not only could the project not have finished without them, it couldn't have *started* without them. The handful of people who started and led the project could not have worked over 15,000 man-hours—even if we had the skills—in a few months. At least 150 people contributed during the restoration; a comprehensive list is included in the appendix. We surely missed some names because some people worked only once, or we didn't record their names. Most volunteers worked regularly. Not a single person was paid. Of course, we paid certain people and companies for professional services, but none of The Crew or the volunteers took a dime for their efforts.

Many came about ten a.m. several days a week and worked faithfully until the regular end of the workday at four p.m.; many worked earlier and later than that. As we approached the finish line, their work hours increased. As more volunteers joined us, the excitement and enthusiasm quickly rose. Most were not pilots or mechanics, and only about a third of them had ever worked on an airplane before. Yet they kept coming.

Not only did they come, they expressed something akin to a higher calling working on the project. Some told us later that the project had pulled them out of a lonely or dark time in their lives; others told us they had never been involved with something so big, so inspiring, so ambitious.

I would try to thank them often, but every time they would brush off my thanks and say, "Thank *you* for letting me work on this airplane." The camaraderie was contagious.

As they left the museum at the end of a day, I would often see them pause before walking out the door to gaze at the old aluminum girl standing proudly with her chin up in the hangar. They weren't doing us a favor, they were learning new things, meeting new people, living beyond themselves, or getting through a difficult time in their own lives. We will probably never know the full impact this airplane had on those who restored her. For some, restoration worked both ways.

Anyone who has ever led a group of volunteers will tell you it is challenging. It is difficult to figure out what each person can do, then find something for them to do and keep them busy. If you don't keep them busy, you risk losing them. Most jobs required parts or supplies. Chasing down parts and supplies, answering questions, and keeping volunteers busy in general kept us scrambling. We learned early on that we should always have some job ready that almost anyone could do. We were mostly awful at this.

To their credit, all of the volunteers were patient with our clumsiness. They could probably tell how disorganized and ill-equipped we were but they didn't hold it against us; we all had the same goal and were part of the same team. They would happily do whatever we needed, and if we didn't have anything for them that day, they would go home and come back another day. Sometimes they would just hang around until something came up, enjoying the camaraderie of working with others and making new friends in the shadow of history.

One of my biggest regrets was that we couldn't take them all with us on the trip to Europe. Many of them had worked so hard and long that it seemed only right that they should get to go along. Of course, it wasn't practical, and the truth was that most of them had no such aspirations. They were content to watch *Miss Montana* take to the skies, follow our progress, and be proud of their part in making new history. We did have all the volunteers sign a Montana flag that we displayed proudly every place we stopped.

There isn't room to tell about all of them, but there were several volunteers who deserve special mention. Kelly Brown and Steve Cooper (Hose Man) are described in the chapter on "Saviors." All of the volunteers are listed in the appendix, along with more details on several who were especially helpful and dedicated to the project. They might be just names to you, but no matter who you are, there was someone like you who helped us in a significant way. As a bonus, we are all now friends.

16

Our Jumpers

ONE OF THE first meetings we had in the summer of 2018 was with Al Charters, Kim Maynard, Keith "Skid" Wolferman, and Shawn Modula. They were all very experienced at jumping out of perfectly good airplanes, and they were confident they could fill our airplane with jumpers who had Montana connections. The story of our jumpers is a big part of the *Miss Montana* story and deserves to be told.

When the D-Day Squadron concept was launched, the main event was always to be the June 5 formation flight from England to Normandy and the dropping of jumpers over an original D-Day drop zone. The jumpers would be dressed as paratroopers in replica World War II uniforms and use round canopies like they did on D-Day. Ours was the only D-Day Squadron plane that had jumpers officially affiliated with it. From my very first communication with the Daks (short for "Dakotas") Over Normandy, the group that organized the 75th D-Day anniversary events in Europe, we made it clear that we had *our* jumpers and they were going to be jumping out of *our* plane.

They were *our* jumpers for two reasons. First, most of them had an affiliation with Missoula or Montana or the smokejumping heritage that was born in Missoula. All fifteen on the final roster actually served in the military or as smokejumpers; there were no reenactors.

Second, many of them helped by working on the plane or in other ways during the restoration. Al Charters and his wife, Kim Maynard, helped significantly, showing up often and doing whatever was needed. Al and Kim were the leaders as well as the heart and soul of our jumpers. They had a significant impact on making the *Miss Montana* story a success.

Al Charters is a retired Special Forces officer and is affectionately known as the "Sky God," with around 13,000 jumps. Anyone who gets to know Al a little wants to know a lot more about what he did in the Army...but he probably can't tell you the best stuff.

Al says he joined the Army so he wouldn't be stuck for life in a menial job such as scraping barnacles from lobster boats in coastal New Hampshire, where he grew up. He served twenty-nine years in the Infantry and U.S. Army Special Forces (aka Green Berets), working his way from enlisted to commissioned officer. He says it wasn't that hard; he just kept showing up, and they kept promoting him. He retired in 2007 but continues to work as a contractor to the Army for military free-fall and tandem, tethered-bundle parachute instruction. One of his active-duty assignments was commander of the Military Freefall School. Al spent time in many of the hot spots around the globe during his career: Lebanon, Somalia, Central America, Iraq, Afghanistan, and others. If it was in the news due to a conflict, Al was probably there, and he was probably falling out of airplanes.

Al organized all of the jumps, including the training jump at Plains, Montana, shortly after our first flight. He coordinated with the restoration crew to make sure the anchor line, jump lighting system, and intercom were installed properly and in the best locations. He then attempted to tutor the flight crew on jump operations and the use of the lighting system, which was mostly futile. It was a good thing that Art Dykstra, an experienced smokejumper pilot, was at the helm during all jump operations.

During the restoration we learned that Al's father flew three missions over Normandy on D-Day as a photoreconnaissance observer.

Like many of us, Al had a connection to this mission that started long before 2018. Al's dream was to fly in the same airspace his father had seventy-five years before.

On one of Al's Army deployments he was on a plane heading to Somalia and sat next to a woman from Montana, also going to Somalia, named Kim Maynard. Al was smitten, looked up Kim when he returned home, and they've been together ever since.

Kim is even more talented and accomplished than Al. Kim is a petite woman but tough and smart, punching far above her weight. Kim fought forest fires in Washington and Alaska before becoming a Hot Shot in Darby, Montana. Hot Shots are elite ground responders to wildland fires. Smokejumpers are elite aerial attack responders who attack fires that can be reached quickly only from the air. In 1982, she applied to be a smokejumper and passed the brutal training to become the first woman smokejumper in Montana. She eventually became the first female spotter (jumpmaster) in the world.

Kim worked as a smokejumper for nine years until getting involved in international disasters. She left smokejumping to earn a PhD in international affairs and spent the rest of her career working in war zones for the U.S. Agency for International Development as well as nongovernmental organizations and the World Bank. She traveled the world helping countries recover from brutal conflict. It's a good bet that Kim was the smartest person on our plane on June 5. Al and Kim were one of the three married couples that jumped from *Miss Montana* on June 5.

All our women were tough. In fact, we regularly joked that if it came to a fight, we would send Crystal and our four women jumpers in first, and it would be settled.

Not surprisingly, the opportunity to parachute into Normandy was extremely appealing to anyone who had ever jumped out of an airplane. The 75th D-Day anniversary would be a historic event, likely never to be repeated. However, there was a significant cost, especially to those coming from the U.S. They had to fund their own transportation to and from Europe and take time off work. They had to buy replica World War II uniforms and acquire military main and reserve parachutes. And, perhaps most challenging, they had to be competent and current jumping with round canopies from a static line at low altitude. All of this took time and money.

Today, most jumps for both military and smokejumping use modern square, highly maneuverable canopies from higher altitudes. These modern tactics and equipment allow the jumpers to land more lightly and accurately, which translates to safety and better ability to complete a mission. In other words, jumping from 3,000 feet or higher allows more time to correct canopy malfunctions, and the wing design in newer, square parachutes is more maneuverable and can be stalled for a light-touch landing. However, the World War II static-line jumps were made from 1,000 feet above the ground or less with round chutes that had faster descent rates and limited maneuverability.

Static-line jumping aims for accuracy by putting the jumpers out closer to their target—close to the ground. In theory, large numbers of combat jumpers can be deployed from multiple aircraft onto a small piece of land and be prepared almost immediately to assemble their unit and start fighting. Since they are being dropped close to the ground, the canopy is deployed automatically upon leaving the airplane. A static line is connected from each paratrooper's parachute to the anchor line in the airplane. Upon leaving the airplane, the static line pulls the deployment bag, or D-bag, off the jumper's back, causing the parachute to open immediately. The canopy snaps open within two seconds after leaving the airplane. Static lines are still used today for smokejumping and by the Eighty-Second Airborne Division, but seldom used by most Special Forces units.

Daks Over Normandy accepted applications and approved qualifications of all the Normandy jumpers. Understandably, they had requirements that all the jumpers be current and competent in round-canopy jumping. When the day of the event finally arrived in England, we had fifteen jumpers on our team who had met all the requirements and were ready to go.

These are the June 5 jumpers of *Miss Montana*:

- Al Charters – Retired U.S. Army Special Forces Lieutenant Colonel, Jumpmaster for first pass
- Kim Maynard – Former Missoula smokejumper squad leader
- Bryan M. – Retired U.S. Army Special Forces Sergeant Major, Jumpmaster for second pass
- Sarah M. – Current U.S. Army Reservist, Lieutenant Colonel
- Keith (aka "Skid") Wolferman – Former Missoula Smokejumper Foreman, Retired U.S. Army Engineer National Guardsman, Sergeant First Class
- Shane Orser – Current Redmond, Oregon smokejumper
- Jon Fuentes – Current Missoula smokejumper
- Andrew Pattison – Current Missoula smokejumper
- Ben Bouchut – Canadian smokejumper
- Shawn Modula – Former U.S. Army Special Forces Major
- Annette Dusseau – Former U.S. Army Lieutenant Colonel
- Amanda Holt – Current Grangeville, Idaho smokejumper
- Jason Junes – Current Grangeville, Idaho smokejumper
- Phil Jameson – Retired U.S. Navy SEAL
- Greg Jones – Current Canadian smokejumper

There were three other jumpers that were assigned to us by Daks Over Normandy on June 5, but they had no prior connection to *Miss Montana*. All of our jumpers are amazing, but a few deserve special mention.

Bryan and Sarah M. were the second of three married couples that jumped from *Miss Montana* on June 5. Al Charters told Bryan about the opportunity; Bryan asked Sarah to contact Al to sign *him* up, but Sarah signed *both* of them up. Both Bryan and Sarah traveled to Missoula several times to help on the restoration, attend functions, make a practice jump out of *Miss Montana*, and organize the June 5 event.

Bryan is a retired U.S. Special Forces Sergeant Major with nearly 3,000 jumps, the majority of which were military freefall jumps. Bryan still works as a contract free-fall parachute instructor for the Army, along with Al Charters. Bryan was the jumpmaster for the second "stick" (or group of jumpers) on June 5. Bryan and Al are two of the most elite military parachute experts in the world.

Sarah served with the 82nd Airborne as a platoon leader and participated in multi-aircraft mass paratrooper jumps at Fort Bragg in the 1990s. Sarah made her first jump at Fort Benning in 1992; her last jump was in 1995 until her refresher jump from *Miss Montana* in May. She was the only person among our jumpers who had served with either of the airborne divisions that jumped into Normandy on D-Day, and she wore her 82nd Airborne patch proudly for the events in England and Normandy.

In the hangar at Duxford, England, where the paratroopers assembled and waited on June 5, some reenactors approached her and informed her officiously that women had not served in the 82nd Airborne Division. Sarah firmly, and correctly, informed them that they were looking at one who had.

Keith "Skid" Wolferman is a Montana guy who retired from smokejumping in 2018 with over 600 jumps, which is quite a lot for a smokejumper. He found out about the project and got involved early on, helping Al procure the jump gear and rig parachutes. Al and Keith initiated the jump lights that we installed in *Miss Montana*, a system of lights and intercom that allow the jumpmaster at the door to communicate with the pilot up front in real time. Most of the D-Day Squadron did not have such a system; it proved valuable for us.

Shawn Modula and Annette Dusseau are the third of our three couples that jumped on June 5. Shawn was a major in the U.S. Army Special Forces, Fifth Special Forces Group Military Free Fall Detachment. His last jump was in 1999, before he left the Army. Annette was a dentist and lieutenant colonel in the Army but got the opportunity to attend airborne school and learned to jump there, where she logged five jumps. The jump on June 5 over Normandy was the sixth jump in her life and the last for both of them. Neither of them plans to jump again because it would be impossible to top their jumps into Normandy.

Shawn and Annette own and operate Family Dental Group in Missoula, and Shawn is on the board of directors for Big Sky Brewery. Shawn convinced Big Sky Brewery to make a custom label for *Miss Montana* and donate dozens of cases of beer for a fundraiser we held in September 2018. The beer was a big hit; we continue to sell it by the case, and occasionally we even drink some.

Amanda Holt was our fourth woman jumper, taking time off from her day job as a smokejumper out of Grangeville, Idaho. She is a private pilot, and, like many others, learned of the mission at the AOPA airshow in June 2018. When Art Dykstra told her about it, she said she would "work like a rented mule" to be on our flight crew. When Art told her that we would need jumpers too, she said, "I would sell my soul to do that." Jumping from the Mann Gulch plane would have special meaning to her as a smokejumper. She signed up with Daks Over Normandy right after the AOPA event.

Amanda flew her Cessna 182 from Grangeville, Idaho, to Missoula when she had time off to work on the restoration, attend functions, and make a practice jump. Amanda started smokejumping with round parachutes thirteen years ago and transitioned to square chutes several years ago. One of the more memorable photos from June 5 is Amanda coolly smoking an unfiltered Camel cigarette after landing in France.

We developed a special affinity for our jumpers. Their military and smokejumping backgrounds made them "doers," not "watchers," and their drive and hard work kept us all motivated. They were also some of our biggest supporters, because their ability to jump on June 5 was largely dependent on our ability to get there in *Miss Montana*.

17

Ground School

WE HAD MADE enough progress by late 2018 that we decided it was time to plan a ground school and begin thinking seriously about our flight crew. At that time, we had exactly zero pilots who were type-rated and current in the DC-3. The ground school allowed us to meet interested pilots, and they got to learn about the plane. By then, we had figured out the legal qualifications required to fly as PIC and SIC both domestically and internationally. We also had a list of pilots who were interested.

Eighteen pilots attended, including many who were career aviators with tens of thousands of hours flying many different aircraft. All of them were hand-selected and invited. Actor Treat Williams, who is also an accomplished aviator with over 10,000 flight hours, attended and was interested in being part of the crew. Skip Alderson (The Ancient One) was planning to teach the ground school, but he suffered an eye injury shortly before the class so he had to be happy with adding important (and usually sarcastic) tips from his chair. Instead, Bill Tubbs led most of the two-day class.

There had been much speculation and rumors about how the crew would be selected, how many would be on the crew, and so forth. This was understandable because we had no idea ourselves. As the vice chair of the project, it seemed some clarity would be helpful, so I made two short presentations to the group.

I told them in the first presentation that I was probably the least-experienced and lowest-time pilot in the room and recognized that many of them had spent a lifetime flying. However, I told them that we didn't really care what they had done, where they had done it, or what they had done it in—because not one of them had ever done what we were aspiring to do. Even if they had flown a DC-3 (most had not), none had flown ours (with our instruments, engines, etc.), and none had flown one across the North Atlantic or participated in formation flights during the historic events we were planning to join. This would be a new experience for every person on the crew.

What we needed were pilots who could commit to the necessary training and competency, be a contributing part of the flight crew, be willing to service oil, fuel the plane, and do any other necessary jobs on the trip. In short, we needed them to be competent, current, committed, hardworking, and pleasant to have around. There were some wide eyes when I finished, but it was an important message.

In the second presentation, I described our crew selection process. I explained the necessary certifications, ratings, and medical certificates that would be required for both domestic and international legs. Each pilot would be required to commit to at least the first crossing and the events in England and France, or to commit to crewing for the events in Germany and the return to Missoula. It didn't make sense to break up the trip any more than that and sacrifice crew cohesion that would develop. They would also be responsible for their own travel expenses to and from Europe. Several of them told me later they appreciated the clarity and candor of the explanations.

Bill Tubbs took us through the systems on the DC-3, flight characteristics, and handling procedures during taxi, takeoff, and landing. Most of us had no experience flying or even taxiing a DC-3, so all the information was new. The ground school was also a requirement for the PIC and SIC type ratings. Some of the attendees were undoubtedly a little skeptical because we still didn't have any engines or props and the airplane was still torn completely apart. We needed to leave for Europe in five months.

18

Media

VIRTUALLY EVERYTHING WE were doing was new to most of us, including much of the mechanical work on the plane, fundraising, flight training, and marketing. And while most of us on the committee knew each other in some way, we had never worked together. A big aspect that was new to us was interacting with the media to promote our project.

Some of the media attention came easily. The local newspaper, the *Missoulian*, had been faithfully covering the museum and various related aviation stories for many years. Kim Briggeman was usually the reporter who covered those stories. Shortly before the AOPA fly-in, we contacted Kim to see if he would do a story. He interviewed Eric, Dick, Mike and Katy Anderson, and me. It was an excellent comprehensive piece on the history of the plane and the mission before us. The story landed on the front of section B, above the fold. The opening line of the article was "It seems preposterous." If only he knew *how* preposterous.[11]

From then until the return from Europe and beyond, the *Missoulian* published many stories on the status of the project. There were twenty-four stories, from the first one on June 3, 2018, to the story reporting our departure on May 20, 2019. The stories quickly moved from section B to the front page, usually above the fold, as the interest in our effort increased. As time went on, Kim said people were captivated and hungry for more information. Kim wrote stories on the AOPA event, our ground school, the Rosie Riveter workday, our jumpers, local veterans, and our numerous setbacks.

After we finally departed for Europe, Kim would call or text us every day or two for an update, and the *Missoulian* published multiple articles following our progress—as well as the link to our satellite trackers so their readers could follow us in real time. His articles would usually include an update on where we were and recent or upcoming events. Twenty more articles were published between the time we departed Missoula and our return. Many of Kim's stories were picked up by other newspapers across the state and beyond, including Canadian papers and the *Washington Times.*

It got to the point that friends—and people we had not heard from in years—from all over the country were contacting us to tell us we were famous. Complete strangers would stop us in public and tell us they were pulling for us. The newspapers weren't the only media coverage we got.

I received an email from Eric Zipkin in December 2018. He told me that Richard Schlesinger with CBS News in New York had contacted him when he heard of the D-Day Squadron and the mission. Richard told Eric he wanted to do a story for *CBS Sunday Morning* on one of the planes that was working hard to go on the trip. Eric told him to go to Missoula and do a story on *Miss Montana.* That should have been our first hint that we were the underdog. We didn't know at that point how far we were behind the other planes, but Eric did. He told me to expect a call from Richard Schlesinger.

CBS Sunday Morning is a long-running special program that is almost always positive, uplifting, and inspirational. To think that our project might be on one of my favorite shows was exciting. A few days later Richard called.

Richard is the same gentleman in person as he is on TV. He is professional and good at his job. He is also a private pilot, which made this story of particular interest to him. He told me that Eric Zipkin had pointed him to us and that he was trying to get CBS management to let him do a story on our plane and the D-Day Squadron to air on the Sunday before the 75th anniversary in June. I told him about our project, our challenges, a rough schedule (because the schedule was always rough), and that we would be honored to be part of his show. We talked about an estimated schedule for them to come out and promised to keep in touch.

CBS came to Missoula on April 10, 2019, and spent the entire day filming and interviewing. It was amazing to watch. They brought two cameramen, producer Alan Golds, and Richard. One cameraman brought twenty large cases of equipment from New York for that one day of filming. Richard interviewed Jeff Whitesell, Eric Komberec, Al Charters, Kim Maynard, Crystal Schonemann, me, and others. It was a very impressive effort.

Being completely new to dealing with national media but realizing how important this could be to getting national and international publicity, we wanted to have something important for them to film when they came. However, our many setbacks and delays prevented us from being able to make our first flight during or before their visit.

I spoke with Richard in the weeks and months leading up to their visit and told him we were hoping to have engines running by then. Richard assured me they did not want us to do anything for their benefit. They wanted to see us as we were, warts and all. His concern for journalistic integrity was refreshing. And they got us, warts and all.

Despite our best efforts, on April 10 we were still a month away from our first flight. However, activity by then was very high every day, and we were pretty sure that we would be ready for our first engine start, a big milestone. We were working hard to be ready for the CBS visit, while also being careful not to do something only for CBS that might set us back. It was just a good excuse to try to move things along. As it worked out, we achieved part of what we had aimed for and CBS got to witness one of our many setbacks.

As CBS was filming and interviewing that day, we were hard at work on the plane, as usual. They filmed around all the activity. I cornered Jeff Whitesell in late afternoon, looked him in the eye, and asked him if he thought we would be ready to start the engines that day. He scrunched up his eyebrows, thought a minute, and said, "I'm pretty sure, yes."

Within a few hours, we pulled *Miss Montana* into the sunlight for the first time since June the previous summer. We put fuel in one of the tanks, pre-oiled the engines, and began the startup procedure on the number one engine. After a few turns of the prop she roared to life, belching fire and smoke. High fives were exchanged all around as the gathered crowd of volunteers and well-wishers cheered the landmark event. It felt very, very good. We then began the startup procedure on the number two engine.

We cranked and primed and cranked and primed, but the engine never even belched. Despite our best efforts, we couldn't get her started. We were disappointed, but CBS was probably convinced we hadn't gone out of our way to do anything special for them. After pulling her back in the hangar, we found the problem on the number two engine in about five minutes. The fuel line to the carburetor had been connected to the wrong port on the firewall, so the actual fuel line had been capped. No fuel meant no start. We fixed the problem and had a successful start the next day.

The *Missoulian* article about the CBS filming on April 10 began with: "Richard Schlesinger is leaving Missoula a believer in *Miss Montana* and the people who've worked mightily to get her airborne." The article ended with another quotation from Richard: "We do a lot of stories about people who do remarkable things. But to pull this off is really a remarkable thing. To pull this off, it's like a triumph of will, you know?"[12] That was very kind of Richard, but he later confessed that he was skeptical we would make it to Normandy on time, if at all. However, his comment that it would be a triumph of will was right on the money.

CBS aired the story on June 2, 2019, the Sunday before D-Day. I was at Duxford, England, and watched it online. They did a great job. The show was about the D-Day anniversary and told about *Miss*

Montana, the D-Day Squadron, and a D-Day veteran in Arizona. They wove together the various aspects of the story to make a fitting tribute for the 75th anniversary. Of course, it would have been nice if the entire story was about our plane, but it would not have had the same impact on the Sunday before the 75th anniversary of D-Day. As we circle the Statue of Liberty at the beginning of the show, Richard describes it, "One stop on an unlikely journey that had *every reason to fail*."

Other local media also covered us extensively and contributed significantly to the local and statewide publicity of our efforts. One of the most enthusiastic was local radio station KGVO 1290 and the iconic Peter Christian. We did several interviews with Peter before and after the Europe trip, and he remains an enthusiastic supporter of *Miss Montana*, the Normandy and Germany missions, and the new missions we've undertaken since returning. He said the *Miss Montana* project was the best thing to happen to Missoula in twenty-five years. We didn't know it initially, but his interviews were shared with sister stations all over Montana, giving us statewide exposure. We remain grateful for his support.

Local TV stations also covered us thoroughly, more so once the momentum was building and it became evident we might succeed. Dennis Bragg with KPAX, Angela Marshall with ABC Fox Montana, and Laurel Staples with KECI all covered us regularly. We made several live call-in reports to these stations, which were very popular. We even did one late-night call-in interview on the national *Jim Bohannan Show*.

The fun part of working with the media was that it was truly a feel-good inspirational story—something that people seemed to need at the time—and the suspense was definitely real. We came within a whisker of failing. Any one of a dozen things could have sunk us. The interest from the media was an extension of those who were following our progress and rooting for us to win. We continue to be surprised by how many people followed us in traditional and social media from all over the world.

Despite all the coverage by traditional media, some of the greatest impact on publicity and notoriety came from social media, primarily Instagram and Facebook. As an old guy, my social media savvy is limited to basic use of Facebook and occasionally Instagram. Fortunately for us, Eric and Tia Komberec were wizards at using these platforms to get out the word. At the very beginning of the effort in May 2018, Eric and Tia started a Facebook page and began posting updates regularly. Our Facebook page has about 8,000 followers, and, during the trip to and from Europe, posts or live video would attract thousands of viewers. The ripple effect was truly remarkable. Many people we met in Europe and from other D-Day Squadron planes commented on our popular social media presence.

We learned much about dealing with the traditional media, and we all got better at it. We learned that it was important to have a simple message and to speak clearly and not mumble. We learned that it was important to be ourselves, genuine and enthusiastic. It was also important to be interesting and have something interesting to say. We learned that you should try to never talk about yourself—let someone else do that. Even if they pester you to talk about yourself, don't do it any more than you must. Talk about the mission, the other folks working on the project, and the big picture. Most importantly, it was critical to avoid stuttering, stammering, and saying "uh" and "you know" as much as possible. If you didn't want to end up on the cutting room floor, you had to be interesting, articulate, and brief. We all got better at it by the end, and it was fun.

19

Our Veterans

THE MOST IMPORTANT people we met during the restoration of N24320 were World War II veterans from Montana and Idaho. We affectionately consider them *our* veterans because they supported our mission in various ways. We included them in events publicizing the project, and we came to be friends. We honored these men because that was the foundation of our mission. It was an enormous privilege to know them and honor them at various functions and parties.

All three of them went ashore on D-Day and fought in the Battle of the Bulge. Two of them also fought in Operation Market Garden. They were the focus of every event they attended. Young and old alike talked with them, thanked them, and asked them questions about their experiences in the war. We had no idea how much time we had left with these amazing men. They clearly enjoyed and deserved the attention.

On June 6, 1944, Verlan Lauder from Rexburg, Idaho, parachuted into Normandy with the 101st Airborne division, bounced off a barn, and landed in a pigsty. He was seventeen years old. Verlan fought through the war in Europe and returned home. He saw some of the most vicious fighting of the war in Europe. After D-Day, he parachuted into Holland for Operation Market Garden and was surrounded for many days in the bitter cold with the rest of the 101st in the Battle of the Bulge at Bastogne, Belgium. He wonders to this day how he survived when so many others didn't.[13]

A friend of the museum knew about Verlan and invited him to two events we were planning. He was unable to come to the first event but arrived in style at our huge send-off gala on May 11, 2019. A generous local businessman offered the use of his jet, so Art Dykstra and Mark Bretz flew to Rexburg to pick up Verlan and three of his family members to bring them to the party in style. Upon arrival, they made a low pass over the museum before landing and taxing up to park near *Miss Montana.*

Verlan was "only" ninety-three at the time of the gala, having gone into the Army at seventeen. He remains very spry and fits comfortably into his original airborne uniform, complete with bloused pants over jump boots. Verlan now lives in an assisted-living facility in Idaho but was driving a truck until he was eighty-nine. His family raised the money and made the arrangements to take Verlan to Normandy so he could be honored at Omaha Beach cemetery on June 6. He was one of only thirty American D-Day veterans to attend the ceremony. Verlan and his family were standing on that hallowed ground when *Miss Montana* flew over with the rest of the D-Day Squadron on June 6.

Ed Siefert was a Montana boy who also went to war on June 6, 1944 with the 101st Airborne. He parachuted into France during the night and went on, like Verlan Lauder, to fight in the Battle of the Bulge and Operation Market Garden. Ed was a big six-foot-one farm boy from the Flathead Valley. He was captain of the football and basketball teams and vice president of Polson High School's class of 1942. He turned ninety-seven years old only a few weeks before *Miss Montana* made her first flight in May 2019. He gets around in a wheelchair now, his knees mostly gone from his paratrooper activities as a young man. He returned to Montana after the war in February 1946 and has lived in the Flathead Valley ever since. Ed was able to join us at the gala so we could honor him and his service.[14]

John Nelson was born a few months premature on December 22, 1922 in Wisconsin, in his home that was heated only by a wood stove. His mother put him in a shoebox and placed him in the warming box on the stove with the door open. John thus survived the first battle of his life. His family moved to Montana when he was five years old, and he graduated from Missoula County High School in 1941. He was drafted into the Army in mid-1942 and was serving in an engineering brigade when he went ashore at Utah Beach on June 6, 1944. Like our other two veterans, John fought in the Battle of the Bulge and went on to help build bridges over the Rhine to keep Patton's army on the move toward Berlin.[15]

During the advance across Europe, John and his unit built a 1,000-foot bridge over the Rhine in less than twenty-four hours, within 400 yards of the enemy, without being detected. John was with one of the units that liberated a concentration camp, a scene that he never forgot. He was eventually wounded and scheduled to be sent home. He didn't wait around for his Purple Heart; his widowed mother who was raising his younger siblings needed him at home. John worked as a heavy equipment operator, building interstate highways and dams during the post-war boom in civil construction.[15]

We found John early in the project because he lived nearby, so he came as often as he could to parties and events at the museum and Kathy Ogren's home. He was always the guest of honor and the life of the party. He told his son-in-law that he didn't know why everyone wanted to hear from "an old duffer like me." Like many war veterans, John didn't think he was doing anything heroic, just trying to do his job and stay alive. Honor and recognition were past due for all of them.

John turned ninety-six years old in December 2018, and Kathy Ogren had a birthday party for him at her house. It was during the ground school, so a bunch of the pilots attended, including Treat Williams. John and Treat hit it off because Treat's father was a paratrooper in World War II and his two uncles also fought—and one died—in the war. We didn't know it then, but we found out later that John's health was failing, and he was in nearly constant pain. He told his daughter, Jeannie, that he was tired and only wanted to live long enough to see the 75th anniversary of D-Day.

We truly stand on the shoulders of giants, and these three friends are among them. Knowing them has been a privilege, and an important reason we restore and fly these old airplanes.

Ed Seifert (photo by Shanna Mae Swanson)

John Nelson, 1922-2019 (photo by Shanna Mae Swanson)

Verlan Lauder at the send-off gala (photo by Amy Myers)

20

Saviors

THERE WERE DOZENS of people involved in getting *Miss Montana* to Normandy and back. You've met some of them. However, a few of these individuals were obviously "saviors" of the project. Were it not for their involvement we would almost certainly have failed. They are described below, in no order of importance.

Kelly Brown

Kelly Brown is a master machinist, jack-of-all-trades, and long-time friend of the Komberecs. Kelly can make about anything you want, and he can do it quickly. There were many times we needed something immediately in order to keep the work moving. Someone would say "Call Kelly," and the call would go out. Kelly would usually be at the hangar within the hour, look at what we needed, ask a question or two, then leave. Within a couple of hours, he would usually return with the shiny new tool or part in hand. It usually worked perfectly the first time. This started when we were removing the propellers in June. We needed a special socket to remove the props. Kelly responded quickly and fabricated a custom-made socket that we still have and use.

As time went on, we made more Kelly calls. From the end of 2018 and into early 2019, Kelly started showing up more often and sticking around longer until he became nearly full-time, like many of us. Sometimes it was to work on something related to the engines. Kelly became especially helpful when Jeff Whitesell came on board in early February. Before we left Missoula on May 19, Kelly was at the museum virtually all day every day. His wife, Janine, was supportive as well, and she would show up and cook meals for the volunteers. Kelly contributed in a hundred different ways. He doesn't say much but neither does he miss much, and his work was always exactly what we needed. Kelly seemed somewhat intrigued with the whole notion of the project from the beginning, and by the end I think he was having a ball.

Dick & Barbara Komberec

Besides being a founder of the museum board and being responsible for acquiring N24320 to begin with, Dick made critical contributions to the restoration. He organized and ramrodded the installation of the new boiler, returning heat to the museum for the first time in many years. Considering it was a record cold and snow year and the work needed to accelerate rapidly in December, January, and February, this was an indispensable contribution.

Barbara worked tirelessly behind the scenes, keeping track of all our purchases and receipts and managing the finances. She wrote thank-you notes to donors and kept us in line financially. She was at the museum constantly and would do anything that was needed to keep the project moving.

In April 2019, Dick purchased and helped fly a *second* DC-3 to Missoula. Dick and Jeff Whitesell located the Western Airlines DC-3 in Mena, Arkansas, then traveled there to inspect the plane and ink the deal to purchase it. Then they flew her from Arkansas to Aurora, Oregon, so she could undergo additional work at Aerometal International, a world leader in DC-3 operation and maintenance.

After the work was completed, she flew to Missoula in early May. This was a significant investment at a crucial time. By this time, it was obvious that *Miss Montana* would not be airworthy in time for us to train and obtain our type ratings. Dick also hovered over all the work from start to finish, encouraged all, and made recommendations where needed in a thousand small ways.

Kathy Ogren

Kathy is one of the most prominent and generous people in Missoula. Her history with aviation and with *Miss Montana* goes back to long before N24320 returned to Missoula. Kathy's late husband, Rik Ogren, was a Missoula pilot who became a local car dealer—mostly because a local dealer needed both a part-time pilot and a salesman. Soon thereafter, Rik bought the Toyota franchise and eventually added the local Ford dealership. Tragically, Rik died in a car wreck with their daughter Kristi Lynn in 1984.[16]

Kristy Lynn Ogren was the reigning Miss Montana USA at the time and was attending an event in Sheridan, Wyoming. Rik flew the company plane to pick her up and bring her home. The plane developed mechanical problems in Sheridan, so Rik rented a car, and they began driving home to Missoula.

Striving to get home for a ten a.m. meeting the next day, Rik fell asleep at the wheel in the wee hours of the morning and both were killed a few miles from home. Recovering from the loss, Kathy took the reins of the dealership, and it became one of the most prosperous and well-run dealerships in the country.

Kathy's connection with aviation started with her husband and her friendship with Dick Komberec, and Kathy was one of the original seven donors who contributed to acquire N24320 in 2001. She served on the board of the Museum of Mountain Flying since its inception and contributed untold time and treasure toward its development and continued operation.

When the project to restore N24320 was hatched, Kathy became an early and ardent supporter, both financially and in other ways. For many nights during the restoration, her home in the south hills was home to pilots, visitors, and mechanics. Kathy was ever present during the restoration and we couldn't have done it without her.

Neptune Aviation

Neptune Aviation is a large aviation company on the Missoula Airport. Both Randy and Eric work for Neptune—Randy as chief mechanic, and Eric as a tanker pilot. Not only did Neptune allow both Randy and Eric time off for the trip, but the company also supplied innumerable parts, supplies, and tools. They donated modern GPS/navigation instruments that we added to the cockpit.

Perhaps most importantly, during the last two weeks when we were scrambling to get the plane flying, they sent over a team of mechanics every day. These included Jay Webber, Cliff Lynn, Nic Lynn, Chad Elliot, Matt Dauenhauer, Chris Smith, and Chris D'Ardenne.

We would not have become airborne on May 12 without their help, nor would we have departed on the mission a week later. There is no way we would have flown at all without Neptune's consistent support. The fact that two of their own had dedicated themselves so completely to the project gave them a vested interest in seeing it done. Yet it was more than that. Neptune is a Missoula business that supports many causes in the community, and as this project gained momentum, they saw it as a worthy cause. They probably also wanted to hear radial engines again, it having been several years since their P2Vs had stopped flying. Neptune employees turned out in force on the ramp to welcome us when we returned on June 24.

Jeff Whitesell

Jeff was part of The Crew, but his contribution to the project before we took flight was essential to its success. When he came to the project in late January and started working in February, we were seriously behind schedule and didn't have any real plan on how we were going to get to the finish line. Jeff showed up and immediately realized how much needed to be done.

To be sure, there were many times when we encountered setbacks that frustrated Jeff as well as the rest of us. Like the rest of us, even though he doubted, Jeff did not quit. His lifelong experience with old airplanes was critical to the project. His knowledge of flying and operating them was indispensable as we got our new crew up to speed.

Steve Cooper (Hose Man)

When you look at a DC-3 with the engines uncovered, access ports open under the wings, and stick your head up in the wheel well, you can't help but notice that there are seemingly hundreds of hoses. They carry fuel, oil, deicing fluid, and hydraulic fluid. Every one of those hoses needed to be inspected, tested, and in many cases replaced. And almost all of them are critical to the safe operation of the plane.

When Jeff Whitesell started on the firewall-forward tasks in February, he had to figure out which hoses went where on the engines, between the engines and firewall, and in the wheel wells. Most of the old hoses had been saved when the engines were removed, and some notes were made about where each hose went. However, most of that was a mystery when it came time to put everything back together. And all the old hoses needed to be replaced.

We knew that we had to figure out how to build new hoses, and soon. Neptune had people capable of doing the work, but they were busy at the time. There are aviation hose shops across the country, but in many cases, we had to make the same hose two or three times as we put everything back together because of problems getting everything to fit. It was a major challenge. Sometime in February 2019, the need was becoming critical, and volunteer Jim Gillan suggested we talk to a local hydraulic shop to see if they could help.

If we used approved aviation materials and Randy or Jeff, as licensed mechanics, supervised and approved the work, we could use a local hydraulic shop. I quickly boxed up a bunch of old hoses and headed over to KLS Hydraulics.

What happened then happened repeatedly during the project. One of us would go into a local business looking for something and tell them that we were restoring a seventy-five-year-old airplane. That alone would usually pique their interest, and, as we got more and more publicity, many of them would be eager to help. They would often donate what we needed or give us a discount. However, it was still early when I put a box of old hoses on the counter at KLS and asked to talk to someone about building hoses for us. They hollered in the back for some guy to come talk to me.

Steve Cooper came to the front and, unbeknownst to either of us, I had just met another savior. Steve looked at the box of hoses, asked what they were for, and immediately recognized it as something he could do. I told him we would provide the hose and fittings if he could build and test them. "No problem. Piece of cake," he said, and quoted an hourly price for his labor. Steve asked what they were for, and when I told him, he asked if the plane was out at the museum. "I went to a fundraiser there years ago and saw that plane," he exclaimed. "That's cool!"

A few days later I took Jeff Whitesell to KLS so Jeff could talk to Steve and determine if he could approve Steve's work. KLS makes hydraulic hoses for all sorts of heavy equipment. The technology is the same, the fittings are mostly the same, and the methods are the same. Jeff left with an enthusiastic endorsement of Steve and his work. Steve was extremely confident he could do what we needed.

A few days later Steve came to the museum after work to see for himself the status of the project. He told me later it was an inspiring experience for him, seeing the plane and all the people working on her. Like many, he got caught up in the notion that not only could we get this plane flying again, but we could take it across the ocean and participate in historic events representing Montana. He knew right away he wanted to be involved.

Before he left that night, he said, "You tell me what you want, provide me the supplies, and I'll make it for you. I'll do it on my own time so there will be no charge to you. If I need to rebuild a hose for any reason, just tell me. This is awesome." Steve had caught the bug. A day or two later he told me the owner of KLS Hydraulics had been in town, and Steve told him about the project. The owner decided to donate all of Steve's time and any parts or supplies.

Steve made many hoses for us. He made some hoses two or three times because we measured wrong. He did it with unbridled enthusiasm and without complaint. On more than one occasion he would work late into the night building (or rebuilding) hoses for the next day so as not to delay the work. He also would come in after work or on weekends to help on the airplane in other ways. Because of his broad expertise, he could do much. Without such an enthusiastic, qualified specialist we could not have completed the project on time. Of the dozens of hoses he made for us, not one has failed or leaked.

Frank Moss and Bob Steenbock

Anyone who has been involved with DC-3s in the last forty years knows Frank Moss and Bob Steenbock. Both will proudly tell you they have been "freight dogs" and fed their families by flying these old planes. Frank is a certified flight instructor with a lifetime of experience instructing for DC-3 type ratings. Bob Steenbock is a designated pilot examiner, approved by the FAA to give check rides for DC-3 type ratings. They make a remarkable pair.

We had intended to have *Miss Montana* flying in February or March, put thirty to fifty hours of flight time on her, and possibly train our pilots in Missoula on her before leaving on the mission. We had no hope of achieving that goal, so with only three weeks or so before we needed to leave, we had no type-rated pilots and no plane in which to train. One piece of the puzzle was solved when Dick purchased the Western DC-3 and brought it to Missoula in early May. Another piece of the puzzle was solved when Frank and Bob agreed to drop what they were doing, fly to Missoula, and train our crew.

Between May 8 and May 17, Frank trained four PICs, all of whom passed their check rides with Bob. Frank also trained two SICs and signed off on their type ratings, which doesn't require a check ride. I was the last one to complete my SIC training, two days before we took off for Europe.

There aren't very many DC-3s available for type ratings; there were even fewer at that time because some that normally offered the service were in the D-Day Squadron and were already on their way to the East Coast. To have these two icons in the DC-3 community help at the last minute to get our crew ready to go was clearly an essential part of our success, and we are enormously grateful. It's been a bonus to get to know them and count them as friends.

Interestingly, Frank and Bob, along with Frank's son Glen, were chosen to fly the brand new N150D from Oshkosh to Europe to participate in the events with the D-Day Squadron. N150D is a brand-new DC-3 restoration by Basler in original military condition and named in honor of the 101st Airborne Division. She proudly sports the screaming eagle logo and *Rendezvous with Destiny* on her nose. We got to see a lot more of Frank, Bob, and Glen in Europe.

Jon Paul De Lucca and Aerotronics

A large and complex part of the restoration was the complete overhaul of the instruments, radios, and navigation equipment. We aspired to have an airplane with modern GPS navigation equipment, modern communication radios, electronic flight displays, and redundancy for each. This required removing at least 200 pounds of old components, wire, and antennas, and replacing it with new equipment. I had a fair amount of experience in avionics from wiring two modern kit airplanes in the last few years, but there were many things I didn't know and tools I didn't have. Another reason Missoula is such a great place for aviation is that we have an excellent avionics shop on the field. Aerotronics happens to be about fifty steps from the museum door.

Jon Paul "JP" De Lucca runs the Aerotronics shop and seems to know everything about avionics. He was understandably skeptical early on when he heard what we were trying to do. Very soon he, like so many others, became caught up in the spirit of our mission. Soon he was helping regularly, or letting us sit in his shop and build wiring harnesses. He loaned us specialty tools a hundred times and often came over to do the work himself. He advised us on the architecture of the instrument panel and helped innumerable times on problems large and small. And he did it with good humor and enthusiasm. Having such an expert close by who was so willing and needed so often made him one of our "saviors."

D-Day Squadron

The D-Day Squadron, especially Eric Zipkin, their leader and visionary, was responsible for getting us started on the mission to return *Miss Montana* to flight. Eric Zipkin's leadership throughout the project made it possible for us (and all the other D-Day Squadron planes) to make the trip successfully. From our first contact with Eric in late March or early April 2018, it was obvious he was professional, experienced, and organized. No doubt, he and his staff learned much as the project unfolded (we all did), but if he had not been so professional and organized from the beginning, we would have been less interested in joining the group.

Eric owns a successful aircraft charter business, Tradewind Aviation, in Oxford, Connecticut. He is also chief pilot and operator of *Placid Lassie*, the beautifully restored C-47 that flew over Normandy on June 6, 1944. He took *Placid Lassie* and two other C-47s to Normandy for the 70th anniversary of D-Day and resolved to bring a bigger American contingent for the 75th anniversary in 2019. The fifteen airplanes that eventually made the trip from the U.S. in 2019 were dubbed the "Mighty Fifteen."

The D-Day Squadron was a loose affiliation of DC-3/C-47s, all of which funded their own preparation and travel to and from England. There was no official agreement and no requirements of any of the planes except that we show up and work together toward the mission in England, France, and Germany. It worked surprisingly well.

When we first contacted Eric Zipkin in early 2018, there were approximately twenty-five American DC-3s considering making the journey. For various reasons, mainly funding, the final number was fifteen. All of the airplanes have a registration number or "N" number, and all but one also have a name. They are usually referred to by their names, except for the one plane (N18121) without. The Mighty Fifteen included the following aircraft, listed by name, registration number, owner, and home base:

- *Placid Lassie*, N74589, Tunison Foundation – New Smyrna Beach, Florida
- *"That's All, Brother,"* N47TB, Commemorative Air Force – San Marcos, Texas
- *D-Day Doll*, N45366, Commemorative Air Force – Riverside, California
- *Miss Virginia*, N47E, Dynamic Aviation – Bridgewater, Virginia
- *Flabob Express*, N103NA, Flabob Aviation Associates – Riverside, California
- *Pan Am*, N877MG, Historic Flight Foundation – Blaine, Washington
- *Betsy's Biscuit Bomber*, N47SJ, The Gooney Bird Group – Paso Robles, California
- *Hap-enstance*, N341A, Golden Age Air Tours – Sonoma, California
- *The Spirit of Benovia*, N8336C, Coffman Companies, Inc. – Sonoma, California
- *Virginia Ann*, N62CC, Mission Boston D-Day, LLC – Newport Beach, California
- *Miss Montana*, N24320, Museum of Mountain Flying – Missoula, Montana
- *Liberty/Legend Airways*, N25641, JB Air Service, Inc. – Denver, Colorado
- *Clipper Tabitha May*, N33611, PDMG Flight Operations – Manassas, Virginia
- *Rendezvous With Destiny*, N150D, Hugo Mathys – Oshkosh, Wisconsin
- N18121, Blue Skies Air, LLC – Aurora, Oregon

Five of these marvelous and historic airplanes are D-Day veterans: *Placid Lassie, "That's All, Brother," Liberty, D-Day Doll,* and *Virginia Ann.* Many of the others also served many years for the U.S. military.

The D-Day Squadron managed the complicated logistics, including the advance purchase of fuel in Greenland, getting many landing and parking fees waived, arranging transportation and lodging at most stops, and a thousand other details. There is no way that, having barely gotten our airplane flying in time to make it to England, we could also have done all the things that D-Day Squadron did for us. Special thanks also go to Kevin Riley and Amandinc Mayle, who did much of the heavy lifting for the D-Day Squadron.

One of the most important resources the D-Day Squadron arranged was custom weather briefings for each airplane. They partnered with the Meteorology Department at Embry Riddle Aeronautic University in Florida, to provide round-the-clock weather briefings for the Mighty Fifteen. Weather over the North Atlantic was not something many of us had experienced, and few of us knew where to look for charts and forecasts or how to interpret them.

Incredibly, Professor Debbie Schaum, Dr. Dan Halperin, Professor Rob Eicher, and Dr. Shawn Milrad always seemed to be awake and ready to give each plane a weather picture for their next leg. It would be great to meet and thank these wonderful folks in person someday. On both the trip over and the return trip, the Mighty Fifteen were spread out over several time zones. ERAU gave all of us current and accurate weather information upon request. They were standing their posts 24/7, and their support was invaluable.

It's unfortunate that we had relatively few opportunities to get to know the crews from the other fourteen D-Day Squadron planes, not to mention the planes beyond those in the squadron. We were there for a mission, we were usually working, and often too tired in the evening to do much but eat and sleep. There were a few opportunities, though, and every time it was a pleasure to meet and visit with other aviators, mechanics, and supporters. All of them were doing it for the right reasons, were serious about their craft, and were personable and friendly.

We like to think that our plane was the most famous plane in the bunch, but only in a certain way. We were the underdog, late to the party, and newcomers in almost every way. Yet we traveled in famous company and were welcomed by the veterans.

The D-Day and World War II veterans among the Mighty Fifteen were incredibly famous and historic aircraft, proudly sporting their authentic green paint and invasion stripes, and it was breathtaking to see them flying in front of us on so many occasions. Their presence brought authenticity to the events and they were—and should be—proud of their aircraft. It was a privilege to meet those folks, and we look forward to seeing them again at future events. We learned much from them.

During the restoration, we discussed painting N24320 green and/or adding invasion stripes (even temporary, removable ones) but quickly dismissed the idea as being inauthentic. We would go to the dance with the girl that brought us, the way she was, proudly displaying her heritage.

21

Empire, Katie, & Tubbs

ONE EXTRAORDINARY GROUP of people who helped us enormously were connected with each other and our airplane in unique ways. Empire Airlines is a private company located in Coeur d'Alene, Idaho, that operates dozens of aircraft for Federal Express. They are a substantial company with a long history. Their CEO, Tim Komberec, is Dick Komberec's brother.

When we started the project, Eric and Dick immediately figured that Tim and Empire might be able to help us. In April 2018 we went to Coeur d'Alene to visit their facility. We were able to meet Katie Lammons, Nolan Wylie, and Bill Tubbs. Katie works for Empire, but Nolan and Bill had other interests in helping us out.

Nolan is a retired FAA inspector and private contractor who has been involved with several commercial aircraft operations over many years. He knows the regulations very well and advised us on various aspects of getting the plane airworthy.

Bill Tubbs is a longtime pilot who worked many years with the FAA. He also worked for JFS in the early seventies, flying DC-3s and other planes. He started at JFS as a flight instructor in June 1970 but quickly moved from flying Cessnas to the bigger planes, including the Beech 18s and the DC-3s. He has almost ninety hours in his logbook flying N24320 and is very knowledgeable about its operation and maintenance. In 1973, Bill flew N24320 coast to coast on several different missions, including one trip to Presque Isle, Maine, to recover a plane.

Bill left JFS in 1974 and went on to fly as a corporate pilot, operate an FBO (fixed-base operator, where noncommercial aircraft get fuel and support), fly contract flights for the Forest Service, and then fly for the airlines for many years. Bill finished his career working twenty-one years for the FAA. Bill's deep knowledge of planes (especially DC-3s), FAA regulations, and aviation in general were a great help to us.

Katie Lammons is a longtime Empire employee and a genius at aircraft records. When we visited Empire in April, she didn't know anything about *Miss Montana* or the mission. After we described it to her, including the history of the plane, the job ahead of us, and the historic mission to Europe, she shivered a little and said, "I just got all goose-bumply." She was in. We got that type of reaction so often that it almost became expected, but that was the first time.

Katie researched and organized all our ancient aircraft records, digitizing them and figuring out what we needed to do to get the plane airworthy in the eyes of the FAA. It was an enormous job, but she did it in a fraction of the time that any one of us could have done it, and she did it perfectly. Empire Airlines also donated a pile of instruments from their surplus and raised money to support us.

Nolan and Bill continued to support the effort, visiting Missoula several times from their homes in Washington. Bill stood in for injured Skip to teach the ground school in December. By that time, we all knew a bit about Bill's connection to the airplane, but we didn't know all of it.

Bill's youngest brother, John, is not a pilot, but he is a good guy nonetheless. He is currently the director of the Montana Department of Natural Resources and Conservation, the agency responsible for Montana's state-owned lands as well as water and timber resources. It's an important and prestigious job. DNRC is also responsible for wild-land firefighting, so they operate a fleet of aircraft and contract for others. But none of that is the most interesting thing about

John...or about Bill.

The most interesting thing about Bill and John is that they grew up at the Gates of the Mountains boat landing on Upper Holter Lake on the Missouri River. Their family operated the marina and the regular commercial boat tours that were offered to...the site of the Mann Gulch tragedy. Moreover, their marina was on the Missouri River, which was the route Lewis and Clark used in the early 1800s to make their way across Montana and eventually to the Pacific Ocean. It may not be obvious how Lewis and Clark connect to our mission, but it was through the Tubbs' connection with two famous authors.

Because they lived on the river, Bill and John had occasion to meet two renowned authors, the late Norman Maclean (author of *Young Men and Fire*) and the late Stephen Ambrose. Stephen Ambrose was a recognized expert on all things World War II, founder of the National World War II Museum in New Orleans, and author of innumerable books on the war in Europe and the Pacific. Ambrose also wrote *Undaunted Courage*, perhaps the best book ever written on the Lewis and Clark Expedition. But John didn't only get to meet Stephen Ambrose, he married Ambrose's daughter, Stephanie.

Therefore, the Tubbs family has specific connections to D-Day through meeting and marrying into the Ambrose family, to the Mann Gulch tragedy through their life at the marina and acquaintance with Maclean, and with N24320 through Bill's career at JFS. You couldn't make this up.

22

Training the Crew

WHEN THE IDEA to restore *Miss Montana* and fly her to Normandy was born, we had no DC-3 pilots or mechanics, and little idea where or how to find them. We knew we had competent pilots in Missoula such as Art and Eric—and others—but we didn't know how much training and experience it would take to become competent to fly the airplane. We kept talking about and trying to figure out who would be flying our plane as the work pressed on.

Art and Eric were obvious choices and my preference from the beginning because of their experience, youth, passion for the mission, and being local guys. Jeff Whitesell eventually joined the ranks as someone who had extensive experience in DC-3s and similar planes. We found Nico shortly before the ground school and immediately hit it off. However, Jeff wasn't current, and the other three had yet to earn their type ratings.

The FAA regulations stipulate that to fly any airplane weighing over 12,500 pounds, a pilot must earn a rating to fly that "type." At approximately 25,000 pounds maximum gross weight, the DC-3 requires a type rating. In the United States a type rating is required for only the PIC in a DC-3. Anyone with a multi-engine rating, tailwheel endorsement, and a few other endorsements can serve as copilot in the United States. However, to fly outside the U.S., the SIC type rating is required for copilots.

It turns out that there are relatively few DC-3 instructors in the world and even fewer examiners who can conduct a check ride and issue the type rating. Two of the best are Frank Moss and Bob Steenbock.

Consequently, for two weeks in May, Frank trained and Bob gave check rides to Eric, Art, and Nico, as well as to Kathryn Burnham, who had traveled from England to obtain her U.S. type rating. Getting the SIC-type rating was a lower priority because any PIC could do the training and sign off for the SIC type rating without a check ride. If necessary, we could get SICs their type ratings on our way across the country. However, both Gman and I earned SIC type ratings with Frank a few days before we left.

Those two weeks in May were hectic. Work continued frantically on *Miss Montana* while Frank and Bob trained pilots in the Western DC-3. I watched and rode along on some of the training flights to learn. The level of ability and professionalism was impressive as I watched Art, Eric, Nico, and Kathryn complete their training and check rides.

The PIC check ride consists of an oral exam and a flight exam. For each of these applicants the oral exam lasted at least three hours and the flight portion nearly as long. As each of them came back from their check ride they looked wrung out. Art and Eric both said it was the toughest check ride they had ever taken. Nico looked at ease. Bob Steenbock grudgingly said Nico was a "check-ride god." Someone jokingly asked Nico if he had taught Bob a thing or two. Nico smiled his trademark grin and said, "Actually, I think I did." If any of them had expected Bob to take it easy on them, they were mistaken.

All four successfully passed their check rides, and Jeff did the necessary training with Frank to become current. Just like that, about ten days before we eventually departed, we had a crew.

23

About Copilots

It's a dirty seat.

— Jeff Whitesell

AS SOMEONE NEW to flying as a member of a crew, there was much for me to learn about the life of a copilot. Many books about flying portray the copilot as a wide-eyed neophyte, new to the cockpit of a particular plane, and in awe of the captain to whom he is beholden for everything. Until he has some experience, he is treated like something found on the bottom of the captain's shoe. Flying as copilot on *Miss Montana* was nothing like that, and I had nothing but respect for the men I flew with because of their patience, experience, judgment, and skills. Ernest Gann says it best in *Fate is the Hunter*.

> "From all these men…I learned something of my craft. Little by little their skills and ways of thinking contributed to my own resources until they built me into a separate entity which was specifically designed to transport and preserve the lives of others. For any professional it was a magnificent opportunity to drain the best from his predecessors."[17]

Most pilots with any experience will tell you that flying the DC-3 takes two adults. The Ancient One claims they used to fly them with one pilot "back in the day," and it wasn't that difficult once you got the hang of it. Nobody flies the DC-3 with a single pilot today. Furthermore, the copilot's job is, in some ways, more difficult and busier than the pilot's. Jeff Whitesell calls it a "dirty seat" because it has so many responsibilities. However, it isn't that hard to be a copilot, and the SIC type rating is vastly easier to earn than a PIC.

The official requirements to obtain the SIC type rating are that the applicant must make three "unassisted" takeoffs and landings, complete some maneuvers in the air, and in general competently acquit himself or herself in the eyes of any willing PIC. After that, it's a simple matter of getting a logbook endorsement followed by a new certificate from the FAA. The truth is that there is no such thing as an "unassisted" takeoff or landing (The Ancient One's myths notwithstanding), but the point is that the SIC candidate must demonstrate the ability to manipulate the controls competently.

In my case, when this project started, I did not have a multi-engine rating or tailwheel endorsement, the two most important skills required for flying a DC-3. The multi-engine rating came in January 2019, and Randy and I obtained our tailwheel endorsements in Missoula in early May. Art Dykstra kindly donated the instruction; Bruce Doering, a local flight instructor and owner of Montana Flying Service, generously donated the use of his Cessna 170.

Anyone new to tailwheel flying beholds it with a certain measure of respect—or they should. Experienced tailwheel pilots wear the honor proudly, and you always sense a slight amount of disdain if they find out you've never mastered tailwheel airplanes. The implication is that you can't call yourself a pilot if you've never mastered a tailwheel plane. It's understandable, because it is indeed a difficult skill to master, and there is a good reason why most new airplanes are built with the third wheel in front. Nosewheel airplanes are inherently more stable on the ground and therefore safer.

The difference between driving tailwheel aircraft and nosewheel aircraft has to do with where the center of gravity is located. On a nosewheel aircraft, the center of gravity is forward of the main wheels and sincerely wants to remain there. If it didn't, the front wheel would come off the ground. On a tailwheel airplane, the center of gravity is aft of the main wheels, which conveniently keeps the tail on the ground during ground operations.

The reason for the difficulty is that your center of gravity is what takes you places, and it always wants to lead the way. In a nosewheel plane, you simply let the center of gravity pull you along, which doesn't require a great amount of skill. In a tailwheel airplane, the center of gravity is always behind you, trying to pass you and lead the way, keeping you literally on your toes. It's a deceitful ploy, but the airplane doesn't know any better.

The best analogy is a shopping cart. If you take a loaded shopping cart into an empty parking lot and give it a shove, it will generally track straight ahead quite nicely, the center of gravity being forward of the main wheels and behind the ones that steer. However, if you shove it backward, something quite different happens. The trailing end wants to pass the main wheels on one side or the other. Once the center of gravity gets outside of the main wheels, whether on a shopping cart or an airplane, it's impossible to stop it from passing you. The result in an airplane is a "ground loop." If it occurs at low speed, it can be embarrassing but relatively harmless; a high-speed ground loop can bend the airplane, or worse.

This issue is a factor only when the airplane is in contact with the ground during taxi, takeoff, and landing. Since landings and takeoffs are the most important and risky portions of any flight, tailwheel pilots always seem a bit nervous, and for good reason. There is absolutely no difference between tailwheel and nosewheel aircraft in flight, except possibly the anxiety the tailwheel pilot always seems to have about getting safely on the ground and in the hangar.

So a tailwheel pilot is constantly trying to keep the center of gravity to the rear, not permitting it to sneak left or right in an attempt to lead the way. This is done primarily by dancing on the rudder pedals, only in a crisis resorting to touching the brakes. Many a hapless tailwheel pilot has touched the brakes at too high a speed and flipped the airplane over onto its nose. Using too much (or not enough) rudder can cause the infamous ground loop, damaging a lot or a little, not the least of which is the pilot's pride.

With all these concepts in mind, Randy and I embarked upon tailwheel training with Art in the 170. Our training would be even more challenging than typical tailwheel training. We would be learning to handle this strange breed of airplane with a new instructor. But Art and Bruce agreed that we would also have to learn it all from the right seat, which would be our domain in the DC-3. It made some sense, given the short time we had available for training, that we should learn our tailwheel skills from the seat where we would be applying them. However, it made an already difficult skill much more challenging for both of us to learn.

For some reason, taking off and landing any airplane from the right seat is a big adjustment from doing so in the left seat. Like most things, it's easier to do on nosewheel planes, and it gets easier with practice. It has to do with your sight picture being slightly different in the right seat from what you are used to in the left seat. But it is enough. For Randy and me it added to the difficulty of learning tailwheel skills. When he started tailwheel training, Randy said he was ninety-five percent sure he was going to break the airplane. When he was finished with the training, he was only fifty percent sure he was going to break the airplane.

Nevertheless, after five or six hours of training, Art believed that each of us had learned the skills needed to drive a tailwheel airplane and endorsed our logbooks. There was some mention about it only being a license to learn, but he didn't need to tell us that.

Flying as a copilot is fun. One of your jobs is reading the checklist for every phase of flight in which you are the pilot not flying. There are checklists for everything: Before Start, After Start, Taxi, Engine Runup, Power Check, Before Takeoff, After Takeoff, Cruise, Descent, Before Landing, After Landing, and Parking. These are only the normal checklists; there is another set for emergencies. They are all important. Some of the items are to be memorized, while the others are to be read and the PIC responds. But of all the checklists, the After Takeoff checklist may be the most critical.

During the takeoff it is the copilot's job to watch the airspeed and engine instruments while the pilot keeps the center of gravity in its proper place with rudder and aileron and pays attention to the engines. The engine instruments can be a sign of an imminent engine failure. The airspeed is important because, beyond a certain airspeed known as V_1, you are committed to taking off, no matter what happens. Any problems encountered after V_1 are to be solved in the air.

When you are still rolling down the runway and slower than V_1, the pilot has one hand on the yoke and the other on the throttles, eyes straight ahead. If an engine loses power on takeoff, he will be the first to know it because the airplane will yaw (twist) toward the failing engine. In that case, he will pull the throttles to idle to abort the takeoff, hopefully before the plane departs the runway. As soon as V_1 is reached, he takes his hand off the throttles and places them both on the yoke, pulling back to put air beneath the tires. The controls in the DC-3 are heavy, so taking off requires a firm grip with two hands on the yoke.

The first thing the pilot not flying (usually the copilot) must do after takeoff is to get the landing gear up quickly as soon as the pilot flying declares, "Positive rate of climb, gear up!" Despite all the power DC-3s have, they don't climb well with the landing gear down, and if you happen to have the gear down at low altitude *and* lose an engine, you could be DRT—dead right there. The heavier you are, the worse both problems become. It's important to eliminate, as quickly as possible, at least one of these potential causes of a DRT situation.

Once the gear is up, the copilot's main job is managing power. The pilot flying still has his eyes straight ahead and hands and feet on the flight controls. Just like on the ground, the pilot flying would be the first to notice a dead or failing engine. This would require extreme rudder input to counter the yaw and keep the plane flying straight. While he is minding his job and the airplane continues to climb, the copilot reduces power in stages.

There are four basic power settings. The first is maximum power, which can usually be maintained for only a few minutes during takeoff or emergency climb before risking damage to the engines. The next highest power setting is maximum except takeoff, or METO, which is the highest power that can be continuously maintained without risking damage to the engines. Most pilots nevertheless limit time at METO power, especially when taking off at lower gross weight. The next setting is climb power, and the lowest normal setting is cruise power. During takeoff, the power settings typically progress quickly from maximum power to METO to climb, and it is the copilot's job to set these promptly and accurately, all the while minding the engine instruments. This critical period with high workload is the reason we found it helpful to have a third pilot or mechanic sitting in the jump seat to make sure nothing was missed.

In fact, on our very first takeoff as we left Missoula, this strategy paid off. As Eric applied power for takeoff, the friction lock on the throttles wasn't tight enough and, soon after becoming airborne, you could hear the power reduce because the vibration had caused the throttles to slip. Randy was sitting in the jump seat, quickly saw the problem, and reached forward to advance the throttles. The crisis was averted.

Once takeoff and climb are complete and you get everything set up for cruise, the pace slows down and there are different things to mind. Engine instruments, navigation, and communication become the focus. You also get to look out the window and marvel at the spectacular views, which we did a lot.

Of course, if both pilots agree, either pilot may execute the takeoffs and landings while the other fulfills copilot duties. This is important to decide beforehand because you both can't do it. It is always briefed during the Before Takeoff checklist.

24

Generator Torment

FROM THE VERY first engine runs in April, our generators were not making power—and we could not fly without them. This was one of the most frustrating setbacks of the entire project.

It started on April 10 when we ran the engines for the first time. We noted the problem and worked on it a bit, along with other jobs on the list. However, the unresolved generator issue soon became priority number one, as all the other barriers to flight were resolved. The issue became such a conundrum that we had at least half a dozen highly qualified mechanics trying to figure it out for about ten days. We could have flown sooner had it been resolved. The amazing mechanics from Neptune spent a huge amount of time on it during the two weeks they were committed to the project.

It was interesting to watch. The proper way to troubleshoot a problem is to stop, sit down with the crew that is working on it, map out a logical troubleshooting path, and then get to work. Despite a couple of efforts to do so, it never happened. It seemed like such a simple problem. We were running around with a million things to do, and this was only one of them. We never stopped and talked about how to solve the problem. We brought in a local guy who worked on automotive generators for a living, but only half of us wanted to listen to him. It was a mess.

We tried everything. We switched out system components if we had spares. We ran new wires to see if it was in the control wiring. We contacted the company that overhauled the generators for ideas. Nothing worked. Aware that too many cooks can spoil the soup, most of us tried to stay out of the fray, but given the desperate nature of the problem, we couldn't remain completely detached. If an idea came to mind, we usually mentioned it to Randy or Jeff. It was starting to feel a little desperate, like we were jinxed.

The answer came out of the blue. It was one of those moments when we felt like laughing *and* crying. On May 10, the day before the send-off gala, we were all still desperately looking for the answer. It seemed like everyone had a different idea and approach, which is never the best way to solve a problem. As the swarm of mechanics worked, we heard someone announce, "Found it!"

Jay Webber, one of the Neptune mechanics detailed to the project, had figured out that the main cables to the generators were connected wrong. It was the simplest of all possible mistakes, but the easiest to fix. The bad news was that the error had cost us about ten days. The good news was that it took about ten minutes to switch the cables and didn't cost anything. The work was done, the engines were started, and the generators started making power as they had been trying to from the beginning. There were shouts of joy and relief all around. We started to think we might pull it off, after all. It was the last mechanical problem we would face until June 18.

25

First Flight

OUR ORIGINAL PLAN was to depart Missoula soon after the first of May, which would have allowed us to make a leisurely crossing of the U.S. and join the bulk of the D-Day Squadron in Oxford, Connecticut, in time to get acquainted and train together. We would also have been able to participate in the AOPA 80th Anniversary Fly-In on May 10-11 in Maryland, where six of the D-Day Squadron airplanes were slated to fly and drop some jumpers. We missed all of it.

We installed our engines and propellers in March and began putting everything back together in earnest. We were finishing the instrument wiring, and it seemed like we were working on everything at once. The workdays got longer, and many of our volunteers started working longer hours. The deadline was nearing, and we all felt the pressure. We started talking about plan B if we couldn't leave by May 6, as we had hoped.

By the first of May it was obvious we weren't leaving by May 6. We hadn't even had our first flight yet, and we still wanted to put as many hours on her after the first flight as possible before we headed east. We started making a list of tasks that were mandatory to complete before the first flight and those that could wait. We even started thinking of things that didn't need to be done at all so that our efforts could focus on the essentials.

Nobody kept a log of what was done every day—we were too busy—but somehow everything got done. We started shipping the parts that we were still buying overnight or second-day air so they would get to us without delay. It's hard to know what everyone was thinking at the time, but volunteers would come up to me during those few weeks and ask if I thought we would make it. My usual answer, and the truth, was that we might pull it off if we kept working and maybe got a little lucky. If we quit, we surely would fail.

The weeks before the first flight were a whirlwind of activity. It's impossible to list all the things that got done between March 1 and the first flight on May 12. However, the following big jobs were completed during that period:

March 2 – The instrument panel was completely empty but had been stripped and repainted, the control yokes were being refinished, and the cockpit seats were out being restored.

March 8 – Installed most of the overhauled round gauges in the instrument panel, along with the donated GPS Nav/Com units.

March 22 – Cockpit seats were upholstered.

March 23 – Both engines, recently back from overhaul, were installed.

March 24 – Two restored fuel tanks were installed.

March 25 – Dick purchased the Western DC-3 in Arkansas.

March 29 – New cabin insulation was installed.

March 31 – Started building the new instrument wiring harnesses.

April 9 – Both overhauled propellers were installed.

April 10 –Engines were cranked and started for the first time.

April 16 – The plane was jacked off the ground for the first cycling of the landing gear.

April 18 – The instrument panel was powered up for the first time.

April 23 – Wheels and brakes were removed and inspected.

April 27 – Engines were run periodically from this time on.

April 29 – The new fabric cargo liner was installed.

May 1 – The brake bladder on the right wheel was replaced.

May 3 – The Western DC-3 arrived in Missoula.

May 10 – The new anchor cable was completed and installed.

May 11 – Send-off gala.

May 12 – First flight.

May 14 – Practice jumper drop at Plains, Montana.

May 16 – The tail was lifted to calibrate attitude instruments.

May 16-18 – Poor weather prevented departure.

May 16-19 – Necessary work for IFR capability was completed.

May 16-19 – Training by Al Charters in jump procedures and pilot-jumpmaster communication.

In addition to these major milestones, there were a thousand small things attended to by dozens of volunteers. The accomplishments of the last forty-five days before our first flight would be a significant achievement for any aircraft maintenance department, but considering we were a group of volunteers with relatively little experience, it was truly impressive.

Once we realized we would not depart on May 6 as hoped, we planned a major send-off gala and fundraiser for May 11 at the museum. It was a huge effort, planned and organized by Kathy Ogren, Barbara Komberec, Eric, Tia, Mike and Kathryn Anderson, and others. By this time, the local interest was at a high, and we sold over 600 tickets to the event. The Ed Norton Big Band played 1940s dance tunes, and many people came in period dress.

We auctioned items to raise money, had a delicious dinner, recognized volunteers and crew, honored our veterans, and generally had a fabulous evening. Many people danced the night away. It was a beautiful spring night, and *Miss Montana* was parked just outside the hangar, behind the big band, offering a surreal image as the light reflected off her shiny skin. If you closed your eyes, it was easy to imagine being back in 1944.

Most of us working on the plane did not work much on the gala. The day before, we had started discussing the possibility of making the first flight the afternoon before the gala, which would have been a pretty dramatic event and given us something big to celebrate at the party. We talked about what needed to be done, who the pilots for the first flight would be, and whether it *should* be done.

One of the things that we did well during the project was group decision-making. This was the first instance where it was put to use. There were three individuals with different perspectives who all had to agree on major decisions such as this one. They were: 1) the plane owner – represented by Dick and Eric Komberec on the museum board, 2) the plane mechanics represented by Jeff and Randy, and 3) the pilots, Frank Moss and Jeff Whitesell. Frank had been in town for a week or more training the PICs and SICs and was even training on the day of the gala. Randy and Eric gave a thumbs-up for a flight that day. Since Frank was out flying, we all agreed to wait until he returned to see if he felt up to it. Other factors were the flurry of activity getting ready for the gala, guests starting to show up, and it was very warm outside. Everyone was admittedly tired but excited to see her lift off at last.

When Frank returned from his last flight, we huddled. Frank and Dick both vetoed a first flight that day. There were too many risk factors, everyone was tired, and it felt like we were in a hurry. It was a good decision made the right way. So we all resolved to enjoy the gala and look forward to the morrow when we thought a first flight could finally happen.

Sunday morning dawned clear and cool, and we arrived at the museum to do final preparations for the first flight. We ran the engines twice, tweaked some settings, and tried to think of reasons *not* to fly. There were none.

CBS had hired Missoula filmmaker Eric Ristau to capture the first flight when it happened. We had one false start the day before, when we told him that it might happen but then it was canceled. We contacted Eric again and told him it was a go.

About five thirty p.m. on May 12, with Jeff in the left seat, Frank in the right seat, and Randy in the jump seat, the engines were started and she taxied out to the runway. Minuteman Aviation donated a fast helicopter with videographer Damon Ristau aboard that hovered behind and alongside her to capture the magic moment, along with four other cameras on the ground. Mike Mamuzich was the helicopter pilot and Art Dykstra was the copilot. Many of us were monitoring the tower and ground radio frequencies and were pleased to hear Frank ask the tower if, instead of N24320, he could use the call sign "Miss Montana" from then on. It was approved.

When the moment finally came, all the anticipation, hopes, and fears of the volunteers, pilots, jumpers, and spectators who were watching came together as Jeff applied power and she started rolling down the runway. It was a magic moment to see air beneath her wheels for the first time. Many tears were shed by the people who had worked so hard for so long. We will never forget that moment.

The flight lasted about twenty minutes as they made several turns around the valley. We heard from many people asking if it had finally happened. With the many training flights of the Western DC-3 in the days before, the public wasn't sure which DC-3 they were seeing until they noticed the bright shiny skin of N24320 glint in the late afternoon light. The weather was perfect, the lighting was perfect, and the flight was perfect. The crew landed flawlessly and taxied back to the hangar to a celebrating crowd.

Eric Ristau later said that the footage they captured was perhaps the best he had ever shot. There are clips of that flight in the *CBS Sunday Morning* story. It was truly incredible quality and lighting, and the angles they captured couldn't have been any better.

After the first flight, we thought we might soon be on our way. But first, we had other business.

26

Practice Jump at Plains, Montana

OUR FIRST FLIGHT was in the books, and things were looking up, but we needed additional flying time to make sure everything on the airplane was behaving properly. On Monday, May 13, we made two short flights, breaking in the engines and looking for "squawks," or problems that needed to be fixed. There were none.

Another ramification of our being so late to get *Miss Montana* airborne was the currency of our jumpers. The Daks Over Normandy organizers in Europe required that every paratrooper have a currency jump with a round parachute within six months of the June 5 jump into Normandy. Almost none of our jumpers had met this requirement. Some of them, mainly the active smokejumpers who lived outside of Missoula, arranged to make their currency jump where they could, but seven of them were counting on us. Moreover, none of us on The Crew, except Art, had ever dropped parachutists from any airplane. The practice would be important for all of us. By this late date we were accustomed to getting everything done "just in time."

Since August of 2018, all our jumpers had been accumulating the correct type of World War II replica uniforms and parachute equipment at significant personal expense and making arrangements to get a currency jump on that parachute. For the currently active or retired smokejumpers on the aircraft, this was a particular challenge because the Daks Over Normandy organizers had required that the parachute systems needed to be military style and use canopies that were olive-drab green, just like in 1944. This type of system was new to most of the smokejumpers. For the former military jumpers, they were familiar with the required canopy types, but it had been twenty to twenty-five years since they had last jumped with one.

All the while that we had been fighting to get *Miss Montana* in the air, Al Charters had been trying to find a suitable place to do a practice jump. He evaluated several of the small, local airfields within an hour's flight time of Missoula. The restoration effort—and our many delays—were by then well known around Montana. Everywhere Al went he was welcomed with pledges to "do whatever it took" to help out. However, the grassy areas alongside all the runways were too small for parachutists to land on. As time was starting to become a factor, Al shared what he had learned with volunteer John Haines.

John Haines, a native of Plains, Montana, got the idea to make the jump over his hometown, a short distance northwest of Missoula. John and Al drove to Plains to check in with the local airfield manager and see if the grassy area was suitable for a practice jump. Once again, the spot on the airport was too small, with too many hazards for parachutists.

So, John went to work. Being a local boy, he contacted nearby ranchers John and Dacy Holland, who owned a large parcel of land very close to the airfield. It looked ideal at 600 acres of alfalfa with no fences—a dangerous feature when descending under a parachute. It didn't hurt that the local hospital was only one block away, the local cemetery was on the other side, and the nearest bar was only two blocks away—perfect attributes for parachute operations.

Within the hour, John had convened a "Montana board meeting" with John Holland consisting of three pickup trucks pulled together nose to nose at a rural intersection. Everyone stood in a circle in the rain. John and Al made the request on behalf of the museum and the *Miss Montana* effort, but no coaxing was necessary.

John Holland granted permission after listening for about thirty seconds. The agreement was sealed with a handshake, no paperwork required. All they wanted was a phone call the day before so the local paper could be there and he could move his cows off the field.

So, with barely two hours of flight time on our newly restored airplane, seven jumpers loaded onto *Miss Montana* on Tuesday, May 14, and set course for Plains, Montana. Eric, Tia, Nico, and I boarded Mark Bretz's helicopter to follow *Miss Montana* and observe the jump. Art Dykstra was the pilot on *Miss Montana*, and Jeff Whitesell was the copilot. Mike Anderson was an observer on *Miss Montana* since he had static-line parachute experience in the U.S. Army Special Forces. Randy and Crystal were assigned to monitor static lines and would haul in deployment bags after the jumps. On board *Miss Montana* as jumpers were Al Charters, Bryan M., Sarah M., Jason Junes, Skid Wolferman, Kim Maynard, and Amanda Holt.

Miss Montana took off about nine thirty a.m. and arrived over Plains, Montana, about forty-five minutes later. Art made two passes over the drop zone to get the proper lineup, and jumpmasters Al and Bryan gauged the winds. The first jump was to be from 1,000 feet above the ground for Kim Maynard and Amanda Holt with round chutes. Kim and Amanda would be the first parachutists to jump from *Miss Montana* in the twenty-first century and the first smoke-jumpers to go out her door in at least forty-five years. It was a beautiful spring day, winds were light, and spirits were high.

While the aircraft was inbound from Missoula, our safety representative on the ground was busy. Shannon O'Keefe, our ground liaison and safety officer for the jump, was a jump colleague and *Miss Montana* supporter who had driven four hours to be there. His specified job was to make sure wind conditions were within limits and that there were no dangers to jumpers on the ground. Nobody had envisioned that he would also be the official "question answerer" for the whole jump event. He and John Haines had to field every question from every five-year-old about why the sky was blue and from every old-timer who wanted to share a war story about his time in

120

the service. Despite the well-intended distractions, Shannon texted the words Al needed to hear as he made the first orbit overhead, "Clear to drop!"

On the third pass over the drop zone, Kim jumped, followed by Amanda. We could see from the helicopter that their canopies opened properly. As they floated gently to the ground, they could hear cheering from the Plains school that was right next door. Small humans were in the schoolyard watching the spectacle. The school superintendent had heard about the jump and let school out so all the children could watch the historic event. The children started chanting, "USA! USA!" and then spontaneously began singing "The Star-Spangled Banner" as Kim and Amanda maneuvered to the ground. After they landed, children ran out into the field to welcome them. The entire population of Plains seemed to be watching from nearby. Ranch trucks, the town's fire engine, and rows of families in lawn chairs lined the drop zone—all waving American flags and blowing their vehicle horns. It was a Norman Rockwell moment, not to be forgotten.

After Randy and Crystal pulled the first two deployment bags back into the aircraft, Sarah, followed by Jason Junes, made the second jump. Skid Wolferman, who had recently retired from a long smokejumping career, was honored with a solo jump on the third and final pass. From the helicopter we could see that all the chutes had opened and the five jumpers were safely on the ground. Then, *Miss Montana* climbed to 3,000 feet above the ground, and Al and Bryan jumped out with square, free-fall parachutes. Soon, all seven jumpers were safely on the ground with big smiles and *Miss Montana* circled to land at the Plains airport a short distance away.

There were additional training objectives that day beyond getting the jumpers current with their parachutes. While Art was an old smokejumper pilot, he had never used military-style procedures, such as would be used in England and Normandy. The rest of The Crew got their first taste of what parachute operations entailed, including the timing sequence, communication with the jump master, and the use of the jump lights next to the door.

Randy and Crystal were performing additional duties they had never seen before—controlling parachutists' static lines inside the aircraft as jumpers leaped from the door, as well as hauling parachute deployment bags back into the aircraft after the jumpers had jumped. This was valuable experience for them. Over Normandy, they would have to wrestle as many as ten deployment bags at once back into the airplane each pass.

The new anchor line had been fabricated and installed only two days before. It worked perfectly. The next time it would be used would be on June 5 over Normandy.

Once the aircraft was on the ground at Plains, it seemed like the entire town turned out to welcome us at the airport and to see *Miss Montana* up close. They brought doughnuts (cleaning out the local doughnut shop) and coffee, and a local retired smokejumper even brought some smokejumper-labeled beer from 1984. Businesses in town closed for a few hours so they could come to the airport. The Plains newspaper interviewed jumpers and The Crew. It was a festive event and a welcome relief to have successfully pulled it off after so many months of frustration and delays. With the practice jump complete, The Crew started packing bags and looking at a date for departure.

After the practice jump at Plains: (L-R) Amanda, Al, Kim, Shannon, Sarah, Bryan, Skid, Jason (photo by Natalie Abrams)

27

More Delays

NOT SO FAST. We were hoping to take off by Thursday or Friday, May 16 or 17, but once again our plans were spoiled. It was cold and rainy with low overcast clouds. The plane could fly in *some* foul weather, but we weren't about to do much of that until we had quite a few more hours on her—and on us. Therefore, we waited, and not very patiently. As often happens when things don't go according to plan, those few days of delay worked out for the best. The most important reason was that we corrected some miscommunication about the instrument flying capabilities of *Miss Montana*.

From my earliest communications with the D-Day Squadron and in all the written information that had been provided to us, we were told that all our flights would be in daytime VFR conditions. VFR stands for Visual Flight Rules and means that you must avoid entering clouds and maintain visual separation from terrain and other aircraft. It's the most basic type of flying. IFR stands for Instrument Flight Rules, which apply when you fly in clouds solely with reference to instruments—because you can see nothing outside the windows. To legally fly IFR, the aircraft must have the proper instruments and the pilots must be current with training. All IFR flight must be conducted on an IFR flight plan filed with air traffic control; ATC monitors your location and, where radar is available, they see you on their monitors for the entire flight.

We had equipped her with the necessary instruments but, because we had been told we would only be flying VFR, we had not gone through the necessary testing and paperwork to be able to legally fly IFR. We were confident that we could do so in an emergency, but we would not do it otherwise. All our pilots were instrument rated, current, and very capable of flying IFR.

At the beginning of this last delay, we had time to go over many details again. One of those things was paperwork we would need for the journey. Jeff asked one day if we had all our IFR certification paperwork in order. My answer was no, we didn't, because the D-Day Squadron had told us we would only be flying in daytime VFR conditions. Jeff hit the roof. He said he refused to fly over the North Atlantic if we weren't equipped and legal to fly IFR. The self-described grouch was right. Off we went to get it done.

The first thing was to huddle with Jon Paul and find out what remained for us to do to get legal for IFR. The list was not too bad and involved only some additional testing on the airplane, calibrating the compass readings on the instruments, and acquiring some additional paperwork on our instrument installations.

Then I called Eric Zipkin. I asked him how many of the D-Day Squadron planes were legal for IFR. He answered, "All of them." Boy, did I ever feel stupid. Then why had he told us from the beginning that we would only be flying daytime VFR? He said, "Weeelll, they would only *plan* to fly daytime VFR, but everyone knew that we would certainly *need* to fly in IFR conditions to make the crossing." Yikes, we had a lot to do before we could leave.

Thanks to Jon Paul and everyone pitching in, along with some help from the *Placid Lassie* maintenance folks on some paperwork, we got it done. When the time finally came to depart on May 19, we were legal and ready to fly IFR if needed. And it certainly was needed.

By Saturday evening, May 18, the weather forecast indicated the conditions would finally be good enough for us to depart the following morning. The word went out to our many supporters and the media. The Crew was packed and ready to go.

28

The Journey Begins

Life without risks is not worth living.
                                                    – Charles Lindbergh

ON MAY 19, we made a short test flight in the morning to check everything one more time, then we assembled to say our final good-byes on the ramp outside the museum. Wives, children, jumpers, volunteers, and supporters were all there on this cold, partly cloudy day. When we finally ran out of things to do, stuff to pack, and good-byes to say, we loaded up, started those beautiful Pratt & Whitney engines, and took off just before eleven a.m. There were six of us on board: Eric, Jeff, Nico, Randy, Crystal, and me.

At the beginning of the D-Day invasion in 1944, General Dwight Eisenhower, Supreme Commander of the Allied Expeditionary Force, issued his iconic order of the day. It began:

> "You are about to embark upon the Great Crusade toward which we have striven these many months. The eyes of the world are upon you. The hopes and prayers of liberty-loving people everywhere march with you."[18]

It was impossible not to think of the opening words of Eisenhower's order the moment when *Miss Montana* broke her bonds with earth and headed east on her epic voyage. A copy of Eisenhower's order was on board for the entire trip.

Eric flew the first leg with Nico as copilot. While the weather was VFR, there were still plenty of clouds to avoid and it was very cold in the cabin. After some fiddling, Randy got the heater working a little better, but that first leg may have been the coldest of the entire trip.

Kathy Ogren had thoughtfully bought six battery-powered heated vests for the entire crew because she was concerned we were going to freeze to death flying over the North Atlantic. None of us knew what to expect in a plane that we hadn't flown before, or even what the temperatures would be on our route. When Crystal told us about the heated vests, I made a wisecrack about those only being for sissies and that I would be plenty warm with the multiple layers and socks I had on. I was tough, a seasoned big-game hunter, and cold weather wasn't new to me.

About an hour into our first leg, the first person to pull out a vest, figure out how to turn it on, and put it on…was me. It was wonderful, and I wrote Kathy a text to thank her. Those vests were amazing, and I wore mine for much of the trip across the pond. Sooner or later, most of us discovered the wonders of battery-powered heat. Mine still gets used from time to time. What a sissy.

We originally planned to fly from Missoula to Rapid City, South Dakota. The overall plan was for us to cross the U.S. to Oxford in a meandering path, stopping at FBOs that sold Phillips 66 products. Tia had helped us get Phillips 66 as a sponsor, and we proudly displayed their logo on our tail. They offered to provide fuel and oil to get us to the East Coast so we wanted to stop where we could get their gas. Rapid City was roughly on our way and had a Phillips 66 FBO. However, Rapid City was badly weathered-in that day, so we called an audible and decided to stop for fuel at Miles City, Montana, instead. On our way to Miles City we diverted slightly to fly directly over Mann Gulch, which more than a few of those following our progress noticed.

There was another reason for taking the long route across the

U.S. When we left Missoula, we had only about six hours on our new engines, propellers…and crew. Statistically, machines fail at a higher rate when they are new—a phenomenon called infant mortality. Some thought we were crazy to embark on such an ambitious voyage with so little time on the airplane and crew, but we were only a little crazy. We took the longer path to Oxford to put more time on the plane while over friendly territory; if something broke while in the U.S., our options for getting parts and help would be much better.

The stop in Miles City after nearly three hours of flight was only a little over an hour but memorable. As at most of our stops, we were greeted by people who had been following our odyssey and cheering us on during the restoration. In Miles City, the local newspaper and radio showed up and interviewed us. We had many miles to go before we slept, so we got fuel and headed to Wichita, Kansas, where we planned to spend the night. We soon said goodbye to Montana, not to return for thirty-six days.

It was about a four-hour flight to Wichita from Miles City. Jeff took the left seat as PIC, and Randy flew in the right. We knew we would be arriving close to dark, but the weather was good and everything was running fine. We landed in Wichita about 7:45 p.m. and were welcomed by the Yingling Aviation FBO. They kindly put *Miss Montana* in a hangar and gave us a short ride to the hotel nearby. We all noticed that the Wichita airport is named after a fairly famous Kansas native, Dwight D. Eisenhower. We were back in my home state and had successfully finished our first day.

We had been keeping track of the rest of the D-Day Squadron over the last few weeks before our departure. Other planes had already started arriving in Oxford on May 12, the day of our first flight. Six of them had assembled in Frederick, Maryland, for the AOPA anniversary flights on May 10 and 11. *Clipper Tabitha May* had left Virginia on May 14 and was leading the way across the Atlantic alone. By May 17, nine D-Day Squadron planes had met in Oxford and conducted flight training, survival training, and a formation flight around New York City. These nine included *Placid Lassie, "That's All, Brother," D-Day Doll, Flabob Express, Virginia Ann, Betsy's Biscuit Bomber, Spirit of Benovia, Miss Virginia*, and *Pan Am. Liberty* arrived at Oxford on the afternoon of May 19. Those ten planes started the Atlantic crossing on the day we left Missoula. On May 19 we were well behind the eleven planes ahead of us, but there were still three behind us—*Hap-enstance*, N18121, and *Rendezvous With Destiny*.

(L-R) Bryan, Nico (in door), Jeff, Crystal, Randy, Eric before departing Missoula (photo by Natalie Abrams)

SUPREME HEADQUARTERS
ALLIED EXPEDITIONARY FORCE

Soldiers, Sailors and Airmen of the Allied Expeditionary Force!

You are about to embark upon the Great Crusade, toward which we have striven these many months.   The eyes of the world are upon you. The hopes and prayers of liberty-loving people everywhere march with you. In company with our brave Allies and brothers-in-arms on other Fronts, you will bring about the destruction of the German war machine, the elimination of Nazi tyranny over the oppressed peoples of Europe, and security for ourselves in a free world.

Your task will not be an easy one.   Your enemy is well trained, well equipped and battle-hardened.   He will fight savagely.

But this is the year 1944 ! Much has happened since the Nazi triumphs of 1940-41. The United Nations have inflicted upon the Germans great defeats, in open battle, man-to-man.   Our air offensive has seriously reduced their strength in the air and their capacity to wage war on the ground.   Our Home Fronts have given us an overwhelming superiority in weapons and munitions of war, and placed at our disposal great reserves of trained fighting men.   The tide has turned ! The free men of the world are marching together to Victory !

I have full confidence in your courage, devotion to duty and skill in battle.   We will accept nothing less than full Victory !

Good Luck !   And let us all beseech the blessing of Almighty God upon this great and noble undertaking.

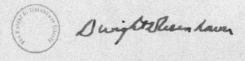

Eisenhower's Order of the Day

29

Wichita to Oxford

AVIATION PIONEER AND record-setting pilot Robert Buck flew all over the world learning about weather and how to predict and avoid it. He authored several authoritative books on aviation and weather. After flying in over a hundred countries, he concluded that the worst weather in the world regularly happens between Kansas City and New York.[19] This was the exact airspace we would be flying through on May 20. Fortunately, the en-route weather was quite nice, but we almost didn't get out before a massive storm cell descended on Wichita.

We awoke early on May 20 and took our time getting ready until one of us looked at the weather. There was a massive storm headed our way, and it was less than an hour away. If we got stuck in that storm, we could be delayed a few days, or the airplane could be damaged. It was a scramble to get to the FBO, get fuel, and head out. We had to do an interview with local media while we were getting fueled and preflighted the airplane, but we made haste and finally launched about eight thirty a.m. The storm hit Eisenhower airport about twenty minutes after we left, and we could feel the winds picking up as we climbed out to the southeast. We read later that the storm spawned several tornadoes and resulted in record flooding. It was a good time to leave Kansas behind.

The flight from Wichita to Rogers, Arkansas was a bit under

an hour and was uneventful—except for a bonehead move by me. As you have seen, the job of the copilot is important. In fact, if you watch a takeoff in a DC-3, you will notice that the pilot appears to do very little, while the copilot is busy moving levers, reading checklists, and waving his hands. As described in the chapter on copilots, despite having an important job, it is fairly easy to be a copilot—at least, if you have a competent captain who keeps you out of trouble. The most hectic moments are on takeoff and climb out.

Raising the gear is somewhat complicated but easily memorized and rehearsed. By this time, I had done it three or four times. It requires moving two different levers in a specific order. It's as easy as A, then B, then C. When we took off from Wichita and Nico called, "Gear up!" I enthusiastically executed A, B, then C…then started to do D, which is done only when *lowering* the gear. Oops. Nico caught my hand and stopped me, but nobody knew if what I had done would prevent us from lowering the gear. I felt terrible. I had visions of landing with our gear up at Rogers and having the whole bloody trip come to a premature and tragic end because of me.

Nico and everyone else handled it like the professionals they are. It probably spooked them a bit, as well, but they didn't beat me up. It had the potential to prevent us from lowering and locking the gear at the next landing. We decided that we wouldn't try to check it or troubleshoot it until arriving at Rogers. Fortunately, it turned out that Nico had stopped me just in time and no harm was done. My first lesson: it is almost never necessary to hurry, and from then on, I talked through each step of raising and lowering the gear and waited for concurrence from the left seat before executing.

Eric noticed that Bartlesville, Oklahoma, the headquarters for Phillips 66 was not far off our planned route to Rogers, Arkansas, so we took a heading for Bartlesville. Arriving over Bartlesville, we did two big circles over the Phillips headquarters. We heard later that the folks at Phillips saw us and cheered us on. From there, it was a short trip to Rogers, Arkansas for more gas.

After a brief stop in Rogers and more interviews with local

media, we launched for Tri-Cities, Tennessee. Nico flew this four-and-a-half-hour leg, with Jeff in the right seat. The stop at Tri Cities was uneventful except that a gorgeous news reporter showed up and we all wanted to be interviewed. Nico got the honors. We took on more Phillips gas and headed for Oxford.

Jeff took this final leg of the day, with Randy riding shotgun. We knew we would be getting into Oxford near dark, so we tried to make haste. We were blessed with screaming tailwinds most of the way, pushing us along the ground at speeds in excess of 215 knots, so we made record time. This was the longest day of our trip so far, totaling a little more than eight hours flight time, until our return from Greenland.

As we passed to the west of Washington, D.C., ATC advised another plane to level off in their climb because there was a DC-3 in front of them. That pilot acknowledged and repeated the command. Then there was a brief pause and the pilot said, "Did you just say a DC-3?"

We landed about eight thirty p.m. local time at Oxford on that Monday night, put the airplane to bed, and headed for the hotel. We were the only DC-3 on the ramp at Oxford that night. Nine other planes in the D-Day Squadron had departed Oxford over the previous two days after a week or more of survival training, formation practice, and a Hudson River flight. Those nine were scattered between Goose Bay and Iceland. *Clipper Tabitha May* had led the way and was already in Scotland. *Miss Montana* missed all that fun, but we enjoyed traveling alone and hustling to catch up.

30

Hudson River & Lady Liberty Flight

OVER DINNER MONDAY night, we discussed plans for the next day. We knew that Nico had to leave us to get back to his day job and that Art would be joining us. We would be stuck in Oxford until at least May 22. We started discussing what we wanted and needed to do while waiting for Art. We had to pick up some oil from Eric Zipkin's company that had been set aside for us. We also had some maintenance checks to do while we were in a place where we could help if needed. Beyond that, we would only be saying goodbye to Nico.

There is a little-known flight that anyone can make around New York City. It is amazing that it is still possible in a post-9/11 world. With no prior permission or advance notice, you can fly down the west shore of the Hudson River, starting at the George Washington Bridge, follow the New Jersey shoreline, turn around the Statue of Liberty, and then return on the Manhattan shore back to the north.

I had made this flight a few years before in my own plane, so I brought it up and said it would be memorable if we could fit it in. The other nine planes in the D-Day Squadron had made the flight together the week before, but we had missed it. Nico's eyes lit up, and he asked more about it. After I described what we could do, he said if he could fly that flight, he would delay his departure. It was decided. Nico would fly as PIC, and I would fly right seat and handle the radios. It would be a memorable flight in several ways, some of which we didn't expect.

I had kept in touch with Richard Schlesinger and producer Alan Golds with CBS after leaving Missoula and had told them we planned to stop in Oxford, Connecticut. They had followed our progress and expressed an interest in coming to see us that Tuesday at Oxford. We invited them to join us on the Hudson River flight, and they were interested.

The weather on Tuesday was blustery, with winds reaching twenty knots or so, but with beautiful clear skies. We probably wouldn't have flown that day except that it was our only opportunity to make this incredible flight. Nico said he was up for it, so we preflighted the airplane and waited for CBS to arrive. They arrived midmorning and shot some video, then we all loaded up for the flight. All six of our crew were on board, plus Richard and Alan from CBS and two of their guys running cameras and sound.

We were also able to arrange for a photo ship flown by a David Tuttle, a friend of Randy's, who happened to live nearby and was available to fly on our wing in his Lake Amphibian plane. We were hoping to get some memorable video and photos from the Lake, but it was going to be a bit dicey; the Lake's top speed is about 100 knots. That's slow for a DC-3 to fly, especially in windy conditions, but we resolved to give it a go. The Lake soon arrived, we briefed our route and procedures, and the Lake took off to get there ahead of us.

We took off about ten a.m., with Richard Schlesinger in the jump seat, and headed south toward New York. It was only about a twenty-minute flight to the starting point of the Hudson River Exclusion route. We joined up with the Lake and pulled the power back to keep from outrunning him.

The flight is a very specific route, with mandatory reporting of your altitude and location at several different points and strictly maintaining an altitude between 1,000 and 1,300 feet. It is some of the busiest airspace in the world. There are dozens of helicopters flying below 1,000 feet and big planes from LaGuardia, JFK, Teterboro, and Newark inhabiting the airspace above 1,300 feet. Following the rules is important in that neighborhood.

We were getting bounced around from the very start due to gusty winds, and Nico was constantly wrestling the plane to keep it straight and level. It was a lot of work. My job was to look good, enjoy the incredible views, and make the radio calls. The cockpit is probably the most comfortable place to be in rough air, so even though we could tell it was rough, we didn't know exactly how rough it was until later.

We joined up with the Tuttle's Lake, entered the route from the north, and headed down the Jersey shoreline, reporting on the radios as required and trying to stay slow enough to allow the Lake to keep up. As we approached the Statue of Liberty, I reported on the radio, "Inbound for the Lady," and we descended to about 700 feet, which is allowed around the statue.

As we started orbiting the Statue of Liberty, Nico announced that this was "pretty freakin' awesome" to be flying a seventy-five-year-old DC-3 around the Statue of Liberty on the eleventh anniversary of his naturalization as a United States citizen. None of us had any idea until that moment, but it explained his enthusiasm to make the flight. It was a poignant moment and even more fun than usual to fly with Nico on that day.

After circling the Lady, humming the tune to "New York, New York," we turned northwest and climbed to 1,200 feet before we approached the NYC shoreline. This is one of the most amazing parts of the flight. You get to fly directly by the World Trade Center site and look down into those marvelous fountains that mark the locations of the Twin Towers. You can see the new Freedom Tower and are well below the top of it, which rises to 1,776 feet at the top of the spire. When flying along the waterline you are less than 400 yards from the tower, so close that you can't capture it all in one photo. We passed it in a few moments, continued north to the breaking off point of the route, then headed back to Oxford.

We hadn't heard any commotion from the rear, and Richard seemed to be enjoying himself in the jump seat, but it got ugly back there. Even seasoned flyers like Eric and Randy were getting uncomfortable and the CBS camera guys had a trash can handy. We made quick time back to Oxford, expecting a "sporty" landing in the gusty winds.

This was one of the most impressive landings anyone made on the trip, and maybe under the most challenging conditions. The winds were over twenty knots, almost directly crosswind to the runway, and gusting. We were getting tossed around as we came down the final approach. Nico is a smart and cautious pilot, so he would not have tried it if he wasn't confident he could make it, but Eric came up to check on him to make sure he could land it. Nico assured him he would abort if he didn't like anything as we came in to land. It was a big deal for Eric to trust Nico with this landing.

Nico was probably the best pilot to land the plane that day. We were getting bounced all around and he was constantly working the controls until we touched down with one squeak from the upwind main tire followed soon by another squeak from the downwind one. That is how it is done, and he made it look much easier than it was. I mostly just sat there and learned.

After parking and unloading everyone, we visited with CBS a while longer, then said goodbye to Nico as he made for the commercial airport. We didn't know if he would be able to rejoin us, but we hoped he would and told him so. When Nico reached the airport, he met Art, gave him the car, and Art soon joined us at Oxford. It had been a memorable day, and we were all glad we had made it happen. We were soon six again, and about to leave friendly territory.

31

Oxford to Presque Isle

THE DAY AFTER the Hudson River and Statue of Liberty flight, we saddled up to head north. This would be the first real leg on our route to Duxford, even though we would still be in the U.S. The flight from Oxford to Presque Isle, Maine, was 440 miles and a little over three hours. Presque Isle is significant because it was the original starting point of the Blue Spruce transatlantic air ferry route used extensively in World War II and would mark the official jumping-off point of our oceanic crossing. With Art replacing Nico on the crew, we launched for Presque Isle at about eleven a.m. Eastern and landed at Presque Isle at about 2:15 p.m. We were several days behind the gaggle of D-Day Squadron planes, so we were not expecting the same kind of welcome they had received. The news reports said at least a thousand people showed up at Presque Isle to greet the nine planes ahead of us.

Shortly after landing at Presque Isle and setting chocks, a long black limousine pulled up next to the plane. We weren't expecting adoring crowds, but we certainly weren't expecting a limo. The limo was owned by Craig Green, an enthusiastic city councilman and local all-around good guy. Craig doesn't work for the Chamber of Commerce, but he should. He was the most friendly, helpful, and energetic person we met on the entire trip.

Craig welcomed us on behalf of Presque Isle and offered to

drive us to lunch and our hotel, where he had already made reservations. It was the Northeastland Hotel, a nice hotel owned by the city, and we were glad to patronize it. We gratefully accepted and piled in. After delivering us to our hotel, he offered to take us to dinner.

However, Randy decided this would be a good time to do a thorough inspection of the plane, as there would be fewer options for help and support after leaving Presque Isle. So Craig took us back out to the airport in the limo. We pulled the engine cowlings and did a scheduled maintenance inspection, anticipating our next flight to Goose Bay and beyond. Jeff, Randy, and Crystal did most of the work while the rest of us pitched in as needed.

Craig didn't want to leave, so he stayed around and watched the work. Jeff asked Craig to write down a bunch of odds and ends that he wanted to buy from local hardware and automotive stores in the morning. By the time we finished, it was about eight thirty p.m. and nearly dark. We asked Craig about dinner options. He said there was a craft brewery and restaurant nearby, but it might be closed. He got on the phone and soon informed us that the owner offered to stay open late just for us. Outstanding.

Craig loaded us all in his limo and took us to dinner at the Northern Maine Brewing Company, where they took excellent care of us, including tasty local beer and fine food. Craig introduced all of us to fiddleheads, a local wild fern that is served steamed or raw. New to all of us, they were excellent. He deposited us at our hotel and told us he would pick us up for breakfast in the morning.

We awoke at a civilized hour, and Craig met us in the lobby for breakfast. Craig kept trying to pay for lunch, dinner, and breakfast, but we couldn't let him after all the hospitality he had offered. We enjoyed a leisurely breakfast and discussed our plans for getting the supplies Jeff wanted.

Except…Craig had already visited half a dozen different stores before breakfast and bought everything on our list. We couldn't believe it, and we unanimously agreed that Presque Isle was the most hospitable stop on our trip thus far, almost exclusively due to the efforts of Craig Green. A return to Presque Isle is on my list.

After breakfast we couldn't refuse a tour of Presque Isle in the limo. Craig took us to the museum at the airport that told the story of Presque Isle and the Blue Spruce route, but not before we went to city hall, where we were welcomed by the mayor.

When Craig delivered us back to the airport, he had one more surprise for us. He had brought us a box of a dozen whoopie pies, a local delicacy somewhat like a MoonPie. A whoopie pie is a sandwich made from two thin chocolate "buns" with delicious cream in the middle. And they are not small. Being the polite people that we are, we graciously thanked Craig for the gift and loaded up for our next leg. The Crew members are all fairly health conscious, and we promised each other that we would abstain from such unhealthy, yet sinful delights. By the time we reached England, they were gone.

As if the hospitality could get any better in Presque Isle, local photographer Paul Cyr came to the airport before daylight the morning of our departure and captured stunning images of *Miss Montana* in the rising sunlight. He also took pictures of the plane as we started engines and took off. Paul's work is spectacular, and he graciously gave us high resolution files of his images. There are some very nice people in Presque Isle, Maine.

We launched from Presque Isle at about one p.m. Eastern and headed for Goose Bay. The real fun was about to begin.

32

Presque Isle to Goose Bay

THE FLIGHT FROM Presque Isle was significant for two reasons. About ten miles from Presque Isle, we left U.S. airspace. We all realized that we had gone international, and the next 500 nautical miles were over very remote terrain. And...we were now officially on the Blue Spruce route upon which our aviation forefathers had flown before us.

We crossed parts of the Canadian provinces of New Brunswick and Quebec before entering Labrador, where Goose Bay is located. A little over an hour into the flight, we started across the Gulf of St. Lawrence, the first sizable body of water we would cross. It was a good initiation. There are some big lakes in Montana, but nothing that big. It was about half an hour across the gulf, and we got a small taste of the long over-water legs to come.

The flight was uneventful, and we landed at Goose Bay at about five thirty ADT. Another thing to learn was that there was a time zone called Atlantic Daylight Time. It's one hour east of the Eastern Daylight Time zone.

Goose Bay is an interesting place. It's historic for many reasons. It was on the Blue Spruce route, and thousands of planes passed through Goose Bay to and from the war in Europe. For many years it was a joint U.S. Air Force/Canadian Air Force base, and during the Cold War was a base for the U.S. Strategic Air Command. During the chaos of September 11, 2001, several planes landed there when the United States closed its airspace, and the 700 passengers were welcomed by local military and civilian residents. A glance at a map tells you how remote it is. Goose Bay is a long way from anywhere—which is sort of the point.

Like many arctic outposts, Goose Bay has a certain feel: austere and functional. The buildings are designed to withstand extreme cold, frost heaves, and strong winds. You don't see a lot of attention to architectural nuance—certainly no art deco or efforts at beautification. There's a feeling of transience, perhaps because few people probably live there for very long. It feels like everything is just good enough. Located strategically on the way across the North Atlantic, it has been an outpost for defense, a waypoint on the Atlantic crossing, and a base for indigenous people in the area.

For us, there wasn't much to see or do there. We figured out soon after landing that we didn't want to spend any more time there than necessary.

The first challenge was finding a decent meal. It looked like there were about five restaurants within walking distance where we could expect to get a good meal. We didn't have a car, so we had to walk if we wanted chow. We settled on Trappers Cabin, which was a short ten-minute walk from the Hotel North, where we were staying. At first glance it looked like a typical bar and grill. On perusing the menu, we found good-looking options for carnivores like us: chicken and ribeye steaks. But there was a catch. You had to cook the meat yourselves. Well, all right, we could manage that. So we placed the order and cooked the meat ourselves over their dedicated customer-operated griddle. It was perfectly fine and another thing to add to the "Well, that's different" list.

After dinner and drinks, talk turned to plans for the next day. Our weather briefing from ERAU predicted lousy weather at Narsarsuaq (*nar-sar-sooack*), Greenland, and between Goose Bay and Narsarsuaq until at least Sunday. This was a Thursday night, and we were aware that we needed to land and depart any airport in Greenland before

Sunday to avoid being stuck—or pay a hefty fee, as their airports are "closed" on Sundays. The weather in Goose Bay looked good for the next two days, but the route to and through Narsarsuaq in southern Greenland did not.

We didn't know much about alternate routes other than hearing about a northern route through some place in Greenland called Sondrestrom. It was too long for us to fly comfortably from Goose Bay to Sondrestrom, plus it would take us through the bad weather hovering around southern Greenland. If we were to go through Sondrestrom, we would need to head farther north into Canada and then jump across the ocean to Sondrestrom.

We went to bed thinking we would check weather again in the morning but would probably be spending another few days in delightful Goose Bay. We wanted to get to Narsarsuaq because we had prepurchased fuel that was awaiting us there *and* it was the shortest route from Goose Bay to Iceland. We also knew that southern Greenland is notorious for bad weather and testing bad weather in the North Atlantic is not a good idea in a very new/very old airplane and a crew with almost no experience in it.

33

Life Aboard

THE TEMPO OF life during the last few weeks before we left Missoula was fast and hectic and filled with suspense. Everyone was working diligently on jobs that needed to be done. Tension was in the air, as the outcome was far from certain. All of us were finishing our flight training. There was all kinds of drama, miscommunications, misunderstandings, mistakes, and probably hurt feelings. Every single person working on every aspect of the project was all in and dedicated to success. It was a whirlwind, right up to the moment on May 19 when six of us climbed aboard, closed the door, and took off. At that moment, everything changed.

Suddenly we had almost no work to do. We had a lot of time for relaxing when we weren't flying. We got to greet people at our stops, do interviews, and tell our story. Between May 19 when we left Missoula and June 24 when we returned, we had over a hundred hours of flight time. Since we traded off flying duties, each of us flew roughly two flights out of three—much of the time we had nothing to do but watch the world go by. So we did. Many people wonder what one does in the back of a DC-3 during those long flights.

None of us had given much thought about how to make the best of these times, but it didn't take long to sort out our routine. Crystal brought a hammock that she quickly figured how to suspend in the cabin. Thanks to Tia, Kathy Ogren, and Natalie, we were well supplied with snacks. We even had the presence of mind to take along a few cases of Miss Montana beer—for the pilots not flying, of course. We had a small trash can in the back that served as makeshift toilet, but it was like doing your business on a bucking horse if the ride was bumpy.

After Randy figured out the heater early in the trip, the front half of the cabin area was usually very comfortable. Due to distance from the heater ducts in front, gaps and holes in the plane, and the leaky main door, the back half of the cabin was much cooler...and a bit breezy. We each figured out our happy place and spent a lot of time there. Crystal normally stretched out on the front port-side seats, propped up against some soft luggage, facing forward. Jeff seemed to be most comfortable stretched out on the seats in the rear of the plane, covered by a sleeping bag. My favorite spot was directly across from Crystal, stretched out on the right seats and propped against soft luggage, facing forward. Eric and Randy couldn't decide, and slept about everywhere. We had great visibility out of the most forward cabin windows, looking out over an engine and wing. Every seat was a first-class seat with outstanding views.

Flying on a DC-3 is almost nothing like flying on a modern commercial airliner. For one thing, it isn't pressurized, so if you fly very high you need supplemental oxygen, which we brought along. We found that we didn't need oxygen up to our typical cruising altitude of 10,000 feet or so, but if we went higher, using oxygen made a big difference in our comfort. One big difference between a DC-3 and modern airliners is that a DC-3 has many holes—a good reason that it's not pressurized. After so many hours on the plane, we can all show you the spot just aft of the cockpit where you can see the world go by through small holes in the belly and a gap in the cargo floor. The main door itself fits poorly, leaks like a sieve, and constantly rattles.

Many of our flights were several hours in length, so we passed the time when not flying by napping, listening to music, watching movies on our phones, or reading books. We updated our trip notes or logbooks. We would also take turns sitting in the jump seats, of which there were two. The best jump seat was right behind the two pilots flying, somewhat higher than the pilot seats but right in the middle. It provided a great vantage point to observe everything in the cockpit and hear everything on the radio and intercom. Many enjoyable hours were spent by all of us in that seat.

The second jump seat was just aft of the first, with the back against the left side of the cockpit. It was very comfortable and has a headset that allowed its occupant to listen to the intercom and radio. It was also a premium napping spot because it was very warm.

During takeoff, the cabin is very loud and it's difficult to have a conversation without a headset. However, at cruise power, the noise is tolerable in the cabin, hardly requiring ear protection for comfort or safety, and allowing conversations without too much difficulty. Nevertheless, for the most part, once we were aloft and in cruise, we all retreated to our favorite places and into our own thoughts. And those thoughts were often about the wondrous places passing beneath our wings. It was fantastic, and I'll never forget it.

Napping on these long flights—and often between flights—became somewhat of an issue. As the uncontested power-napping expert, my ability to catch ten or twenty minutes of shut-eye seemingly at will drew attention. It is a finely honed art after many years of practice that has served me well, and the truth is that those not blessed with this skill are simply jealous. Always being well rested is important for performing consistently at a high level. Rumor has it that there are many candid pictures of me in various napping positions and locations, and there is talk of producing a calendar. For the record, there are also pictures of every other crew member slumbering, and I would happily contribute them for the calendar.

34

Goose Bay to Iqaluit

WE MET TO discuss options over breakfast. Eric had done some sleuthing and identified Iqaluit (*ee-kha-loo-eet*) as a possible stop farther north in Canada. None of us had ever heard of it. We all dutifully opened our iPads and looked at Iqaluit. The first thing we noticed was that Iqaluit didn't have aviation gas, or avgas—the 100-octane low-lead fuel for piston engines such as ours. Eric made a disparaging remark about all of us and, touting his experience bush flying in Alaska, said, "Everybody has avgas. You just need to talk to the right people."

Sure enough, he made a call to the FBO at Iqaluit, and they said they had several pallets of avgas in drums in a warehouse that they could sell us…and it was cheap, about six dollars per gallon. As soon as we found this out, and that the route from Goose Bay to Iqaluit avoided the low-pressure system defending Narsarsuaq, we quickly checked out of the hotel, called for a ride to the airport, and prepared to launch—thankful that we didn't have to spend another night in Goose Bay.

We were airborne by 11:45 ADT, with Jeff as PIC and me as SIC. We plotted a course for Iqaluit, which looked to be about a five-hour flight. The maps didn't show much in the way of civilization between Goose Bay and Iqaluit. That turned out to be optimistic.

During the five-hour flight from Goose Bay to Iqaluit, we saw some of the largest unending vistas of some of the most remote territory any of us had ever seen. Snow, ice, rock, and the first icebergs awaited as we approached Iqaluit. During the entire flight—and we were looking—we saw exactly one piece of evidence that humans exist. It was the Voisey's Bay nickel mine, a large mining complex with an airstrip, a road to a bay, and a dock where they could bring in supplies and ship out ore. There might have been other human presence during that five-hour flight, but we never saw it. Not a town, a road, a house, a building, or anything to indicate that humans had been present. It was probably the first time that it had sunk in exactly where we were heading, and it wasn't *toward* civilization.

The flight from Goose Bay to Iqaluit was our first time flying IFR. Jeff and I flew in and out of clouds for an hour or two as we approached Iqaluit. We were thankful to have IFR capability, and to be *legal*. It would not be the last time we needed it.

Iqaluit is the native name for the capital of Nunavut (*new-na-voot*) Territory. The population of Iqaluit is about 8,000; most of the people work for the airport or the government. The former name of the town was Frobisher Bay, and it is on the Davis Strait on Baffin Island—one of those islands that is so huge it's hard to think of it as an island. Nunavut Territory is the newest, largest, and most northern Canadian territory. That's saying a lot, because Canada has some very large and very northern territory. It was named after Sir Martin Frobisher, the first European to visit it, in 1576, when he was looking for the Northwest Passage.

It was established as a trading post in 1914 and later became an air base in World War II. During the Cold War, it was a Defense Early Warning radar station designed to alert North America if the Russians sent bombers over the North Pole. The Inuktitut name was restored to the town in 1987.

Iqaluit is north and west of Goose Bay. In a way, we were going backward by diverting to Iqaluit. However, we wanted to keep moving because we had to be at Duxford by June 2, and nobody knew what additional delays might lie ahead. We were also very happy to get out of Goose Bay. We kept moving, burning more gas, and flying more miles than we otherwise might have. But it was the right decision.

We landed in Iqaluit about four p.m. local time and were amazed at the size of the runway for such a remote town. It is 8,600 feet long and 200 feet wide. Somebody told us the U.S. had enlarged it to serve as an emergency landing spot for the space shuttle. We taxied to a corner of the airport where they had our fuel drums waiting.

In most of the arctic, aircraft burn jet fuel. They are either jets or turboprops, which are essentially jet engines driving propellers. Jet engines are more reliable, more powerful, and have a better safety record than piston engines. Finding avgas for a piston engine in the far north can be difficult. Also, since it is used somewhat infrequently, they often don't have a fuel truck dedicated to avgas. They often order it, store it, and pump it out of sealed drums. This was also common during World War II, so we were excited to get the full legacy experience of flying the North Atlantic in a DC-3—and refueling from fifty-five-gallon drums.

The stamps on the drums said the fuel was about a year old, which was probably acceptable. Randy carefully inspected each drum and watched like a hawk as the fuel was pumped to make sure no water, rust, or crud got in our tanks. The fuel was fine, and with all hands pitching in we were soon done.

Due to our quick departure from Goose Bay, we hadn't made any plans for lodging or transportation at Iqaluit, which was common on the journey. The FBO helped by ordering a taxi and recommending some hotels. We picked one, which was perfectly fine, and then headed out to look for food and drink.

In many northern outposts, alcohol is banned because of rampant alcoholism that is common in northern climes. Fortunately, Iqaluit wasn't one of them. We quickly stumbled across, of all things, a small barbecue restaurant. It looked clean, and we couldn't resist the idea of barbecue in such a remote spot. Having grown up in Kansas City, I was skeptical that it would meet my standards, but it was very good. Unfortunately, they did not serve adult beverages at the barbecue restaurant. One of the locals suggested we should try the Canadian Legion Hall across the street.

We learned three things that are true in a Canadian Legion Hall: you don't go in the back door (even though it was open), you don't wear hats inside (they barked at us immediately), and they don't take U.S. dollars. We made our way into the legion hall in search of the illusive adult beverage. Of course, we hadn't had time to get Canadian cash in Goose Bay, so we had only credit cards and U.S. cash. We didn't know if only members were allowed, if we had to be Canadian or U.S. veterans (none of us were), or if we would be thrown out on our ears as imposters.

We decided that if it came to it, we would tell them the truth— that we were on an epic mission flying a restored warbird to Europe to honor all veterans at the D-Day anniversary, in hopes that they might at least throw us out gently. We had nothing to worry about. After apologizing for entering the wrong door and obediently re-moving our hats, we found our way to the bar and were welcomed.

Surprisingly, they had a pretty decent selection of beer, and we all found one we liked. However, none of us had any Canadian money and we couldn't get the ATM machine in the lobby to cough up any local currency. They also didn't accept credit cards. After or-dering a second round of beer and smooth-talking the bartender, we got him to accept U.S. dollars at about twice the price in Canadian dollars. After such a long day, that seemed like a pretty good deal.

We had a good chuckle about our experience in the legion hall, made our way back to the hotel, and turned in for the night. The next day our sights were set on Greenland.

35

Iqaluit to Sondrestrom

Nobody wants to die a coward.
— Eric Komberec

ALTHOUGH WE HAD covered many miles since leaving Missoula on May 19 and flown over extremely remote territory since leaving Presque Isle, the next leg was something special. We were about to fly 560 miles, most of which was over the cold, gray, remote North Atlantic Ocean. The plane was running great, we were working together well as a crew, and the weather was forecast to be very good.

We had fueled up the night before so we were ready to go... except we weren't. As we were to learn so well in the coming days and weeks, nothing was as easy as it was in the United States. Even though our airplane was parked on the ramp, we had to get an escort from security to get through the gate and to our airplane. We were there too early, so we had to wait in the commercial terminal until the security folks got to work. Then we had to wait for the *right* person to show up. Then, he had room in his vehicle for only four of us, so he had to make two trips to get us all to the plane.

Another thing we learned, starting first in Iqaluit, is that many international airports require that you wear a high-visibility vest when on the ramp. Since we didn't have any, we required a security escort anytime we moved anywhere on the ramp. Nothing was easy, but we finally all got to the plane, preflighted, and loaded up. We broke a few rules, I'm sure, but we weren't planning to stick around for long. Eric and Randy flew this leg, and the rest of us sat back to enjoy the view.

The flight was about three and half hours, about two hours of which were over water. For the first hour or so we flew over parts of Baffin Island. It was incredibly beautiful and desolate, and we saw no more evidence of human existence.

Many people ask if we were scared flying over such inhospitable territory and water in a seventy-five-year-old airplane that had only about twenty-five hours of time on new engines and props. None of us was too concerned. We were more excited about landing in a place as mystical as Greenland. How many people do you know who have been to Greenland? This was the beginning of the big crossing, we had executed a good plan to avoid bad weather at Narsarsuaq and continue on our way, and the plane was running great.

In late May there was still plenty of ice on the ocean, especially close to land, and the patterns and colors we saw seemed infinite. Soon we went "feet wet," leaving land and flying on a heading of about eighty-seven degrees toward Sondrestrom. From about 10,000 feet, we could see Greenland nearly an hour away. As we approached Sondrestrom, we flew over land and down a beautiful fjord for about thirty minutes before landing.

Like Iqaluit, Sondrestrom also goes by another name—Kangerlussuaq (*gang-er-loose-sue-arc*). When it was built by the U.S. in 1941, the base was named Bluie West Eight. It was one of the two largest airports on the Blue Spruce route. After the war it was renamed Sondrestrom, which is still used by people like us who have difficulty pronouncing Kangerlussuaq. However, the official name is Kangerlussuaq, which means *Big Fjord* in the Greenlandic language.

There are some things about Greenland that you should know if you ever aspire to fly there. They have very different rules that govern their airports. First, every single airport in Greenland of any size was originally an air base built by the U.S. and eventually transferred to Greenland. Don't expect them to give you any breaks because of it. Second, they have odd hours. In the U.S. the towers at many airports close in the evening, but you can still land there at any time. In Greenland, the airports are closed between five p.m. and eight a.m. You can't land there outside of their operating hours without prior permission and paying a large fee. They are also closed on Sundays and national holidays. This just doesn't happen in the U.S.

To be fair, there probably isn't a lot of air traffic to Greenland airports. However, they have some unnecessary rules: the tower must be operating and firefighters must be on duty for any airplane to land. That isn't the case in the U.S., and we seem to manage just fine. Nevertheless, those were the rules, so when we landed at Sondrestrom on Saturday, May 25, we knew we either must remain there until eight a.m. Monday, or pay the hefty fee to depart on Sunday. None of that detracted from our elation upon landing at Sondrestrom.

To begin with, the approach into Sondrestrom is stunning in its beauty. It's impossible to describe and photographs don't do it justice, but the vistas of rock and snow and ice and icebergs were so vast they challenge the senses. There was some relief that we had made our first long over-water leg, but nobody thought much about it. As we approached the airport, we had to spiral down to lose altitude before landing straight in from the west. We taxied over to the mostly deserted parking area, and the fuel truck and ramp staff came to greet us.

Greenland is an autonomous territory of the Kingdom of Denmark. Most of the workers there are Danish. As with most of the places we stopped (except for Scotland), they all spoke fluent English. This was a good thing because our Danish and Greenlandic language skills were nonexistent.

By this time, we had developed a good rhythm as a crew. Somebody put in the gust locks, gear pins and set the wheel chocks. Somebody else serviced the oil and refueled. As usual, we scurried about doing our jobs when someone said, "Do you realize we just landed in freakin' Greenland?" That caused us all to laugh and contemplate for a moment what we had accomplished.

Since this was our first major international destination, we were prepared to clear customs but weren't sure what to expect. Nobody mentioned it or asked to see our passports, so we didn't bring it up. It would have been nice to have a passport stamp from Greenland, but we couldn't figure out where to get one. Maybe they don't even have them. Apparently, that's just the way it works. No paperwork, no declarations, no stamps.

When we landed, the wind was blowing steadily, and Eric skillfully handled some wind shear right before we touched down. One of the other D-Day Squadron planes had advised that we should be sure to have mosquito repellent handy when landing there, but we didn't see any bugs. We scoffed about how that advice was bogus—and of course we had no bug juice. Then, not long after we landed, the wind died down and the bugs came out in hordes. We hopped into the crew vehicle to get a ride to the hotel—and ran inside to avoid the swarming mosquitoes. We had scored rooms at the best hotel in Sondrestrom...also the only hotel in Sondrestrom.

About 500 people live at Sondrestrom. It is a major airport in the country, but it isn't much of a country. The entire population of Greenland is less than that of Missoula, even though Greenland is nearly six times larger than Montana. You can't help but wonder what they do for entertainment, work, and recreation. Fortunately, we didn't stay there long enough to find out.

After landing, refueling, and paying for fuel, we had a discussion with the airport officials about how much it would cost to take off the next morning. They informed us it would cost about $1,200 in U.S. dollars to "open" the airport, and they would need three hours' notice. We cringed at that but were ready for a cold drink and a warm meal, so we tabled the discussion for later.

We checked into Hotel Kangerlussuaq, which was a clean but fairly spartan hotel; we guessed that it was originally military housing from when the U.S. owned the facility. There was no air conditioning, and the rooms were warm. You couldn't open the windows because the bugs were still on the prowl and there weren't any screens. With nothing else to do, we cleaned up and headed to the bar.

Surprisingly, the bar was fairly well stocked, and we shared some celebratory drinks as we looked out at *Miss Montana* sitting on the ramp not far away. It was still soaking in. We were north of the Arctic Circle for the first time (and the only time on our trip), having left Missoula only six days earlier.

Just outside the window of the hotel was one of those poles with signs pointing in different directions with mileage to various places. I noticed it showed four hours to New York and three hours to the North Pole. We agreed that if we had to spend another night there, we would covertly add a sign with the DC-3 flight time to Missoula.

Soon we were ready for a meal and headed to the restaurant. The only choices were a cafeteria and a pretty nice-looking restaurant, the Muskox Restaurant. We were skeptical about what the menu would offer. Much less remote places in the U.S. certainly have few quality dining choices.

Much to our surprise we got a fairly good bottle of wine. The dinner consisted of an appetizer of shrimp with green onions, lentils, and some kind of vegetable puree. The main course was a delicious muskox steak with au jus and some kind of local vegetable. Dessert was a combination of crème brûlée, whipped cream, fruit puree, and berries. The presentation was top drawer, the quality was outstanding, and we were suitably impressed—and full. It was surely one of the best—if not the best—meals we had on the entire trip.

We retired for the night after discussing whether to leave the next day. Since we had eaten at all the restaurants in town, the hotel bill for the six of us would be about $1,200, and the meal was $500, we decided we were better off to pay the airport fee and be on our way to Iceland.

When we went to bed we were all reminded that we were north of the Arctic Circle in late May, when the days are almost twenty-four hours long. The light never faded, and sleep was elusive.

Nevertheless, we managed to get some rest, and we woke the next morning ready to go.

When we got up, there were three planes on the ramp that hadn't been there the night before. Maybe we were in luck and the airport was already open for a bit. If we hurried maybe we could take off before the airport closed again and we had to pay the fee. The FBO then informed us that *every* plane had to pay the fee. We were starting to feel a bit shaken down; when the rest of the crew heard the news, we all agreed to get out of Greenland.

We checked out of the hotel and got a ride to the airplane. Our driver was an airport firefighter, so Randy and Crystal requested— and we received—a tour of their firefighting equipment before we made our way to the plane. Since we were all fueled and ready to go (and had paid our exorbitant fees), it was a short preflight before we were loaded and taking off.

Next stop, Iceland.

Art photobombing Eric in Sondrestrom (author photo)

36

Sondrestrom to Reykjavik

THERE WERE MANY things we didn't know about Greenland. One of them was that the ice cap, which we were about to cross, rises to over 10,000 feet above sea level. Since Sondrestrom is at sea level, we had to circle and climb after takeoff to get to 12,000 feet to clear the ice cap. It was a clear, beautiful day as we departed Sondrestrom, heading east. We had a gorgeous view of Sondrestrom and the airport, as well as of the bare hills that rise to where the ice cap starts.

The flight from Sondrestrom to Reykjavik is 840 miles, the second longest leg on the trip but not the longest over-water leg because 330 miles is over the Greenland ice cap. An emergency landing on the Greenland ice cap is no more attractive than ditching in the North Atlantic. Well, maybe a little more attractive because you don't have to get wet. However, there are relatively few rescue options in that remote neighborhood, so whether you go in the drink or land on the ice cap, you should plan to be there for a while. Even with the advent of satellite beacons that tell search-and-rescue teams exactly where you are, getting rescued is often another matter entirely.

Fortunately, none of that happened after we took off from Sondrestrom. Instead, we were treated to about two hours of flying over absolutely nothing but snow and ice as far we could see. It's easy to see why pilots in poor visibility could lose the view of the horizon above such a vast sea of white. There is a story of a bomber crew flying above Greenland in poor weather during World War II who suddenly noticed a strange vibration and noise. They had unknowingly descended until the plane landed very smoothly on the ice cap with its gear up and under full power, eventually grinding to a stop. Fortunately, thanks to our modern equipment and clear skies we avoided such a mishap.

The transition from ice to ocean is much more abrupt on the east coast of Greenland. We saw numerous glaciers extending all the way to the water and thousands of icebergs of all sizes floating in the bays and inlets. For the second flight in a row, we saw almost no sign of human habitation.

The only possible human artifact we saw over the ice cap, an hour or so into the flight, was an odd straight line in the snow. As we followed it, we speculated on what it might be. An expedition of researchers on a snow cat? Indigenous people hunting polar bears? We soon reached the end of the line and saw a herd of muskox plodding their way across in a perfectly straight line. It's hard to imagine what they were doing up there because there was nothing to eat.

Soon, we were once again "feet wet" over the cold, gray ocean for another 415 miles into Reykjavik, Iceland. We later realized that we never saw a single ship below us during any of the flights between Canada and Scotland. We were above clouds for some of those miles, but for the most part we had clear weather and could see the water. Those were the times when we noticed those holes in the belly. It was much different than flying on Delta.

Arriving at Reykjavik was another memorable moment. Iceland is far different from Greenland. Many people say that the names should have been switched. Greenland is mostly ice, and Iceland is predominantly green. Iceland is small compared to Greenland but has several population centers, a busy international airport, and many things to do.

There were two airports for us to choose from: Reykjavik and Keflavik. The Reykjavik airport is within the city of Reykjavik, while

Keflavik is about forty miles away. Reykjavik had waived landing and parking fees, while Keflavik had not. However, Keflavik was open twenty-four hours a day, while Reykjavik closed at around eleven p.m. local time. It wasn't an issue because we arrived at Reykjavik at 6:20 p.m. local time. It was slightly under six hours flying time, our longest flight yet. Everyone except me got some time in the seat; Art and Jeff did most of the flying.

As pilots, we frequently use Greenwich Mean Time, also known as Zulu time. It is the time zone where the prime meridian (zero degrees longitude) crosses through the town of Greenwich, England. GMT is used in aviation instead of trying to deal with multiple time zones. For instance, 1600 Zulu is the same moment in time in Missoula as it is in Moscow. It simplifies communication and planning for pilots, who are not good at math.

It turns out that all of Iceland is on GMT. This was my first time being *in* GMT as opposed to using it for reference. The prime meridian doesn't cross Iceland, but Iceland is close enough to it that it falls in that time zone.

Upon landing at Reykjavik, there was still plenty of daylight, which is normal at these latitudes in May. We had sent the required customs and immigration forms in advance and were assisted by the helpful folks at the Ace FBO. As in Greenland, we didn't know what to expect from customs, so we waited on the ramp until they showed up. They looked around the airplane, asked a few questions, and welcomed us to Iceland. Once again, there were no passport stamps to be had.

We got a ride into downtown Reykjavik and checked into a hotel right next to the harbor. Reykjavik struck all of us as a clean, modern, vibrant city. The downtown isn't that big, and we enjoyed walking around the town with shops, restaurants, and sights to see. Once again, after landing, someone thought to remind us, "You do realize we just landed in freakin' Iceland!"

After checking in, we started in search of food and beverage, and everyone but me voted for sushi. I made the mistake of admitting that I had never had sushi, so of course it was decided. We found a lovely sushi restaurant, and everyone ordered what sounded good; some of them were kind enough to order something for me. It was delicious.

After our fine dinner, we turned in, looking forward to our last major leg, the longest overall and the longest over water—to Prestwick, Scotland.

37

Reykjavik to Prestwick

THE NEXT MORNING, we met for breakfast and to discuss the weather briefing from ERAU. That day's leg would be a serious bit of flying and nothing to take lightly. The weather looked good for getting to Prestwick but not so good for making it to Duxford. We returned to the Reykjavik airport, got our customs matters in order, and filed an IFR flight plan to Prestwick, Scotland.

Once again, nothing was as easy outside the U.S. It was more difficult to get fuel, to pay for fuel, or to get a cab somewhere. In some ways, it was the product of the very different general aviation world outside the United States. In some ways, it was simply cultural. We had not refueled the plane upon landing, so it was time to do that when we arrived at the airport. For no obvious reason, it took over two hours to get a fuel truck. If that happened in the U.S., an FBO wouldn't last long.

Fueling complete, we finally launched for Prestwick at 10:45 GMT, with Jeff as PIC and me in the right seat. Randy filled in after a couple of hours. Then, with about an hour and a half to go, we entered IMC (instrument meteorological conditions) so I got back in the right seat for the rest of the flight. It had been a while since I had flown IFR for very long without the benefit of an autopilot, which *Miss Montana* does not have. After a little adjusting and some tips from Jeff, it all came back to me, and it was a ball, especially with such a big, lumbering plane. There's something remarkable about flying a legacy airplane over the North Atlantic using, if not primitive, at least fairly unsophisticated equipment. I couldn't help but think of those youngsters making the crossing seventy-five to eighty years earlier who had even less to work with.

We landed in Prestwick after about four and half hours. We cleared customs (again no passport stamp) and celebrated the completion of our first Atlantic crossing. The folks at Prestwick airport were some of the most friendly and helpful of any place on our trip. They allowed us to store our survival suits and raft in a secure hangar, they arranged for a hotel and transportation, and chatted with us about the trip and our mission. They don't get to see DC-3s there very often, and, now that we were in Europe, more people knew about our mission and the approaching D-Day anniversary.

The Scots were certainly a friendly lot, although it was the only stop on our trip where we had a language problem. The Scottish brogue is very hard to understand and they don't seem to soften it any for Yanks; in fact, I suspect they work harder to make it unintelligible for our benefit.

We had a pretty significant range of flight time and experience on our crew, but this was a significant accomplishment for all of us and even more rewarding to have done it as a crew. It was May 27, so if we didn't crash and burn the next day on the short flight to Duxford, we would be nearly a full week ahead of our June 2 deadline.

After dinner, we turned in, anxiously anticipating what the next few days would bring. We were all a bit excited, on the verge of completing what so many had labored so long for.

38

The D-Day Clock

ONCE IN A while, something happens for which there is no logical explanation. On May 12, the museum was a flurry of activity, with everyone getting ready for the first flight. It was one of the busiest days of the last several months. A stranger came in the hangar and stood there, looking around. This happened often by this time. If any of us had a moment, we would welcome them, ask what brought them in, and encourage them to look around. If we weren't too busy, we would give them a tour.

This gentleman approached me and introduced himself as Jim Notaro, from Stevensville, about thirty miles south of Missoula. He said he didn't want to bother me, as he could see we were busy, and he had heard about the deadline we were up against. He was right, we were busy, and anxious to make our first flight, but saying so would have been rude, so I assured him I had a few minutes. He had something in his hand and this is the story he told.

Jim's father, Phil, was a tail gunner on a B-26 Marauder in World War II. Phil and his crew flew many missions over Europe, including during the D-Day invasion. At the end of the war, his crew was somewhere in France and they were ordered to taxi their bomber to the end of the runway, open the fuel valves, and light her on fire to destroy the plane.

This they reluctantly did, but not before Phil salvaged a small, windup "eight-day clock" made by Elgin. The clock was mounted on the instrument panel and was used for a variety of navigational tasks, besides showing the time. It was designed to run for eight days after a single winding, hence the name. As a standalone instrument with no electrical or pitot/static connections, it was easy and quick to remove from the B26.

Phil Notaro kept the clock after the war as a family keepsake, and Jim inherited it when Phil passed away. It had stopped working, so Jim had it repaired at one of the few remaining shops that could repair such a clock. Jim's son would eventually enter a career in aviation, rising to the position of captain for Alaska Airlines. Jim had heard about our project and had come with a request. He asked if we would take the clock with us and fly it over Normandy once more on the 75th anniversary of D-Day, then return it to him so he could give it to his aviator son.

What a story! Yes, I said, we would be honored to do it but… where would we put it? It would be our luck to be entrusted with such a keepsake, put it in a cubbyhole somewhere on the plane, and then lose it. Then, standing there with Jim, a thought came. Having worked extensively on the instrument panel I was familiar with the whole layout. I told Jim to follow me; we climbed into the plane and walked up to the cockpit.

In the process of rebuilding and modifying the instrument panel, we had a new eight-day clock, very similar to his old Elgin and exactly the same size. However, there were other openings in the instrument panel that formerly held instruments, but which were no longer needed and covered with blank plates. One of them was a perfect fit for Jim's clock. I pointed at the spot and asked if we could install it there, because it would be the safest place for it. He readily agreed, and, in a few minutes it was done. Jim wrote a small description of his story that we carried with us on the trip in a notebook, along with other similar stories we had collected. Before departing Missoula, somebody set both the new clock and the D-Day clock to Missoula time, wound them, and we promptly forgot about them.

Fast-forward to somewhere over the North Atlantic between Iceland and Scotland. Jeff Whitesell and I were flying. The legs over the North Atlantic mostly, and fortunately, consisted of long hours when not much happened. Believe it or not, the view even gets a bit monotonous over the cold, gray water with nothing else to see. As it happened on that leg, I was looking around the cockpit for something else to think about.

That was when I noticed that the two eight-day clocks were not showing the same time. The new one was still set to Missoula time, but the D-Day clock was not. My first thought was that it was too bad Jim had fixed his clock and now it wasn't keeping proper time. I said something to Jeff, and he looked at the clocks.

Jeff is a career airline pilot accustomed to bouncing from one time zone to another and keeping track of the time where he is as well as the time at other places in his head. I started to reach over and reset the D-Day clock to Missoula time, when Jeff stopped me. He looked at me, then at his watch, then at me again, and then at his watch again. He said, "The D-Day clock is set to Normandy time."

Look, I'm just telling you what happened.

The D-Day clock in the instrument panel (photo by Keely Flatow)

39

Prestwick to Duxford

MAY 28 DAWNED partly cloudy, but the weather forecast looked good for making the approximately two-hour trip to Duxford. Rain was forecast at Duxford, but we expected to arrive before it did. We launched about noon from Prestwick, with Eric as PIC and Art in the right seat, and made our way in a nearly direct line to Duxford. For the first time since leaving Missoula, we stayed low—around 3,000 to 5,000 feet. It was enough to clear the hills but low enough that we could enjoy the view of the countryside.

It was everything you expect of Scotland: small towns, rock fences, rolling hills, and green, green, green. We saw sheep and other livestock and a few lochs. It certainly made us want to return and spend more time getting to know the land and people.

After we crossed into England, the land became increasingly more populated. The terrain was still incredibly green but became flatter. We started to notice old airfields the closer we got to Duxford. Most of them had long been abandoned and some had even been converted into housing developments, but the shape of long, crossed runways on the earth was unmistakable.

On this most significant day of our trip thus far, there were two amusing stories that both involved ATC. None of us, except maybe Jeff, knew exactly what we were doing flying in the United Kingdom, and his experience was flying commercial planes at 40,000 feet.

The rules are quite a bit different from the U.S., and the airspace is complex.

We avoided many complications by staying low, but we also filed an instrument flight plan to try to stay out of trouble—because we would be in constant radio contact with ATC. In the U.S., when you file a flight plan, you remain on the flight plan until you cancel it or land. When we filed at Prestwick and took off, we were on the instrument flight plan for a while, then suddenly we weren't—and for no apparent reason.

There were some puzzled looks among us when the controller asked us what "services" we wanted. In the U.S., there is only one service on an instrument flight plan, but in England you have four choices: basic, traffic, deconfliction, and procedural. We're still not completely sure we know the difference between them. They send you a bill for the service you request, so we assumed "basic" was the least expensive, and requested "basic."

At one point not long after leaving Prestwick, as we approached a large bay named Solway Firth near the border with England, the Scottish controller asked us to report…something unintelligible. Part of it was that we had never heard the term he was using; the other part was his Scottish brogue. We eventually figured out that we were to report "coasting out," or leaving land. Presumably, we would be asked to report coasting in as well.

As we approached Duxford, we tuned to the Duxford tower frequency and reported "*Miss Montana* is ten miles west, inbound to land." The tower controller came back with an approval to land, then a pause, and, in a very proper British accent, added, "And if you were to request a low fly through…it would be approved." We all had a good laugh and accepted his invitation.

We made a low pass down the runway, catching our first glimpse of the Duxford Aerodrome, as well as the ten D-Day Squadron sister planes already parked on the grass, before we came around to land. We had arrived. And we were six days early. It was the only deadline we had met during the entire year of preparation. Yet it was the only one that mattered and we were thrilled.

The second funny story from that day happened later. We had all joked about how we had done such a poor job with ATC on the trip from Prestwick. We even wondered if we had violated some rule or airspace and might get a letter from the authorities. Imagine our surprise when Tia got a nice message via social media that evening.

The sender said he was a controller with Scottish ATC and had the pleasure of working with *Miss Montana* that day (we never used *Miss Montana* as a call sign until arriving at Duxford). He wanted us to know what a pleasure it had been to work with American pilots who had done such a fine job navigating complex U.K. airspace. We had another good laugh. We seriously thought we had made a hash of it, but we had obviously fooled somebody.

Duxford is a beautiful and historic airfield near a small town, about a two-hour drive northeast of London. It existed before World War II and was a key base during the war. It retains many of the original buildings from—and before—World War II and houses one of the finest World War II museums in Europe, the Imperial War Museum. It has a hard runway as well as a grass strip and a large amount of parking on the grass inside the fence. There is a quaint old control tower that overlooks the field. All the people there, including the many volunteers, were polite, friendly, and helpful. From the looks of it, the tower dated back to the war.

After landing, we taxied over to our spot, which happened to be next to the *Spirit of Benovia*, a DC-3 from California. We piled out and took care of the necessary chores, but not before celebrating and taking pictures. Eric started a Facebook Live broadcast, which was watched by thousands from all over the world who had been following our journey. It truly was an extraordinary moment that most of us had wondered if we would ever see—and will never forget.

Almost at once, other D-Day Squadron crews started coming over to welcome us. This continued for the next two weeks. Without exception, they all said they had been following our progress on the restoration and—don't take this the wrong way, they said—they were pretty sure we weren't going to make it.

They said, "You guys pulled off the impossible," "You're heroes," and "We can't believe you really did it." Coming from these guys, some of whom had been operating DC-3s for decades, it opened our eyes to the fact that our entire gang of volunteers, donors, supporters, and flight crew had accomplished something extraordinary.

Since we arrived several days before June 2, when the official events would begin, we had some time on our hands. We toured the extensive museum facilities, ate in the diner, and Eric rented a beautiful house in the country. By this time Tia, Taylor, Avian, and The Ancient One had arrived, and we all settled in at the rental house, about twenty minutes from Duxford. Eric, who had spent some time in England, got driving duties and showed us around a bit. We shopped for groceries, got much-needed haircuts, and relaxed.

One day, Jeff, Eric, Randy, and Art were eating lunch in the diner at the Imperial War Museum. One of the other DC-3 crews introduced themselves, congratulated us on making it to Duxford, and inquired how things were going. At one point the subject of pilot training came up, and one of our guys mentioned that all four of our PICs had been type-rated the week before we left and that we left Missoula with about five hours on the freshly restored airplane. There was a moment of silence as the other crew processed the numbers. Once again, we got the distinct impression that they thought the *Miss Montana* folks might be a little crazy.

After we arrived in Duxford, Peter Christian or Kim Briggeman or Dennis Bragg would contact us almost every day asking for an update. We were usually able to respond and bring them up to speed on events. They said that people back home were clamoring for news and the update reports were very popular. That made us all feel very supported, and we kept them informed as much as possible.

When we arrived at Duxford on May 28, there were ten other

D-Day Squadron planes that had arrived: *Placid Lassie*, *"That's All, Brother,"* *D-Day Doll*, *Liberty*, *Miss Virginia*, *Flabob Express*, *Virginia Ann*, *Betsy's Biscuit Bomber*, *Spirit of Benovia*, and *Clipper Tabitha May*. *Pan Am* was still enjoying Prestwick, *Rendezvous With Destiny* and N18121 were in Iceland, and *Hap-enstance* was bringing up the rear in Manitoba, Canada.

40

Formation Flying

FROM THE VERY beginning of the project and first conversations with Eric Zipkin, formation flying was a topic of discussion and concern. One of the early requirements for each crew was that we have at least one pilot who was certified in formation flight. Two organizations issue such certifications. The one closely affiliated with warbirds is the Formation and Safety Team. FAST is "a worldwide educational organization that promotes safe formation flying in restored, vintage military aircraft and civilian aircraft." FAST is the gold standard for groups like ours, and most of the other crews had one or more pilots with FAST cards.

We also learned early on that it would take either a very intensive (and expensive) course or repeated attendance at scheduled clinics over a period of more than a year to earn a FAST card. This was not a skill that could be mastered in a weekend. It is more akin to an instrument rating that requires a good bit of instruction followed by much repetition, then a check ride by an approved examiner. An additional complication is that if you are going to practice formation flying, you obviously need at least one other airplane, and preferably two.

None of us had the time or money to get the training, and we were unlikely to achieve the level of skill required for a FAST card in such a short time, anyway. When the topic came up, our prospective PICs dismissed the need for FAST training. Our prospective PICs all had experience with various types of precision flying, but not the specific and unique training required for formation flight. I began discussing with Eric Zipkin early on whether we could get a waiver after some training flights together in the D-Day Squadron. Our prospective PICs were confident that they could handle the formation flying with no problem. In fact, parodying a popular movie, the mantra became "We don't need no stinking FAST cards."

I had no experience in formation flight, and I certainly didn't know its rigid rules. Yet I thought our plane's more experienced pilots were a little too cavalier about it. Pilots are by nature confident, which is a good thing, but any experienced pilot will caution against being overly so. From my perspective, it seemed that all our PICs (who were all instructors as well) were displaying an attitude that they would probably have warned me against as their student.

Formation flying is truly an art, as well as a perishable skill. Flying in formation requires a "lead," which is the plane in front and then one or more additional aircraft that follow the flight lead. These aircraft form an element, usually three or four aircraft, and they perform all sorts of maneuvers while maintaining proximity and holding precise alignments known as "holding station." The Blue Angels and Thunderbirds are the gold standard of formation flying and the highest level of the art.

Obviously, this type of flying is very dangerous—which is why it is so exciting to watch. As pilots, we are taught from the very beginning to "see and avoid" other traffic, and now these crazy pilots are getting, and staying, very close to other aircraft while performing extreme maneuvers that are difficult even when flying solo. The smallest mistake can result in catastrophe—and has—even with the most highly trained pilots and high-performance planes.

Formation flying in a DC-3 is basic formation flying. There are no loops, rolls, or other maneuvers that are common at airshows. DC-3 formation flying generally consists of joining up in a "Vic" (short for Victor, or V), which is a three-ship element, then flying straight and level, or perhaps making large gentle turns. The plane in front is "Lead," the plane to the right is the "Number 2," and the plane to the left of Lead is "Number 3." Sometimes a fourth ship (Number 4) will be added directly behind to form a diamond. It doesn't look that hard to join up with two other planes and fly straight and level for a long distance—especially if nothing changes much, or quickly. Looks are very deceiving.

First, just *getting close* to another plane—but not *too close*—requires great skill and a fine touch. Second, there are all sorts of dynamics that interfere with this seemingly simple exercise. The lead is never exactly steady. He might be drifting up or down in thermals, or he might drift slightly left or right due to winds. The smallest change in the lead position has a ripple effect through the element. Even if your lead is perfectly steady, those forces can affect the wingmen.

Holding your station requires constant effort, even when everything else is static. The planes that are following must make constant small changes to pitch, bank, and power, trying to keep two points lined up on the plane they are following. Those two points on a DC-3 are the top of the air intake scoop on the engine and the bottom of the cockpit window for a wingman. And you must do all this while flying within a wingspan (100 feet) of the plane you are following.

Straight and level flight is only the start. The other standard maneuvers are turns and changing from a three-ship Vic or four-ship diamond to echelon formation. Echelon formations are formed when the lead is followed by his wingmen in a line, all on the same side. An echelon forms an offset line instead of a V, like one side of a Vic extended to include all three or four planes.

The echelon can be right or left and is commonly formed when preparing to drop paratroopers or preparing to land. The *right* echelon is formed for dropping jumpers because most DC-3s have their jump doors on the left, and a right-echelon formation makes it unlikely that jumpers will fall in front of a following airplane. Oftentimes, the following planes are also "stepped up," or flying fifty or a hundred feet higher than the plane they are following for the same reason, as well as to avoid turbulence from the planes ahead.

Formation flying has cardinal rules. One of them is you rarely turn into or toward your echelon, and *never* without prior agreement. In a right echelon formation, the lead should always make left turns and vice versa for a left echelon. The reason for this is, if you turn *into* your echelon, the airplanes on your wing must bank away from you and may not be able to see you as you turn their way. As the formation turns, each plane's belly goes up and it makes it difficult, if not impossible, to see the plane ahead of them. If you can't see, then you can't avoid.

One of the ironies of formation flight is that it is much easier to hold station the closer you are to the plane you are following. This seems counterintuitive but makes sense and it is most obvious in a turn. Whenever the lead plane of a Vic starts a left turn, say, the plane on the left (Number 3) has less distance to fly in the turn and must slow down and descend a bit to hold station. The Number 2 on the right has farther to fly in the turn and must climb in order to hold station as the Vic banks slightly away. This requires changes to power, pitch, and bank all at once. And, the farther you are away from your lead, the greater the changes because you have much less (Number 3) or much greater (Number 2) distances to fly to remain on station. Therein lies a fundamental difficulty of formation flying.

We never quite resolved the issue of whether a FAST pilot would be required on every plane. The D-Day Squadron leaders probably figured they needed every plane and they could probably work with crews who were not FAST trained—and we weren't the only one. On our second day in Duxford, we began briefing for the upcoming formation flights. We had been late leaving Missoula, so we had not been able to fly and train with the other nine planes at Oxford. We were the new guys. We were about to be baptized into formation flight in a big way.

Our crew had decided before arriving at Duxford that our most demanding formation flights—such as the photo flight and para-trooper drop flights—would be flown with two PICs in the front office. It made sense to have the most experienced guys driving on those missions.

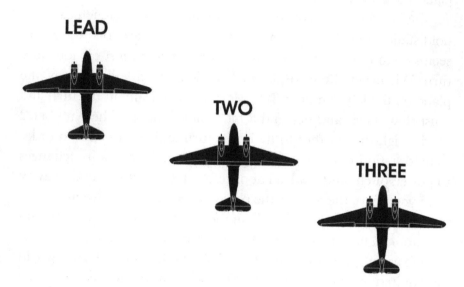

A 3-ship right echelon formation

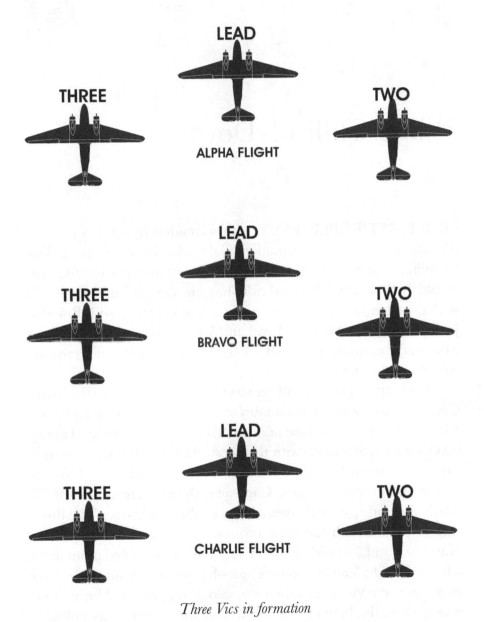

THREE

LEAD

TWO

ALPHA FLIGHT

THREE

LEAD

TWO

BRAVO FLIGHT

THREE

LEAD

TWO

CHARLIE FLIGHT

Three Vics in formation

41

White Cliffs of Dover

OUR FIRST EXPERIENCE with formation flying was on May 31, when we made a formation flight with most of the D-Day Squadron planes to the White Cliffs of Dover for a photo shoot. Art would fly PIC, and Jeff would ride shotgun. We briefed it extensively with the other crews before we took off and joined up with Brandon Jewett's gorgeous *Liberty* as Lead and John Session's Historic Flight Museum's beautiful *Pan Am* DC-3 as Number 2. As the new guys, we would be Number 3.

The plan was to fly south in several three-ship Vics to the White Cliffs of Dover, with a few minutes of separation between Vics. Each Vic would orbit over a fixed point at 1,500 feet above sea level until it was their turn to join up with the photo ship. When it was our turn, we would descend to 1,000 feet, move to left echelon, and join up with the photo ship, a Cessna Caravan with the left rear door off. We would then orbit several times so they could get photos of the three-ship formation with the cliffs and the sea as backdrops. Then the Number 2 and 3 would break off to orbit over the fixed point again while the flight lead got some single-ship photos by the cliffs. Each plane in each Vic would then get solo photographs. The weather was perfect, the lighting was ideal, and the scenery was unforgettable. Those of us riding in the back were treated to incredible views, and the images made that day were stunning.

The left echelon formation for the three-ship photos would be challenging, especially since we were in the third slot. That would make us holding station on John Sessions's *Pan Am* DC-3 to our right. Art had flown everything until we moved to left echelon. It made sense for that portion of the flight to be flown by Jeff from the right seat, as he had better a better view of the planes we were following. While he was polite about it, John Sessions had bluntly told Jeff that he would let us fly on his wing, but he didn't want the new guys flying too close.

This was perfectly understandable, given our lack of formation experience and the demanding nature of the flight—and John knew nothing about our flying abilities. However, it meant that we would be the tail end of the whip and we would be getting cracked. When the echelon turned away from us, we would have to add a lot of power to hold station, then when we straightened out we would have to reduce power to stay in the right spot. It all had to be done just right, or we would constantly be struggling to get and stay in position. Our extra distance from *Pan Am* made us effectively in the fourth spot in a left echelon, with a gap, or "missing man," between us and Sessions.

This was the first time for both Art and Jeff flying formation in the DC-3, and they both did well considering how new it was for them. Art handled the takeoff and the formation flight from Duxford to Dover. Appropriately, Art took his time moving into position but kept a comfortable distance from the lead and Number 2 as he got the hang of it. Art is a very cautious and safe pilot, and it was the right thing to do. However, it meant that we were significantly out of position for most of the flight and he had to work harder. But he was learning.

The photo flight was probably the most dangerous of all the flying we did. We were in formation for most of it, at low altitude over water for some of it. We were trying not only to hold formation but to be in the right location for the photographer, paying attention to the photo ship. Being at 250 to 500 feet above water poses extra risk because it's harder to gauge your altitude. More than one plane has ditched unintentionally because they lost depth perception over water and didn't keep an eye on their altitude. The pilot of the photo ship was also constantly talking to his subjects: "Number 2 is too low," "Number 3 is too far back," "Number 2 is too far forward." The flying was very demanding, and we were all on high alert to ensure we did it safely.

Once we moved into the left echelon formation and took our turn for the three-ship photo passes, Jeff took the controls from the right seat. It was every bit as hard as he expected, and the photo ship was chiding us, like the previous flights, but at least we were prepared for it, having listened to the other guys get scolded.

That day was harder for Jeff than we knew. He later confided that his brother Bruce had died in a horrible airline accident on May 31, 1984. Since that day Jeff had never flown in any airplane, in any capacity, on May 31. This was the first time he had taken to the skies on that date in thirty-five years, and the additional stress of having to fly formation as left wingman from the right seat was something he had never done.

As the time approached for our first pass in the three-ship formation for the photo, Jeff started to worry that he was going to screw it up. This was going through Jeff's head unbeknownst to us. He told me later that he heard a "still small voice" telling him, "Be still. This is finally your missing man formation for Bruce." And then he was fine.

We made several turns in the three-ship, then several by ourselves. One of our three-ship photos shows us in exactly the right position. Art joked that it was probably the only three seconds we were in the right spot all day. And it was the missing man formation for Jeff's brother.

When it was our turn for our single-ship photos, Art took the controls, and they got some amazing images. The photographer, Rich Cooper, graciously gave us the high-resolution files. They are spectacular images and one of the favorite souvenirs of the trip.

Art later mused about the photo flight over Dover. He said the experience was so amazing that all the work he had done over the last year, all the time off of his day job, the setbacks, and the other difficulties…were worth it to be able to fly that one day over the White Cliffs of Dover. We later realized this was true for almost every day of our five-week trip.

Our crew's first experience with formation flying was, to say the least, humbling. There was no more chest-beating and "We don't need no stinking FAST cards." Instead, conversation turned to how hard it was and how we could learn and do better. There were not-so-subtle comments in the debriefing by the other crews about making sure everyone was holding station properly. They were talking about us. We learned and got better but were a long way from being proficient when the formation flying came to an end.

Our next experience with formation flying was on June 3 when we started practice flights in preparation for the main events of June 5 and 6. We flew some flights with two Vics, again with Art as PIC and Jeff as SIC. Another decision we had made was that Art would fly all paratrooper jump flights because he flies smokejumpers for a living and therefore was the most qualified. It also meant the most to him personally. On that June 3 flight, we practiced joining up after takeoff, holding station, and moving from a Vic to an echelon formation. Art was generally very frustrated and even uttered some rare (for him) "blue" words. We all thought he was doing fine and probably too hard on himself.

After the flight, the squadron held another debrief, and the performance of *Miss Montana* was again a topic. Everyone knew that we had no FAST pilots on board. There was some discussion about how *Miss Montana* was going to get up to speed. To his credit, when Art was asked how he thought it went, he said, "We're working hard and happy to be here." Art's humble attitude seemed to go a long way toward getting the squadron to accept us despite being new to formation flight. That said, the squadron decided that we must have a FAST pilot on board for the next flight or two in order for us to participate.

Andy Maag, a pilot on "*That's All, Brother*," kindly agreed to fly right seat for the next flight on June 4, when it was Jeff's turn to fly PIC. Andy was extremely helpful and knowledgeable, and his willingness to help was very much appreciated. After that flight, our performance improved, but we still had a lot to learn. It would have been a steep hill to climb for anyone.

Art told me once that a flight instructor is the only teaching job where your student is constantly trying to kill you. In fact, Art has become known for saying—after a difficult flight—no matter how scary, dangerous, or unskilled the flight might have been, it's a success if "nobody died." We said that many times during our trip. There were some close calls, and the formation flights were challenging and dangerous. While there was plenty of risk, and in some cases little margin for error or mechanical problems, we all made it home safely and nobody died. *Miss Montana* had seen enough death in her time.

42

Shuttleworth/Old Warden Excursion

DURING OUR WAIT for the beginning of official events, we had the opportunity to do some memorable things. By this time a tour group, consisting mostly of Montanans and some of our supporters and donors, had arrived and we were able to take a load of them on one of our practice flights over England. Then we were told that the squadron had been invited to fly to the Shuttleworth Collection, a museum a short distance away for a tour and barbecue for all the crews. *Miss Montana* was grounded that day for our fifty-hour inspection, so we were able to hitch a ride on *Placid Lassie*, the flagship and lead of the entire D-Day Squadron. It was quite a treat, and there was even room for several of our tour members/supporters.

The Shuttleworth Collection at the Old Warden Aerodrome is another world-class museum mostly consisting of pre-World War II aircraft. In fact, we were told that the newest plane in the collection was a Spitfire. Perhaps more remarkable is that all their planes are maintained in flying condition *and* fly regularly. Both museums are outstanding and well worth a visit.

On June 1, seven of the D-Day Squadron planes made the flight, landing at the gorgeous Old Warden Aerodrome. It is a short but beautifully maintained grass strip, and all the planes made spot-on landings one after another for the adoring crowds. It was reminiscent of C-47s landing at English airfields after missions across the channel during the war. This mass arrival of seven American Dakotas at Old Warden Aerodrome was later voted the number one airshow moment in England in 2019.[20]

After a tour of the museum, we were shuttled across the airfield to an estate owned by a D-Day Squadron supporter who treated all the crews to a fine outdoor barbecue dinner on his lawn. The evening was beautiful, the temperature mild, and the assembled group enjoyed our first real opportunity to socialize together.

After dinner, each crew was invited to say a few words. By this time, we had learned that most of the other planes were owned either by individuals or by foundations. The other crews were invited to introduce themselves, and they thanked their generous owners, benefactors, and foundations for supporting them on the mission.

It was different for us because our airplane is not owned by a wealthy individual or foundation. It is owned by a modest museum with little in the way of resources, but enthusiastically supported by our community. When our crew was introduced, we proudly thanked our supporters—the entire state of Montana—for making the dream happen.

Long after dark, buses arrived to take us back to Duxford—much beer and wine had been consumed so nobody was in condition to fly. The crews of the seven planes returned the next day to fly their planes back to Duxford.

43

June 2 – It Begins

JUNE 2 WAS the day we had been anticipating for many months. The Duxford airfield was the site of two days of airshows, flying demonstrations, and thousands of visitors. We quickly learned that in England and France, the public is not usually allowed to walk out on the flight line and get close to the aircraft, like in the U.S.

Our DC-3s were parked on the beautiful grass infield at Duxford, and the public had to view them from behind the fence fifty or a hundred yards away. Credentialed crewmembers could cross the fence to access the aircraft and were allowed to escort small groups of people to our plane, which we did as often as we could.

By June 2, all of the Mighty Fifteen from the American D-Day Squadron had arrived at Duxford, and eight other DC-3s from elsewhere in Europe had arrived. The European DC-3s included the following airplanes, listed by name, registration number, owner, and home base:

- *Aces High*, N147DC, England
- *Gamle Dame*, OY-BPY, *Foreningen for Flyvende Museumsfly*, Denmark
- LN-WND, Dakota Norway, Sandefjord, Norway
- *Finnair*, OH-LCH, DC-Association, Helsinki, Finland
- *Swiss Air*, N431HM, Switzerland

- HA-LIX, Karman Todor, Budapest, Hungary
- *Daisy/Scandinavian*, Veterans Flying Association, Stockholm, Sweden
- KLM *Prinses Amalia* (PH-PBA) DDA *Classic Airlines*, Netherlands

We soon found out that the British are crazy about Dakotas, and that many of them had been following the *Miss Montana* story and wanted to meet us and see her in person. The Imperial War Museum sold guidebooks with a story about each of the D-Day Squadron DC-3s, and all of our crew were asked to autograph the *Miss Montana* page.

One day we were invited to park *Miss Montana* on a hard ramp that was right up against the fence, with four or five other D-Day Squadron planes. They put up a second fence around our planes and, for several hours, allowed the public to come out and see our planes up close. We opened our plane for them to go inside and spent the entire day giving tours and talking to the enthusiastic aviation fans from the United Kingdom and Europe. We much preferred this to being parked out of reach of the visiting public.

Another important thing about June 2 was that it was the day when our lodging, meals, transportation, fuel and oil, would be paid for by the Daks Over Normandy organization. We moved into hotels that had been prearranged, and started eating together at Duxford Aerodrome on a regular basis. Up until that time we had been operating on the funds we had raised, so it was a relief when someone else started paying most of the bills.

The Crew at Duxford: (L-R) Jeff, Eric, Giuseppe, Art, Bryan, Randy, Crystal, Skip (photo by Chris Rose, AOPA)

44

D-Day Squadron & Daks Over Normandy

WE SENSED FROM the beginning that the D-Day Squadron would take good care of us and we would be in capable hands as a group. However, the quality of planning and logistics, not to mention goodwill and friendship, that we encountered from the D-Day Squadron only became more exceptional during the Atlantic crossing and during our time in Europe. Even though we made the crossing alone, we received weather briefings, information from the planes ahead of us, and discounted fuel prices and landing fees that had been arranged by the D-Day Squadron.

Upon arrival in Duxford, the D-Day Squadron and Daks Over Normandy began officially working together, with the operation of our Mighty Fifteen under the leadership of Eric Zipkin of the D-Day Squadron, and the organization and logistics of the events under Daks Over Normandy. Daks Over Normandy had raised the money to fund our lodging, transportation, meals, fuel, and oil, and organized all the events with the authorities in England and France. Their job was a monumental one. In addition to our fifteen planes, there were eight to ten other planes from Europe that participated in the events.

Daks Over Normandy started strong. Fuel, oil, lodging,

transportation, and food were provided as promised. Daks Over Normandy had done a lot of work with authorities in England and France to obtain approvals for the various flights, paratrooper drops, and landings. However, when it came to execution of the bigger details, things started to break down.

Once we joined up with the D-Day Squadron, we became part of a unit. We had to adjust, partly because we were a bunch of proudly independent Montanans. None of us had flown in a squadron, in the military or otherwise. We had also been flying on our own for over a week and had enjoyed the independence and freedom of it. After we became integrated into the D-Day Squadron and Daks Over Normandy, we had work to do—flying safely and precisely with other big airplanes.

To their credit, both D-Day Squadron and Daks Over Normandy did a great job preparing briefings in advance of every squadron flight event. They weren't all perfect, and it was a tough crowd to be sure, but the information was detailed and thoughtfully prepared. Various opinions and questions were aired, and good solutions were usually the result. We would meet in a large conference room or briefing room, whatever was available. They would present slides and graphics depicting our taxi and flight order, our route, and various airspace considerations.

Equally important but more difficult were the debriefings after most flights. They were important because that was where lessons were learned and mistakes corrected for the next flights. They were difficult because we were usually tired and often grumpy. As one of the crews with little or no formation flight experience, we were often mentioned in the debriefings, but it was usually done professionally and with an offer to help us in any way they could. The other crews generally made us feel like we were part of the team.

There were often more than a hundred people in the room at one of these briefings. One of the most remarkable things about those briefings—it was mentioned once or twice—was the concentration of DC-3 experience sitting in those chairs. As one of the newest DC-3 pilots—maybe *the* newest—the sum of DC-3 experience and knowledge surrounding me was amazing. Those briefings might have been the last time in history so much DC-3 talent and experience would be together in one place.

45

Big News

FROM THE VERY beginning of the planning and organization of the D-Day Squadron events, the actual D-Day anniversary of June 6 was expected to be a no-fly day, with the D-Day Squadron on the ground at Caen-Carpiquet airport in France. This surprised nobody because multiple heads of state and leaders would be in the area and the entire Normandy area would be under a presidential temporary flight restriction.

A TFR can be placed over any area for many reasons, such as stadium events, active aerial firefighting, and to protect VIPs. Depending on the nature of the TFR, an aircraft violating a TFR can be subject to severe penalties. Presidential TFRs are the most strictly monitored and enforced. There are always armed fighter jets patrolling the area or ready to launch on short notice should an unauthorized plane stray into the TFR. A presidential TFR is a very serious thing.

Not only would the Normandy airspace be locked down for the day, but we found out later that virtually all roads would be closed off to civilian traffic. If you wanted to be somewhere that day, you needed to get there early and plan to be there all day.

The VIPs in Normandy for the day included President and Mrs. Trump, French President and Mrs. Macron, U.S. House Speaker Nancy Pelosi, French Prime Minister Edouard Philippe, Canadian

Prime Minister Justin Trudeau, Britain's Defense Secretary Penny Mourdaunt, Dutch Defense Minister Ank Bijleveld, and others. The area was loaded with VIPs, and we never expected to fly on June 6.

However, a few weeks before departing the U.S., on one of our last conference calls among the D-Day Squadron, Eric Zipkin mentioned that he had been contacted by the U.S. military about the possibility of the D-Day Squadron participating in a presidential flyby on June 6. It was a teaser that got all of us excited. He said nothing was firm yet, but he would keep us posted.

After arriving in England, he mentioned it a time or two in briefings, but still nothing was official. Then, on June 3 he announced in the afternoon briefing that we had been officially invited. We would be participating in the June 6 flyby at the Omaha Beach cemetery in front of Presidents Trump and Macron, and their wives, and with all the assembled crowds!

It was a rare honor, indeed, since civilian aircraft are almost never allowed to fly near the president, much less fourteen very large, very old, civilian aircraft. The event would be scripted in detail, from the number of crew members on each plane to our routes, sequencing, and the altitude we would be flying. We would be the only civilian element in the flyby along with six military elements from the U.S. and France. The flyby included the following aircraft, in order: four French Rafale fighter jets, a French Airbus A400, our flight of fourteen DC-3s with a Coast Guard C130 in trail, eight U.S. C130s, four U.S. F15s executing the missing man formation, the *Patrouile de France* (the French precision aerobatics team) Alpha jets, then a final pass by the *Patrouile de France* executing a missing man formation. We started to get a sense of how big a deal it was to fly in such company. It was the big league.

The U.S. Secret Service informed us they would only allow five crew members on each airplane. All prospective crew members for that flight had to provide their information to the Secret Service immediately for vetting. We must arrive at the Caen airport very early and expect to be busy all day.

This raised a question for our flight crew. There were six of us at that point, but only five would be allowed on the June 6 flight. Art volunteered that the June 5 jump flights would mean much more to him because of his background dropping smokejumpers, so he volunteered to sit out the June 6 flight. Jeff was happy to sit out the June 5 flight if he could make the morning flight across the channel and fly the following day. It was decided.

46

June 4

THE PLAN FOR June 4 was to make two flights as an entire squadron to practice dropping jumpers at Duxford as a dress rehearsal for the Normandy jumps on June 5. By this time, all the jumpers were on site and ready to go. Many, if not most of them, had never jumped out of the plane they would be assigned to, so it was a good idea to have a practice run or two for them. It would also serve as a practice run for the crews that had never dropped jumpers from a formation—like us.

By June 4, another European DC-3, *Daisy* (registration SE-CFP), owned by Veterans Flying Foundation in Stockholm, Sweden, had arrived at Duxford, bringing to twenty-two the total number of DC-3s. It made for an impressive parking lot on the grass.

By the night of June 3, the forecast for June 4 was for wind and rain. The day dawned damp and dreary with a modest wind, so we began to question whether we would be able to complete the practice drops. We also couldn't help but worry that weather might prevent the main paratrooper drops over Normandy on the following day, June 5. Daks Over Normandy, the D-Day Squadron, and the British Civil Aviation Authority would decide whether the practice jumps would happen.

Parachutists have standards for safe jumping conditions. They consider the jump altitude, the size of the drop zone where they are to land, the number of jumpers, and the type of equipment they use. For these jumps with round canopies and limited maneuverability, low altitude (1,000 feet), and a drop zone the size of the Duxford infield, the maximum allowable wind would be ten knots and the cloud ceiling must be at least 1,500 feet. As the day progressed, the weather did not improve; winds were blowing at twelve to fifteen knots and cloud ceilings were 2,000 feet.

Nevertheless, the jumpers got suited up and, at the appointed time, mustered cheerfully out to the flight line. By that time the British aviation authority had decreed that the jumps were off, but we would proceed with the practice flights. The first load of jumpers for *Miss Montana* was a boisterous bunch from Finland and Norway. Several of them spoke serviceable English, and we enjoyed meeting them as they prepared to load up. Despite the canceled jump, they were enthusiastic and happy to be there. We like to think they were particularly happy to be assigned to our plane. After loading up, we took off, made a practice pass over the field in echelon elements, then broke off one by one to land. Several of the jumpers told us they had jumped out of DC-3s before, but never *landed* in one.

The weather failed to improve before the second jump window, so it was destined to be another scenic flight with paratroopers on board. However, this time the jumpers were to be *ours*. These were the men and women, mostly from Montana or with ties to Montana, many of whom had worked on the restoration, who would be jumping out over Normandy. For most of them it was their first ride on *Miss Montana*, and many of these jumpers also commented on how infrequently they had actually landed in a jump plane.

Although it was a disappointment not to be able to make the two practice drops, everyone agreed that we would much rather get weathered out on June 4 than on June 5. The weather for the next day was forecast to be somewhat better in both England and France, but still not ideal. We would know more in the morning.

47

D-Day, June 6, 1944

THE INVASION OF Normandy on June 6, 1944, marked the beginning of the end of the war against Germany in Europe. Until the invasion, Germany had mostly had its way with every country on the continent and occupied countries in every direction. Only British resilience—and the English Channel—had prevented the conquest of England. Hitler had even invaded the Soviet Union in 1941, splitting his forces in what is widely considered his biggest mistake of the war. After the United States entered the war in December 1941, the Allies began planning an invasion of the continent to take back Europe and defeat Nazi Germany.

Planning and preparation for the invasion, code-named Operation Overlord, took several years. The American military had to vastly increase its size and capability after downsizing significantly following World War I. Massive amounts of personnel and equipment then had to be transported to England and the troops had to be trained. Finally, all the Allied leaders had to agree on the strategy. These parts didn't come together until late 1943. Planners originally aimed for the invasion to commence in May 1944, but delays pushed it back until early June.

Two of the most critical considerations were the tides and the weather. The beaches at Normandy are shallow sandy beaches, so when tides are low there can be several hundred yards of beach between the waterline and the German defenses. At low tide, invading soldiers would be exposed to fire for much too long. Weather was a major factor because the entire invasion force, except for the airborne troops, would be coming across the channel by ship. Bad weather could prevent the crossing or, upon reaching the beaches, complicate the landing of men and equipment. High winds and low clouds or rain would also make it much more difficult to drop airborne troops accurately and safely, or for bombers to hit their targets ahead of the invasion. A visible moon was also preferred so pilots could see their targets and drop zones at night. The tides and moon phases were well known, but the weather was not.

The first date for the invasion was June 5, the first day in a narrow, three-day window with acceptable tides and a full moon. This would mean the airborne assault would start shortly before midnight on June 4. General Dwight "Ike" Eisenhower, Supreme Commander of Allied Expeditionary Forces, would make the final decision to go or wait. Eisenhower met with his top generals and Winston Churchill in the early morning of June 4 and reviewed the weather forecast. It was not good, predicting low clouds, rain, and heavy seas. Eisenhower decided to postpone the invasion twenty-four hours.

All of Operation Overlord had been planned with the utmost secrecy. The Germans knew an invasion was coming, but they could only guess where. Without knowing where it would come from, they were forced to harden the defenses along a vast length of the French coast. German Field Marshal Erwin Rommel was tasked with building this "Atlantic Wall." The fortifications and defenses he constructed, much of it with slave labor, were massive and exquisitely planned. There was no easy place to invade France, but the Allies chose Normandy because they believed it had the greatest chance of success.

The shores of Normandy were divided into five beaches for the invasion. From west to east, they were Utah, Omaha, Gold, Juno, and Sword. The Americans would go ashore at Utah and Omaha beaches. Sword and Gold beaches were assaulted by primarily British troops, and Canadians assaulted at Juno. Airborne troops from each country would land inland, behind the German defenders and before the beach assaults began.

On June 4 the team of Allied weather forecasters differed on whether June 5 or June 6 would have better conditions. The head of the weather forecasters, British Captain James Stagg, urged a delay, and he was correct. The next day, Stagg advised Ike that the weather of June 6 would be less than ideal, but it would be good enough for the invasion to begin. The next window of tides and moon conditions would be several weeks away, increasing the chance that the Germans would discover the secret invasion location. Ike gave the order for the invasion to begin. Ike drafted two statements that night, one that praised the Allied forces for a successful invasion and a second one in which he took full responsibility for the failure.

The invasion started before midnight on June 5, 1944, when more than 800 C-47s carrying almost 22,000 Allied paratroopers took off from airfields in England. Many C-47s were also towing gliders that would land in France, carrying elite troops, jeeps, and light artillery. Due to the marginal weather in France and anti-aircraft fire from Germans, the airborne assault did not go as planned. Units were dropped in the wrong places, scattered over large areas, and even dropped into the sea or areas that had been flooded by the Germans, where many drowned. It took several days for most of the paratroopers to find their units, but the disarray had an unintended benefit.

The very first contact with the enemy was between British commandos and Germans defending Pegasus Bridge near Caen. The bridge remains today and is a popular tourist destination. Our drop zone near Sannerville was near Pegasus Bridge.

The Germans had seen much of the same weather information that the Allies had. They were convinced that the invasion could not happen until mid-June, and many left their coastal defenses and generally let down their guard. Field Marshal Rommel was so convinced the invasion was not imminent that he had returned to Germany to celebrate his wife's birthday. When the invasion started, the Germans were caught off guard. The disorganized airborne assault also convinced many of the German defenders that it was a feint intended to draw their forces away from the real invasion elsewhere. By the time the Germans figured out that it was the real thing, Operation Overlord had secured a beachhead and the Allies were on the way to Berlin.

Operation Overlord was the largest amphibious assault in history. Due to the changing nature of warfare, it's unlikely to ever be surpassed. Approximately 6,000 ships and 11,000 planes were involved in the invasion. More than 150,000 troops from the United States, Britain, Canada, France, and Norway went ashore the first day.

The airborne component on D-Day was critical to the success of the amphibious assault. Even though it was disorganized, the paratroopers completed most of their objectives, which included seizing bridges and crossroads, and preventing German tanks from engaging Allied troops coming ashore. By June 11, the Allies had secured the beachhead and started fighting inland. Germany would surrender eleven months later in May 1945.

The goal of the D-Day Squadron was to reenact, commemorate, and honor the pilots, crews, paratroopers, and ground troops that put their lives on the line for this historic invasion. June 5 was to be *our* D-Day.

48

June 5 – The Best & Worst Day

NEARLY EVERYONE ASKS about our favorite part of the entire journey. The question itself implies that there could be several to choose from—and there were. Picking one is hard because of the variety of experiences in so many places, all of which were once-in-a-lifetime historic events. As Art said about the Dover photo flight, all our efforts would have been worth it for that one day alone. Nevertheless, we all pretty much agree that if you made us pick one, it had to be the flights of June 5.

The June 5 event was the goal from the very beginning. It was the primary focus of all our efforts. We were the D-Day Squadron, after all. Five of our planes actually *flew* on D-Day in 1944. The entire mission arose out of Eric Zipkin's vision for repeating—and improving—the American DC-3 presence on the 70th D-Day anniversary. The sole motivation of the entire effort was to drop jumpers over Normandy on June 5. We were not disappointed, but none of us could have predicted the true story of that day. It was the best and the worst day of the entire trip.

We had been told several weeks before the trip that two private parachute teams had asked the D-Day Squadron to conduct some additional drops on the morning of June 5 in France. Because *Miss Montana* was one of the planes equipped to jump with an anchor line, we were invited to join the morning drop in Normandy on June 5.

After reviewing the flight times and logistics, Eric Zipkin determined that, weather permitting, we could cross the channel in the morning, pick up the jumpers at Cherbourg, France, make the drop over Carentan, then return to Duxford in plenty of time to make the main flight across the channel for the main event at Sannerville. The private teams had paid for the planes in advance, so it was an opportunity to earn some additional funds.

We awoke on the morning of June 5 anxiously anticipating the big day. We all immediately looked at the weather and were cautiously optimistic that it would cooperate. The winds in Normandy were forecast to be light, with a broken cloud layer at 3,000 feet or so. We left the hotel at five a.m., made our way to Duxford Aerodrome, and got ready for the morning flight. Excitement was in the air over the entire airfield. We would be flying across the channel in excellent company, with *Placid Lassie*, *Betsy's Biscuit Bomber*, *D-Day Doll*, and *"That's All, Brother."* All four sported military livery with invasion stripes; we were the only plane not similarly dressed, but we were honored to fly in their company.

We launched by seven a.m., with Jeff as PIC and me in the right seat and joined up for the flight to Cherbourg. Since this was to be our last day in England, we had loaded up all our luggage, along with The Ancient One, Tia, Taylor, Avian, and Gman, who had joined us in England. To carry a full load of jumpers, we had to unload all our luggage, our passengers, and most of our flyaway kit at Cherbourg, where we were told it would be transported to the Caen Airport by the end of the day. Skip, Tia, Taylor, Avian, Gman, and Jeff Whitesell would be bused to Caen, where we would meet them at the end of the day.

After departing Duxford, we flew south, to the west of London, and over the English Channel directly toward Cherbourg. Flying over the channel that morning was an incredible experience, especially in our position in the rear following four DC-3s in military livery, including three D-Day veterans. We imagined the same flight seventy-five years before. We flew low, at 2,000 feet above the water or so, and the view was marvelous. Part way across, the four planes ahead of us joined up in a diamond formation, making for a historic photo opportunity. By this time our sense of wonder had been regularly exercised. Still, that was amazing.

We landed in Cherbourg and scurried to get our gear and passengers unloaded, clear customs, and get ready to load our jumpers. We removed our jump door and got ready to take on the parachutists. We were joined by *Drag 'em Oot*, a British-based DC-3 (and a fourth D-Day veteran) that would lead the way for the drop over Carentan. The other planes also unloaded passengers and gear and loaded up with paratroopers in their World War II uniforms. We waited for our assigned parachutists, but none ever showed due to some mixup. We weren't going to let the lack of jumpers keep us from making the flight with the rest, so we took off without a load. We followed the other planes from Cherbourg to Carentan at low altitude and got a great view of the beautiful Norman countryside.

Carentan is only a short, twenty-minute flight south from Cherbourg. It is a small town at the base of the Cotentin peninsula, between the American landing beaches of Utah and Omaha. Carentan was at the center of the American paratrooper drop zone seventy-five years earlier, right between the 101st airborne and the 82nd airborne. It was one of the first French towns to be liberated, so this flight had special significance for the five American DC-3s. There we were, bringing up the rear behind five historic DC-3s painted just like they were in 1944, flying over a historic American drop zone on the 75th anniversary of D-Day. As we circled around getting set up for the drop run, we could see thousands of vehicles parked near the drop zone and thousands of people standing in parking lots and fields to watch.

We made two passes over the drop zone to gauge winds, then paratroopers began jumping out of the planes ahead of us. As the last plane in the formation, we had a front-row seat to see approximately one hundred paratroopers jump out and drift toward the ground. The canopies were graceful as they floated silently beneath us. As soon as the jumpers were out, *Drag 'em Oot* left our group to go home, and our group of five turned north toward England. We were the only planes that would get to invade France twice on the same day. We have the passport stamps to prove it.

Until then, it had been a fabulous day. The events of the next few hours would be the most unfortunate, dramatic, and painful of the entire trip.

Daks Over Normandy was the organization that accepted and approved applications from prospective jumpers from the beginning. Several World War II reenactment teams applied. These were parachutists who regularly jumped into historical events, though none had brought their own aircraft to Duxford. Daks Over Normandy had a difficult job because it wasn't clear exactly how many planes would be available or even how many paratroopers each plane could carry.

By virtue of their registration and other specifics, each plane is permitted to carry up to twenty-eight jumpers. Every plane was different, and it can be complicated. Our plane could carry nineteen passengers in addition to the flight crew. Daks Over Normandy had to vet and approve enough jumpers to fill all the planes that *might* show up, but not too many. They didn't want more jumpers than planes, either. No question it was a balancing act from the beginning.

By June 5, the number of planes was certain, along with the number of jumpers for each plane. However, there were no contingencies if a plane were to drop out. Daks Over Normandy had found a spot for all of the approximately 220 jumpers who had been approved and had been waiting at Duxford over the past three days.

From our first communication with Daks Over Normandy in mid-2018, we had emphasized that we had our own jump team and were adamant they would jump out of our airplane. These were Montana-affiliated jumpers, many of whom had put in long hours working on our airplane. We were the only airplane in the D-Day Squadron that had come with its own specific jumpers. However, it wasn't until the morning of June 5 that we got confirmation that it would happen as requested. The fifteen *Miss Montana* jumpers, plus three more assigned to us by Daks Over Normandy, would be jumping from *Miss Montana* over Normandy. We appeared to be set.

Then, on the morning of June 5, two airplanes broke down at Duxford. With no extra airplanes, Daks Over Normandy suddenly had the unenviable task of scrubbing twenty-two jumpers from the afternoon jump. We had no knowledge of this as we flew to France in the morning and returned to Duxford. Shortly before we landed back in Duxford at about two p.m., I got an urgent text from Al Charters, *Miss Montana's* jumpmaster, telling me the short version and urgently asking me to come to the hangar, where the jumpers were assembled. He needed me to tell the organizers that our jumpers would not be scrubbed and would be flying on our plane.

When we landed back at Duxford, we were amazed at the huge number of spectators who had arrived to see the entire squadron depart for Normandy. We later learned there were 12,500 people that day (a new record for the museum), and they were crowded along the fence, snapping pictures as our five DC-3s taxied to our parking spots in a graceful line. Many of the visitors had been awaiting this day for years.

As soon as we parked and shut down, I made a beeline for the large hangar where the paratrooper operations were staging. Al and our jumpers were standing around looking grim, and Al gave me the full story. The leader of Daks Over Normandy was in a lobby with a few others, and they were writing numbers on 220 pieces of paper and a corresponding number next to each name on the jump roster. They had decided to hold a lottery to randomly select the twenty-two jumpers who would be scrubbed from the jump.

Nobody would dispute, either then or now, that this was just awful, including the organizers. The enthusiasm and patriotism of the men and women parachutists who had worked toward this event for over a year was amazing. They were in replica uniforms, complete with period combat boots, all the way to period helmets. Many of the men sported Mohawk haircuts that airborne troops had worn in

1944. They had spent thousands of dollars to buy their uniforms and parachutes, make practice jumps back home, and get to England. For many, it would be a once-in-a-lifetime event and they were all in. Some of them were active duty or retired military. To think that twenty-two of them would be denied was a gut punch for all of us.

Eric Komberec was away somewhere, so an urgent text went out to get him to come to the hangar. Randy and Art were already nearby. If we were going to stand up for our jumpers, it would be a team effort. Art and I found the Daks Over Normandy leaders preparing the lottery and sat down to try to persuade them to leave our jumpers out of the lottery. I explained that *Miss Montana* was the only plane that had preselected its jumpers. I explained that many of our jumpers were also volunteers who had worked on the plane and helped make the *Miss Montana* restoration happen. I explained that the owner of the airplane (the Museum of Mountain Flying represented by board president Eric Komberec) was adamant that *all* our jumpers were going to jump out of our airplane, or we might not fly. I didn't know if Eric would agree, but I went with it.

The Daks Over Normandy organizers shrugged and said they had no other choice, that a lottery was the only fair thing to do and that all jumpers and planes would be included. The organizers appeared to be in a state of shock. They weren't any happier than we were, and none of us could change the facts. We went back and forth, and they finally suggested that we go ahead with the lottery. Maybe *Miss Montana* wouldn't lose any spots. In hindsight, an ultimatum that we wouldn't fly without *all* our jumpers would probably have worked.

On one hand they needed us badly because we were equipped for jumpers. Both the *Miss Montana* crew and our jumpers had been clear from the very beginning that the plane came with designated parachutists. Also, it wasn't our plane that had broken down. Still, we were part of the squadron and this was a team sport. Demanding that *Miss Montana* be eliminated from the lottery would cause the other jumpers to suffer disproportionally. It was a tough choice.

Art and I reluctantly agreed to wait for the results of the lottery and left to join the jumpers in the hangar. The atmosphere among the paratroopers in the hangar was somber. We were already hours behind schedule. Over 200 men and seven women dressed in World War II uniforms, some with Mohawks and camo paint on their faces, were anxiously waiting next to their gear with their teams. The only items missing from the authentic scene were weapons, which was probably a good thing. They were trying to comprehend the elimination of ten percent of their assembled number. *Would it be one of ours, or me?* It was written on every face, and it was dreadful.

We waited until the Daks Over Normandy leaders showed up with the numbers in a bowl and the roster of names. All 220 people moved in close so they could hear, shoulder to shoulder, most huddled with their own jump team. You could hear a pin drop. I was standing next to Al Charters, our jumpmaster, the Sky God, and heart and soul of our jumpers. Nearby were several others from our group.

As the names were read, groans and gasps came from the crowd. A guy from another team who was standing next to me reacted to a name that was read, "Oh no, that's our jumpmaster. We can't lose our jumpmaster." Men were crying, both inside and out. Someone later offered $2,000 to buy a seat.

We had seventeen jumpers on our manifest before the lottery. The lottery would eliminate ten percent of the jumpers, so if the scrubbed jumpers were evenly distributed between the planes, we should have lost one or two jumpers. We lost three. Al Charters was standing right next to me, and his name was about the fifth name read. My skin went cold and the hair on my neck went up. Al didn't blink. This was the leader of our team, our jumpmaster, and the coordinator between the flight crew and jumpers. No way could we lose Al. I leaned over and whispered to Al, "That is not going to happen. You *will* be on our airplane." Al nodded stoically, and we continued to listen to the angel of death read the names. By the time it was mercifully over, we had lost two more jumpers, Phil Jameson and Greg Jones.

Phil is a retired Navy SEAL who came to be involved with our group through a mutual contact, but had never been to Missoula. His wife was waiting at the drop zone for him in Normandy. Greg is a Canadian smokejumper who got on our team as a fellow smoke-jumper. Phil and Greg were not very familiar to us. They had never been able to come to Missoula to work on the plane or meet us. Still, they were members of our jump team, and we were determined to get them on the flight.

About that time, Eric Komberec made it to the hangar, and we brought him up to speed. His first words were music to my ears. Without hesitation he said, "Well, we just won't frickin' take off with-out our jumpers." I wanted to hug him. We were in perfect agree-ment that we had an obligation to fight for our jumpers. They were as much a part of *Miss Montana's* team as anyone.

As soon as the lottery was over, Kim Maynard, Al's wife, spoke to the Daks Over Normandy lead organizer. She told him that *Miss Montana* couldn't jump without Al, who was essential to our entire jump operation. The organizer acknowledged the truth in that but claimed to be helpless. Kim asked him how many seats they now had assigned to *Miss Montana*, and he said, "Eighteen." She said, "Well, we have seats for nineteen. Al will take the last seat." All he could say was, "Okay." We had official approval, but Al would have been on the plane without it.

We had started with fifteen jumpers from our team, and Daks Over Normandy had assigned us two more that morning for a total of seventeen. We lost three in the lottery, and they assigned four reenactors to us from the broken airplanes. That put us at eighteen seats filled. We had nineteen seats available. Al Charters got the nineteenth seat. Then the discussion revolved around how to get Phil and Greg on board.

This was another time when our decision-making process was valuable. We had the airplane owner, represented by Eric. Randy, as mechanic, would address the weight and balance issues. Art Dykstra would be our PIC for the flight. We huddled there in the hangar while jumpers around us were gearing up and considered our options. The first question was: with our current fuel load and other weight on board, could the airplane handle the weight of twenty-one jumpers on board? Randy said it could. Art agreed that the airplane could carry a lot more than twenty-one jumpers and that he could fly it. The real issue was our legal limitation of carrying only nineteen jumpers.

This raised an interesting issue. Paratroopers aren't legally considered passengers, maybe because they usually jump out and don't land with the plane. The rules governing this issue are complicated and somewhat gray. We were required to have a seat belt for everyone on board, and we only had nineteen seats with belts. Some of the airplanes use some pretty sketchy straps that pass for seat belts; we probably could have rigged something as well.

All of us wanted to get Phil and Greg on board. The question was how we could do it. After some discussion, we decided that to put them on board would be a real gray area. Physically we could do it, but the regulations might not allow it. We might do it if we were dropping them over Montana, but this was a foreign country and a very public event. On this day, the entire world would be watching, and it wasn't worth the risk. We all dearly wished we could have done it. I told Phil and Greg of our decision and the reasons and expressed our sincere regret that we couldn't get them on. Both were understandably disappointed.

The repercussions of not being able to jump were even bigger for those two guys because the ride they had arranged for getting to France—*Miss Montana*—had fallen through and they both needed to figure out a way to get there. Phil's wife was waiting for him at the drop zone. In the end, they both took the ferry and eventually made it to France. We were able to make it up in a small way to Phil and his wife, but it still stung.

At least four men gave up their seats that day for jumpers who had lost the lottery. One of those who had been scrubbed was to jump with his father; an unnamed hero gave up his seat so the father and son could jump together. There were also many jumpers approved to jump that day who lived in Europe and had made this jump before. Many of them would probably do so again and many would jump in Normandy again over the next few days. You would think that those jumpers would be the first to offer their seats to those from far away for which this was a once-in-a-lifetime opportunity. Sadly, most did not.

By this time, the schedule for taking off had slipped about two hours. As we all filed out to the plane, the assembled crowds cheered the flight crews and the paratroopers, who had their helmets, uniforms, and parachutes. We had a few minutes to snap pictures of our jumpers and savor the moment before loading up so that we could meet our takeoff time. It was starting to get late, and we had nearly three hours of flying ahead of us. At the last minute, another paratrooper came up to the plane and asked Al if Daks Over Normandy had given him the briefing on the drop zone conditions. They hadn't. Thankfully, the jumper gave him the basic, but critical, information. The awkwardness and disappointment of the last few hours were over. We were eager to put it behind us and carry on with the reason we were there.

49

June 5 – Mission Accomplished

Nobody died.

– Art Dykstra

BY FIVE P.M. we prepared to launch for Normandy. On this flight there would be a total of twenty DC-3s, nine of which would drop jumpers over Sannerville, near Pegasus Bridge. *Flabob Express* and *Dakota Norway* (LN-WND) would remain behind at Duxford with mechanical problems. A pair of P-51 Mustangs and four T-6 Texans would provide roaming top cover and two C-45s (also known as a Twin Beech or Beech 18) would bracket us on the left and right as photo ships. The squadron of twenty-eight aircraft would be an impressive and historic sight.

In the days leading up to June 5, the squadron had developed and practiced an efficient mass takeoff procedure. All the planes had to get off the ground in quick succession to join up in formation rapidly once we were airborne. By this time, we were good at it.

Every plane was assigned a position in the flight during the briefing. For instance, on this day *Miss Montana* was the number three plane in the third, or Charlie, Vic. We would be Charlie Three. The Vics would be designated Alpha, Bravo, Charlie, Delta, and so on. Every plane would assume its position in the line as we taxied for takeoff, then keep that position throughout the flight. The goal was for a DC-3 to be airborne every ten seconds or less.

The lead plane in Alpha flight, normally *Placid Lassie*, would taxi out, obtain a takeoff clearance for the entire squadron, take the runway, and taxi forward far enough for Alpha Two to pull onto the runway behind it. Alpha Lead would apply power and begin its takeoff roll. As soon as Alpha Lead started rolling, Alpha Two would pull forward to allow Alpha Three to take the runway behind it. As soon as Alpha Lead's tail came up, Alpha Two would advance partial power and hold its brakes. As soon as Alpha Lead's main gear came off the runway, Alpha Two would advance to full power, release its brakes, and begin the takeoff roll. We could get the entire squadron off the ground within a few minutes. It was beautiful to watch and the crowds always loved it. Images went through our minds of hundreds of bombers performing mass takeoffs during the war.

That was the way we practiced it, but on the day it mattered most, we didn't do it quite that way. Instead of *Placid Lassie* as our flight lead, *Aces High*, piloted by the leaders of Daks Over Normandy, took the lead position. The reason for this was that they had planned the jumper drop in Normandy, worked with the authorities in France to make it happen, and they supposedly knew the way to the drop zone. It turned out not to be such a good idea, and it nearly ended badly.

The route from Duxford to Normandy had been published weeks in advance, and it was not intended to be a direct route from Duxford to the drop zone for good reason. The organizers wisely intended to put on a show for the assembled crowds on the ground. After takeoff and joining up in the largest formation of DC-3s in many years, we headed southeast to Colchester, on the English coast. Then we turned south along the coast, passing *Southend-on-Sea* and *Maidstone* before starting across the English Channel near *Eastbourne*. Flying in such an amazing group, at 1,000 feet above the ground, was thrilling. Everywhere we looked, we saw thousands of spectators witnessing history.

The first sign that *Aces High* was not up to the job as lead was their radio silence well into the flight. One of the jobs of the flight lead was to call roll before taxi, before takeoff, and after joining up. *Aces High* never called roll. *Placid Lassie*, our usual lead—and Alpha Two on this flight—tried to contact them after we took off, but there was no answer. *Placid Lassie* tried various frequencies and finally contacted *Aces High*. *Aces High* had just headed out and expected the rest of us to follow.

Shortly before we got to the drop zone in France, the two P-51s asked where the lead wanted them during the drop and were told by *Aces High* to "knock off the chatter," so the P-51s broke off and landed at Caen. This was not the type of leadership we were accustomed to, and it was happening on the most important flight of all.

The entire flight from Duxford to Sannerville to Caen was estimated to take two hours and forty minutes. Because we would be dropping our jumpers at Sannerville, we had removed our jump door and made the entire flight from Duxford across the channel with the door off. All the jumpers were in their seats, and most of them seemed introspective for much of the flight, contemplating the significance of this historic day. Some of them, like Al Charters, had relatives who had made this very trip seventy-five years before. His father made three trips to Normandy that day as an aerial reconnaissance observer. As Al said, to occupy the same airspace as his father had, seventy-five years on, would be…perfect.

During the flight, the jumpers all signed my logbook, we took many photos, and the jumpers stood up and walked about the plane, at least as much as possible, given their heavy loads. Despite the engine noise and the wind noise from the open door, it was possible to have conversations about the significance of what we were doing. You should have been there. Words fail.

With Art flying PIC and Eric in the right seat, we rumbled across the channel in this famous group. It was impossible not to think about what it was like seventy-five years earlier for those young paratroopers and aviators. The similarities were remarkable, but the differences were more so. There we were, in daylight, with good weather, a highly experienced flight crew, and modern navigation avionics and radios. In 1944, it was dark, the weather was foul, the navigation equipment was inadequate, the flight crews were inexperienced and…upon reaching France, the Germans shot many of them out of the sky. What we were doing was easy in comparison. Except it wasn't quite.

The GPS coordinates of the drop zone had been distributed to all the planes in the briefing. I had them in my iPad so we would have a backup if needed. When we reached land at Le Havre, France, we turned inbound to the drop zone and headed straight toward the coordinates on my map. I was in the jump seat with a headset on monitoring the action. Based on our destination and groundspeed, we were less than ten minutes out from the drop zone. At that point, the three-ship Vics moved to right echelon, the red standby light near the door was turned on, and Al motioned for the jumpers in the first stick to stand up and snap their static lines onto the anchor line.

It was a fabulous view out the front windscreen as we anticipated the drop zone, and as we approached it, we saw…nothing. There was no field, no drop zone large enough for us to drop nearly 200 jumpers.

Pretty soon, *Aces High* announced on the radio that the coordinates for the drop zone were wrong. We were about twenty miles away from the correct spot. Everyone in the squadron had the same thought at once, "Are you kidding?" But it was true. And at that moment it started to get dangerous.

Immediately after announcing a change of plans, *Aces High* turned *right* into our *right* echelon formation. *Placid Lassie*, which was number two in the first element, yelled into the radio, "What the hell are you doing?! You *don't* turn into your echelon!" The entire squadron heard the exchange. *Aces High* responded back, "We're doing what we were told. We're headed to the correct drop zone." With that, we all headed off to the correct drop zone about twenty miles away. We all remained in right echelon.

Fortunately, that turn was gradual enough that the entire squadron was able to adjust, but there were more than a few curses in more than a few cockpits. Our jumpers in the back didn't know exactly what was going on, but they knew something was amiss. Al was on the intercom in the back. It was clear to him we were not where we were supposed to be, as the area we were over didn't look anything like what had been briefed back in Duxford. Al, who would lead the first stick out the door, gave no further commands to our jumpers until the mess was sorted out. Once the first stick was standing and snapped onto the anchor line, they remained so until we found the correct drop zone.

About that time, one of our Missoula volunteers who was waiting patiently on the ground at Sannerville sent me a text. He had been following our GPS satellite tracker and asked, "Are you guys lost?" I didn't reply.

Unbeknownst to us, there were other jumpers from another group also jumping at the correct drop zone. These were free-fall jumpers, jumping from several thousand feet high, unlike our D-Day Squadron, which would be dropping from 1,000 feet above the ground. As we approached the drop zone, the planes in the front of our squadron saw that the free-fall jumpers were still descending over the drop zone. Fortunately, they were trailing red smoke so they were easy to see. It would have been disastrous for our squadron to fly right through the middle of the descending jumpers.

In response, *Aces High* started another big turn, again to the *right*, but this time much sharper and again with no warning. The reaction was swift and violent. *Placid Lassie* banked hard right to avoid being hit by *Aces High*. *D-Day Doll* decided they had had enough, banked right, and dove to get out of the formation. Airplanes scattered everywhere to avoid a collision. In front of us, *D-Day Doll* disappeared from view as she dove to get away. After the formation straightened out a few minutes later, *D-Day Doll* slid right back into position for the rest of the flight. There was more condemnation of *Aces High* over the radio, but no response.

After flying one or two big circles north of the drop zone, we finally started our inbound run. The jumpers in nearly all the planes had remained standing for about twenty minutes during the confusion and were more than ready to get out. When we were less than five minutes out from the correct drop zone, they began their final gear checks. Because the drop zone was not large, we would make two passes to get the jumpers out in two sticks of nine or ten jumpers each so they could all land within the designated area. At least that was the plan.

Randy and Crystal were in position in the back, with parachutes on, ready to pull in the D-bags after each stick. I was standing behind the jump seat to watch all the jumpers go out.

Finally, after so many months of effort by so many people, the hazardous Atlantic crossing, and preparing for this day, it happened. Our first stick moved to the door, the green light came on, and, when Al Charters decided it was time, out he went, followed by Kim Maynard and the rest of the first stick. All nine jumpers in the first stick were out the door in as many seconds. Crystal and Randy and our second jumpmaster, Bryan M., pulled in the D-bags against the slipstream's drag, and we started a big turn to come back around for the second stick.

As we approached the drop zone for the second drop, Bryan M. told the second stick to stand up and hook up. At the appointed time he gave the signal and out they went, Bryan in the lead followed by his wife, Sarah, and the rest of the stick. He was a little early, and most of the jumpers in the second stick landed in a gorgeous wheat field. They said later it was the softest place they had ever landed. The good news was that despite the poor leadership, confusion, and near misses…nobody died or was even injured.

Miss Montana, which had not participated in the D-Day invasion, had finally accomplished the mission she had been built for—we had dropped paratroopers into the historic air space over Normandy.

After the drops, the squadron turned toward the Caen airport a few minutes away. We lined up for landing, each plane breaking off from the formation about seven seconds apart to come around and land. All the planes landed without incident. I suspect there was a heated discussion between the pilots of *Placid Lassie* and *Aces High*. In the debriefing that followed, Eric Zipkin apologized and announced that Daks Over Normandy would have no more involvement in flights with the D-Day Squadron. Nobody argued.

We joked that we had actually been trying to simulate the events of June 5-6, 1944, when planes got lost, entire units were separated, jumpers landed far from their designated drop zones, and in general everything that could go wrong, did. Indeed, like the Germans in 1944, nobody on the ground at Sannerville had a clue that day, the parachute drops were spectacular to see, and it was by all accounts a stunning success.

That day was one of the very few days when I wasn't entirely sure whether it was better to be in the airplane or on the ground watching. Of course, it was better to be in the plane, but seeing it from the ground would have been magnificent. Fortunately, there were many cameras recording and many videos of the event were made for us to see later.

Two hours after we landed at Caen, our jumpers showed up to claim their gear. We later found out that much of their luggage had been left behind in England, and, due to financial issues with Daks Over Normandy, some had no accommodations or transportation in France. Some of them slept in the hangar that night.

This was the end of our time with our jumpers. They would not be jumping again, and most of them would soon head home or off to enjoy Europe. The ending was bittersweet, but we had accomplished what we had come for, and for that we were all proud and pleased. Yet, there was no time to celebrate, as we had to brief for the next day, find our lodging, eat, get some sleep, and prepare for June 6. As we parted, we were treated to a beautiful sunset behind *Miss Montana*—a fitting end to a momentous day.

Two more DC-3s joined our group after we arrived in France. KLM *Prinses Amalia* (PH-PBA) DDA Classic Airlines, Netherlands, arrived at Caen on June 5. *ChalAir*, owned by Dakota sur la Normadie (F-AZOX), from Caen, France joined us on June 6 or 7. This final addition brought our number to twenty-two total aircraft on the ground in France.

Jumpers out over Normandy (photo by Keith Wolferman)

Our jumpers before boarding, June 5 at Duxford (photo by Al Charters)

Amanda & Kim (L-R) relaxing at Duxford (photo by Al Charters)

Kim and Al over the channel on June 5 (photo by Shawn Modula)

Scrubbed jumpers being selected at Duxford (photo by Greg Jones)

Second Jumpmaster Bryan, Sarah, and family in Normandy (photo by Bryan M)

Shawn Modula and Annette Dusseau, Duxford (photo by Shawn Modula)

50

June 6 – Presidential Flyby

THERE IS NO question that June 6 was a close second to the historic and memorable events of June 5. We were humbled and honored to join the presidential flyby, and none of us wanted to screw it up. Coming on the heels of June 5, it was destined to be another long day. None of us thought much about that; we were just thrilled to be there.

On the evening of June 5, we got a glimpse into how detailed the event had been planned when we mustered in the hangar at Caen. The military organizers had prepared an extremely detailed electronic briefing and slideshow for the events of the next day. It choreographed each element, with routes and altitudes to be flown, times over target and so on. There was even a second-by-second animation of each pass. We were to be the third element in the flyby, following shortly behind and below a huge Airbus A400, which is a military transport that is only slightly smaller than the Boeing C5 Galaxy.

We arrived at the Caen airport before 0600 as instructed, before all the roads in Normandy were locked down. Two polite Secret Service agents checked our identities before admitting us into the hangar. We then waited at the hangar until President Trump landed in Air Force One and departed again by helicopter for Omaha Beach Cemetery. The Secret Service then cleared us to go to our planes and prepare to launch. We originally planned for fourteen planes from the D-Day Squadron to participate, but *Flabob Express* was still broken down in Duxford and unable to make the flight.

The historic flight of thirteen DC-3s would include eleven from the D-Day Squadron and two from the European contingent, in flight order: *Placid Lassie*, *"That's All, Brother,"* *D-Day Doll*, *Virginia Ann*, *Betsy's Biscuit Bomber*, *Rendezvous With Destiny*, *Miss Virginia*, *Swiss Air*, *Miss Montana*, *Liberty*, *Pan Am*, *HA-LIX*, and *Spirit of Benovia*. *Clipper Tabitha May*, N18121, and *Hap-enstance* from the D-Day Squadron did not participate for various reasons.

Our flight of thirteen, which was designated "Dakota 44 Flight" by someone with an appreciation for history, would be trailed by a U.S. Coast Guard C130. We speculated that the C130 was there to deal with any of us that might go rogue. Actually, none of the other services wanted them along, so they were stuck with us. During the briefing, we were instructed not to descend below 1,000 feet for any reason...*or bad things would happen.* They never specified exactly what that meant, but we could guess.

After we launched from Caen, we flew in formation to the west of Omaha Beach cemetery and orbited, following orders from the U.S. Air Force plane overhead, appropriately designated "Overlord." Overlord's job was to tell us when it was our time to turn inbound for our target pass. Most impressive of all was that they expected us to fly past our target in smart formation within ten seconds of a designated time—"time over target," or TOT. The original TOT was something like 10:38:00 a.m. Our familiar lead, *Placid Lassie*, was back in her rightful place, the mistakes of the previous day forgotten, and the whole world was watching.

According to our previous arrangement, Jeff flew PIC and Eric flew SIC for this flight. Randy, Crystal, and I got to watch from the back and the jump seat. *Miss Montana* was once again assigned the third spot in the third Vic, as Charlie Three, making us the ninth plane in Dakota 44 Flight. The leader of Charlie Vic was Karl Stoltzfus's *Miss Virginia* and on our right was the gorgeous *Swissair*.

After takeoff, we listened to the frequency assigned to Overlord and orbited for about two hours west of Omaha Beach.

Orbiting at that location had incredible historical significance. We were 1,000 feet above the water, in a formation of thirteen DC-3s, and every orbit took us past Utah Beach, then past Point Du Hoc, past the west end of Omaha Beach, and back again. It was history in every turn for two hours on the actual 75th anniversary of D-Day. And all of it by invitation in a presidential TFR.

As we orbited, Overlord kept us updated with changes to our TOT. Not surprisingly, the TOT slipped twice, probably because the speeches lasted longer, or there were more babies for the presidents to kiss. However, the time came when Overlord told us to expect our ten-minute warning shortly. The trick at that point was to orbit so that we were never farther than ten minutes from our target. Eric Zipkin, in *Placid Lassie*, was leading the way and did a great job of setting us up to make the target run on time. When we finally got the call from Overlord for "ten minutes to TOT," *Placid Lassie* turned inbound on the target run, and we all followed as if we had done it before.

The target run itself was stunning and unforgettable. We turned left, flew just off shore from Point du Hoc and down the full length of Omaha Beach, right over the waterline. Our target was directly offshore from the overlook, where the presidents and their wives would be watching at the Omaha Beach Cemetery. We were a few seconds behind our ten-second window, so we updated Overlord, and the elements following us adjusted slightly. We weren't quite perfect, but it wasn't bad for a bunch of civilians.

Flying in close formation is demanding work. Another complicating factor when you're in a large formation is that the turbulent air from the planes ahead of you can bounce you around quite a bit, making your job even harder. It's called "dirty air," and we tried to avoid it whenever we could, usually by flying about fifty feet above the plane in front of us to avoid the turbulent air coming off their wings. Still, after orbiting in formation for two hours, Jeff was pretty worn out. Of course, he wasn't going to miss the big moment, so he soldiered on until the big moment was over.

From the right side behind the wing, I saw Omaha Beach Cemetery come into view, with its rows and rows of perfectly aligned brilliant white grave markers. Then we passed the overlook point and could see the two presidents and their wives looking up from the appointed spot. We could also see the thousands of attendees to the ceremonies that had just concluded.

In just a few seconds, it was over. Well, not quite. As we passed the target, our entire formation was buffeted by very turbulent air. The turbulence bounced all the planes around, and for a moment we were concerned we might collide, but every plane did the right thing and immediately widened the spacing to give everyone space to recover. We had just flown through wake turbulence from the enormous Airbus passing above us moments before.

After our target run, we were required to orbit to the east of Caen until President Trump had arrived back at Caen by helicopter. This took an hour but was fun as well. When *Placid Lassie* asked Overlord where we should loiter, we were told that we were the only aircraft approved to be in the presidential TFR, so we could do whatever we wanted as long as we stayed clear of Caen.

So, we made the best of it, touring the famous spots at the east end of the invasion area. We flew over Pegasus Bridge and along Sword, Juno, and Gold Beaches, then out over the water multiple times. Many great photos and videos of our squadron that day were taken by folks attending ceremonies at many spots along the beaches, and those passes were huge hits at the memorial events.

Finally, we were cleared back to Caen, where we all landed without incident. The two biggest days were over. The crews that had made the historic flight assembled in the hangar and celebrated a day that none of us would ever forget.

There were two meaningful epilogues to that historic day. Some of us had been housed in a college dormitory in Caen, but Eric had rented a house on Sword Beach for the rest of the crew and his family. After landing, we all headed to the beach house for a cookout and relaxation.

When we arrived, one of our volunteers, Natalie Abrams, showed us an amazing photograph. She had been walking on the beach after sunrise that morning and happened across a bouquet of flowers placed in a pile of rocks in the sand. Next to the flowers was written in the sand, "Merci." Her photo was one of the favorites of the entire trip. That anonymous gesture powerfully expressed the gratitude that the people of Normandy have for their liberators to this day.

Late that evening, while we were cooking dinner on the grill in the yard of the beach house, we noticed that the neighbors were watching a movie on a big-screen TV. Their blinds were open, and we couldn't help but see the movie they were watching. Mind you, we were fifty yards from Sword Beach on the 75th anniversary of D-Day. They were watching *Saving Private Ryan*. Perfect.

About this time, Jeff told us that he had decided to take ten days off to go on a river cruise with his wife, who had joined him in France. We had other pilots showing up, and by this time he evidently felt we could fly the airplane without breaking it. The plan was for him to catch up with us for the trip home after the events at Berlin.

Dakota 44 flight on June 6, 2019 Miss Montana is third in line on the right, Charlie 3 (photo by Mecky Creus, Sound Off Films)

Anonymous bouquet, Sword Beach, June 6, 2019 (photo by Natalie Abrams)

51

Friends in France

JUNE 6 WAS on a Thursday, and we spent the next two days mostly relaxing in Normandy. The weather was damp and overcast with some rain, not very conducive for scenic flights. Our luggage and flyaway kit had still not been brought to Caen from Cherbourg, so when we heard that *Placid Lassie* was flying over to Cherbourg on Saturday to retrieve their stuff, we asked to tag along. They kindly agreed to let us go along and retrieve our stuff as well. Fortunately, everything had been kept secure and we were able to bring everything back. Once again, *Placid Lassie* had come through.

The folks from Montana who were in the tour group were still in France, and we wanted to get them in the plane for a scenic flight over the Normandy beaches. However, the weather on Friday and Saturday was not good for a scenic flight. We took turns being at the plane for Friday and Saturday, when there was a sizable crowd on the field at Caen. Those among our crew who had never been to Normandy visited the famous places such as Omaha Beach and the iconic cemetery there, Point du Hoc, Arromanches, and St. Mere Eglise.

As in England, the French did not open the infield at Caen, so the public could not get close to the planes. About half the planes were parked on the opposite side of a big grass taxiway, and half were parked close to the fence. All the crews had credentials to get to their planes, and we were able to escort people to our planes whenever we wanted. We enjoyed it much more when we could invite hundreds aboard for tours. Nevertheless, we met some people at Caen who enriched our time there.

Before we left Missoula, one of our supporters told us about a woman named Lilli who had some sort of connection to Montana, World War II, and our airplane. He said that she might track us down in England or France. Lilli contacted me while we were in England, and I arranged to meet her at the Caen Airport. Her story is worth telling.

Lilli was born in May 1944 in Holland and is a small woman with a very big heart. Many Americans know about the American cemetery at Omaha Beach, the largest American cemetery in Europe, with 9,380 Americans buried there. Most people, including me, did not know that the American cemetery at Margraten in the Netherlands is the second largest, with 8,291 Americans buried there. In addition to those buried, they have a section called Tablets of the Missing on which are carved 1,722 names of Americans who died in the war but were never found.[21]

Lilli explained that in the Netherlands, the Dutch have a tradition of "adopting" the graves of Allied servicemen who are buried in their country. They have an organization called the Foundation for Adopting Graves at the Netherlands American Cemetery and Memorial that manages the program. The Dutch take this very seriously; every single grave has been adopted for many years...and there is a waiting list. Those who adopt a grave regularly decorate it with flowers and research the life of the fallen, to remember them and honor their sacrifice.

A few years ago, the foundation decided to open the names on the Tablets of the Missing for adoption as well. Lilli applied and adopted two names of the missing. One of them was Robert "Uncle Bob" Lammers, a Montana boy who went to war but didn't come home. He was a bombardier/navigator in a B-26 that was shot down over the English Channel on February 25, 1944, after an extremely successful attack on a Nazi aerodrome at Venlo, Holland. His body was never recovered. Twice every year, Lilli drives to Margraten to honor Uncle Bob and place flowers by his name on the wall. That isn't all she has done.

Lilli researched Bob's life and eventually found and contacted Bob's family, some of whom still live on the family ranch near Hedgesville, Montana. Lilli has traveled to the U.S., met Bob's family, visited the family ranch, and shared what she learned in her research. She even was able to find the name and a photo of the German fighter pilot who shot down Bob's plane that day. She has prepared a detailed presentation telling of Bob's life, his wartime service, and his death. Several of Bob's relatives have traveled to Margraten with Lilli to honor his name on the Tablets of the Missing and place soil from their Montana ranch in the planter by his name.

In another remarkable coincidence, Doc Lammers, the man who told us about Lilli, is a former smokejumper, and Bob Lammers was his uncle. Doc was an early donor to our project and avid supporter throughout. He said that from the time Lilli adopted his Uncle Bob, their family has also adopted her.

Lilli's devotion to someone she has never met is moving and instructive. We should hope that if the United States was ever liberated from tyranny by a foreign power, we would show the same devotion to those who were lost in the cause; the Dutch have indeed set a worthy example.

One of the biggest national holidays in the Netherlands is Liberation Day, May 5, which marks the anniversary of the Dutch liberation from the Nazis by the Allies in 1945. Liberation Day 2019 had only recently been celebrated, and Lilli brought some lapel pins with the Liberation Day symbol for each of our crew. Each one was mounted on a card on which Lilli had inscribed a verse from the poem "In Flanders Field," "To you from failing hands we throw the torch; be yours to hold it high."

I was the only one of our crew who got to meet her, but she is planning to return to the U.S. again, and we will find opportunities for her to tell her story. Like us, she wants to inform the next generation about what happened long ago.

Another pleasant encounter at Caen was with Phil Jameson and his wife, Jeanne. After getting scrubbed from the jump list at Duxford, Phil had made it to France, met up with his wife, and they were seeing the sights in Normandy. We had kept in touch, and we very much wanted to try to do something for them. They stopped by Caen and got a tour of the plane. The debacle on June 5 was still fresh, but Phil brushed it off and said he was over it. I invited them both on a scenic flight over Normandy if weather allowed. They eagerly accepted.

Standing watch at the plane those two days in Caen, I met many strangers who would come to the fence, wave me over, and ask questions. Several were active duty U.S. military serving in Europe. Anybody who wanted one got a tour, but every active duty serviceman got the deluxe tour. Many of them brought "challenge coins," a long military tradition in which units make heavy metal coins signifying their unit. These coins are given as tokens of honor or appreciation, and several of these coins were my reward for giving tours for two days. My favorites are from SEAL Team Two and the 82nd Airborne. The guy from the 82nd Airborne said that showing that coin in St. Mere Eglise (which the 82nd liberated on D-Day) would get me free beer. Yet another reason to go back.

We were still hoping for favorable weather to make the scenic flight over Normandy, but were scheduled to depart Caen on Sunday afternoon, June 9, for Germany, so time was getting short. The weather on Friday and Saturday was poor, but Sunday morning dawned with broken clouds and high ceilings. Art and Nico made a short flight to Cherbourg in the morning to pick up another private parachute team and drop them nearby. Then they headed back to Caen.

We assembled the Montana tour group Sunday morning at the plane. The group included a number of volunteers who had worked on the plane; fortunately, we had room for Phil and Jeanne. Art and Nico did the honors in the cockpit, and I gave a spellbinding airborne tour of the Normandy beaches, Pointe du Hoc, Omaha Beach Cemetery, and the remnants of the mulberries (man-made temporary harbors) at Arromanches. Everyone had a great time, many of them commenting that it was the highlight of their trip.

Phil told me it meant the world to him to be able to go on that flight with Jeanne. He said he had made thousands of jumps during his career, but to be able to go on that flight over Normandy with his wife meant much more to him than the June 5 jump would have. They also presented us with a commemorative bottle of local wine for us to drink together as a crew.

The friction between the Daks Over Normandy leaders and the airplane crews and jumpers came to a head on Saturday, June 8. One of the two main Daks Over Normandy leaders suffered an apparent heart attack in the morning and was taken to the hospital. He eventually recovered. Many of the jumpers were into their second day in France with no luggage or accommodations. Tempers flared. Toward midday, word circulated that their luggage was en route from England. The other primary Daks Over Normandy leader resigned and returned to England in *Aces High*. At around noon, Eric Zipkin announced that the D-Day Squadron was assuming leadership over all future operations for the Berlin Airlift events, including all flight operations. Any European Dakotas would be welcome to join us.

June 9 marked the end of our time in France, and we were anxious to be heading to Germany. Our parachute operations were over, but we had more formation flights ahead of us in Germany. N18121 departed our group to continue a trip around the world. *Gamle Dame* left to return to Denmark. On June 10, KLM *Prinses Amalia* left to return to the Netherlands. *Clipper Tabitha May* also left the squadron to tour Europe on their own. We would run into them at Reykjavik, Iceland, and Narsarsuaq, Greenland, on our way home. On June 10, we would have eighteen Dakotas on the ground in Wiesbaden,

Germany. Thirteen were from the D-Day Squadron, and five were from Europe.

The schedule for the events in Germany had been somewhat vague until this point. D-Day Squadron had told us there would be three stops in Germany between June 10 and June 19: Wiesbaden, Fassberg, and Berlin.

52

Luftbrucke

THE PURPOSE OF our time in Germany was to commemorate the 70th anniversary of the Berlin Airlift, including reenactments of the candy drop, and many activities and celebrations. Americans seem to be unusually ignorant about the Berlin Airlift. This is partly because it came five years after the war, early in what later became known as the Cold War. It also required relatively few resources from the U.S., especially compared to what was required of war-torn Britain.

The airlift was a consequence of the war and how Germany was divided, but it was also an early hint of the future relationship between the Soviets, Germany, and the West. One of our objectives as the D-Day Squadron was to promote awareness of this historic event.

After the defeat of the Nazis in May 1945, Germany and its capital, Berlin, were divided among France, England, the Soviet Union, and the United States. Each of the four Allied powers received a portion of Germany and of Berlin to govern. The eastern portion of Germany and the east side of Berlin were given to the Soviets. Unfortunately, the entire city of Berlin was located about a hundred miles *inside* the Soviet sector of Germany. West Berlin was effectively an island surrounded by communist rule. There were only a few land and rail routes into West Berlin from West Germany.

What could possibly go wrong?

The Soviets and the French had each been attacked by Germany twice in the last thirty years, so they were both keen to prevent Germany from ever becoming a major power again. The Soviets were also eager to expand their communist system throughout Europe and the world. These factors set the stage for an epic dispute between the Soviets and the Western powers over the future of Germany. The Soviets wanted East Germany to become a communist satellite country, which it eventually did. They also wanted to have all of Berlin as the capital of East Germany.

By 1947, the British, Americans, and French were combining their three sectors of West Germany and West Berlin to form one country, and they proposed to introduce a new currency that would be used in all their zones. The Soviets, who were concerned about a reunified Germany with a new robust currency, regarded this as a threat; the Soviets also had plans to take West Berlin into the communist fold without firing a shot.

On June 24, 1948, the Soviets closed the roads and rail routes from West Germany into West Berlin. West Berlin was instantly isolated, preventing import of virtually everything needed for life and commerce. West Berlin was home to more than two million Germans, plus 25,000 Allied occupation personnel. The Soviets did not expect the Western powers to resist, partly because the Western powers had demobilized most of their military after the war. The Soviet military in and near Germany outnumbered the Western forces more than sixty to one. Moreover, the Soviets did not believe the Western powers would, or *could*, supply West Berlin by air. They were wrong.[22]

The reaction to the blockade in Washington, D.C., and the capitals of England and France was nearly unanimous: West Berlin could not be saved. The reaction was *nearly* unanimous because the only person that mattered, President Harry Truman, disagreed and declared, "We shall stay, period." And so it was, the military forces of the United States and England started what would become the most heroic aerial rescue mission in history, bringing in everything needed by West Berliners from coal to flour to baby formula to food—for nearly a year.

The U.S. military calculated how many calories each person would need and very quickly developed an aerial chain of transport planes that brought in the necessary nutrition and supplies every day. The operation was code-named Operation Vittles by the U.S. military and became known as the Berlin Airlift (to the Germans, *Luftbrucke*, or *Air Bridge*). As time went on, the airlift got progressively more efficient, breaking new records for tons delivered each month, even during the brutal winter weather over Berlin.[22]

Because of their presence nearby, the very first transport planes enlisted for the airlift were C-47s, most of which were tired veterans of the recent war. Many had been sitting idle since 1945. They were worn out, and in many cases broken down, but they could be cobbled together, and each could carry three tons. They worked. Two days after the blockade started, thirty-two C-47 flights brought eighty tons of supplies into West Berlin. There were only forty-eight C-47s in Germany and only ninety-eight in all of Western Europe, but they were all being recalled for duty in a hurry. On day two of the airlift, 295 tons were delivered; on day three, 384 tons, all flown into Tempelhof airport in West Berlin, around the clock. And so, it began.[22]

The U.S. initially determined that *4,500 tons* was the minimum daily amount necessary to sustain life for the two million residents of West Berlin. They revised that amount to 5,620 tons by October 1948. In the beginning, the airlift was far behind this number. However, by July 1948, the average daily tonnage had increased to 2,000 tons per day. One year later, the average daily haul had reached over *8,000 tons*, having increased nearly every month of the airlift, and showed no signs of slowing down.[22]

American pilots, mechanics, air traffic controllers, and other military personnel were recalled to active duty, after only having been home from the war for a few years. Eventually, the chief pilots of

United Airlines, American Airlines, and TWA were all called to fly in the airlift. The U.S. soon started bringing in the much larger C-54 (DC-4) transport planes from all over the world, even robbing important military capability elsewhere. At the start of the airlift, there were only two C-54s in Europe. By the end of the airlift, there were 225 C-54s working around the clock. The C-54 could carry ten tons of cargo and was much more efficient than the C-47. Nevertheless, both planes continued to fly into West Berlin for the duration of the airlift.[22]

The Berlin Blockade lasted for almost a year from June 24, 1948, until the Soviets conceded and reopened the roads and rails on May 12, 1949. The Berlin Airlift was a monumental achievement that was larger than any airlift in history and is unlikely to ever be matched. The official records of the airlift credit the Allies with delivering 2,325,809 tons, of which 1,783,573 tons were flown in by the Americans and 542,236 tons were flown in by the Royal Air Force. There were 277,569 flights. Thirty-nine British citizens and Royal Air Force personnel lost their lives during the airlift, along with thirty-two Americans and nine German airlift employees.[22]

Transport aircraft landed at three airports in West Berlin approximately every *three minutes* for over a year. Aircraft continued to bring in supplies even after the land and rail routes were reopened—stockpiling supplies in West Berlin in case the Soviets reneged. The final flight of the airlift arrived at Tempelhof on September 30, 1949.[22]

The U.S. space program resulted in a multitude of advancements and inventions, from the powdered orange drink Tang to advances in science and medicine. The Berlin Airlift produced similar unforeseen but valuable advancements. For example, all the flights to and from West Berlin were flown under Instrument Flight Rules in order to maintain precise separation, maximize safety, and to allow flights in all weather. However, flying so many planes in such poor weather around the clock had never been done before—the current air traffic control system we have in the United States wasn't started until 1956. By necessity, methods were developed during the

Luftbrucke that were eventually used in the air traffic control system in the U.S. and around the world.

Montana also played an important role in the training and preparation for the airlift. The flight route in and out of Tempelhof was narrow and busy, so there was little room for error, especially in bad weather. To prepare new pilots to fly the Berlin route in all types of weather, a training area was established at Great Falls, Montana, that duplicated the route, navigational aids, and runways at Tempelhof. Air traffic controllers would guide pilots, who were training to fly only by instruments, along this route before they deployed to fly in the airlift.

The Berlin Airlift also demonstrated that, as the official Air Force summary stated, "Given the tools of personnel, equipment, aircraft, and the steady flow of supplies, cargo can be moved from any point in the world to any other point in the world, regardless of geography or weather."[23] We take this capability for granted in the twenty-first century but it was a revolutionary concept in 1949.

53

Rosinenbomber

THE CANDY BOMBER is one of the most famous stories associated with the Berlin Airlift. Allied pilots were flying into Berlin several times each day and occasionally would layover in Berlin where they would go out into the city. They observed firsthand the poverty, devastation, and ruin brought on first by World War II and subsequently by the Berlin Blockade. Virtually everyone in West Berlin was starving.

One U.S. pilot, Lieutenant Gail Halvorsen from Utah, was visiting West Berlin on a layover and saw a crowd of children outside the fence near Tempelhof airport watching the airplanes land. He took out a few sticks of gum and handed them to the children. The children split the gum among themselves, even licking the wrappers to enjoy the flavor. Most of them had been born after the war started and had never tasted candy of any kind. Halvorsen pondered how he could get more candy to the children and resolved to smuggle more in on his next flight.

He told the children that he would wiggle his wings as he came into land and would drop candy for them from his C-54. The next day, the children anxiously waited for the pilot who would become known as "Uncle Wiggly Wings." When he arrived, they scrambled for the candy falling from the plane suspended on little parachutes. Halvorsen had donated his entire candy ration from Wiesbaden

Army Air Base and fashioned the parachutes from handkerchiefs. It was a small gesture by one pilot that quickly grew into a campaign.

Halvorsen enlisted other pilots and crews to donate their candy rations, and soon they started dropping parachutes with sweets as well. His commanding officer also heard about it. The commander at Wiesbaden had been flooded by letters from West Berlin thanking the United States for the gifts from the *Rosinenbombers (raisin bombers)*. To Halvorsen's surprise, not only was he not reprimanded, he was ordered to continue and expand his efforts.

This humanitarian gesture by one U.S. pilot grew into one of the most famous goodwill missions in history. U.S. pilots and crews were risking their lives to feed people who had only three years before been trying to kill them. Not only did they supply their recent enemies with loads of life-saving cargo, they added a small act of kindness.

After World War I, Germany was humiliated and punished by the Treaty of Versailles, setting the stage for World War II. In contrast, after World War II, the Marshall Plan, aided by human gestures such as the Berlin Airlift and the Candy Bombers, established and strengthened the relationship between defeated Germany and her former enemies that lasts to this day. The strong relationship between modern Germany and the West is hard to imagine without the heroic efforts to save West Berlin.

The airplanes coming to West Berlin landed at Gatow, Tegel, and Tempelhof airports; Tempelhof was in the American sector on the south side of the city. It was a remarkable architectural achievement for its time, massively remodeled by the Nazis in the mid-1930s. The beautiful circular concourse was innovative, and the large overhang where planes could park and be protected from weather was unique. Tempelhof operated until 2008. However, the runways and concourse remain, and the runways are in usable condition.

From the beginning of our discussions about the events in Germany, we advocated for and hoped to somehow be able to drop candy over Tempelhof...even to land there and celebrate with the

German people. As we began our time in Germany, we started to ask about what would be happening in Berlin for the reenactment of the Berlin Airlift and the candy drop. We soon found out that the authorities in Berlin had refused to grant permission for us to land at Tempelhof.

While disappointing, it wasn't a huge surprise. Reopening a closed airfield is a big bureaucratic effort, and a city as large as Berlin surely has a giant bureaucracy. They had many months of notice, but at this late stage there wasn't much we could do about it. Twenty DC-3s dropping candy and landing at Tempelhof would have been amazing to see. Sadly, it was not to be.

What *did* surprise and anger us was when we learned we had not been given permission to land anywhere near Berlin. Candy drops over Berlin were also verboten. As word trickled out, we even learned that the Berlin Airlift 70 group, which organized the events in Germany, had known about it for some time. They had not informed the D-Day Squadron because they were afraid we wouldn't come to Germany if we knew. That probably wouldn't have happened, but we all felt more than a little deceived. However, by the time we found out about it in Wiesbaden, we were all committed to continuing our schedule. There were some last-minute efforts by Eric Zipkin and BA70, even getting the U.S. Ambassador involved, but to no avail. Other than that one incident, BA70 did a good job organizing the events in Germany.

On a positive note, the German people we met, without exception, were embarrassed, angry, and terribly disappointed in the Berlin government for missing a historic opportunity. They were also shamelessly grateful for our efforts. Everywhere we stopped, Germans would apologize, shaking their heads at the inept Berlin politicians. They told us that the government in Berlin was a socialist bunch, and they didn't want to celebrate or honor the herculean effort by the Allies that saved West Berlin. At Fassberg, a kind woman gave us a bottle of Tempelhof Champagne that she had been hoping to present to us in Berlin.

After we headed for home, several of the other D-Day Squadron planes continued to Tannheim, Germany. At Tannheim, local citizens presented them with a written apology for the actions of the Berlin government that was signed by at least 500 local citizens. We all received copies of these signed apologies for our records.

The first and the last major twentieth century events in the history of Berlin and Germany bear striking similarities and significance. The Berlin Airlift was the first de facto battle in the Cold War. The last Cold War battle was the confrontation between the U.S. and the Soviets in the late 1980s, which soon led to the fall of the Soviet Union and reunification of Germany. Two U.S. presidents, one from each party, nearly single-handedly brought about these victories.

When West Berlin was blockaded in 1948, every advisor, cabinet member, and the Joint Chiefs of Staff advised President Harry Truman to give up West Berlin to the Soviets. Truman stood his ground, saving West Berlin, and possibly all of West Germany. In 1987, every advisor to President Ronald Reagan pleaded with him not to provoke the Soviets at the Brandenburg Gate in West Berlin. Like Truman, Reagan refused, and gave one of the most famous speeches in modern history, telling General Secretary Gorbachev, "Tear down this wall!" Reagan's determination led to the end of Soviet domination and the end of the Cold War. To be sure, there were other factors in both cases, but the will and principles of these two presidents largely determined the outcomes.

54

Wiesbaden

WE TOOK OFF from Caen on June 9 at about seven p.m., with Nico as PIC and Gman in the right seat, and headed to Wiesbaden in formation with *Placid Lassie*, *D-Day Doll*, and *Daisy/Scandinavian*. The weather was gorgeous, and we flew at about 1,500 feet above the ground. Out of so many memorable flights, it was one of the most relaxing; the scenery we saw was different than anything we had seen yet in Europe. We flew across northern France, the southern tip of Belgium, Luxembourg, and into Germany. *Placid Lassie* had the historical IQ to adjust course slightly and lead us over Bastogne, where the famous Battle of the Bulge was fought. The terrain looked beautiful from the air, with thick forests, small towns and villages, rivers, deep gorges, and even castles. The terrain was reminiscent of many parts of Montana.

After all the activities and drama in England and France, we were all happy to move on to Germany. As Eric Komberec had warned—and we all witnessed firsthand by that time—everything had been harder outside the U.S. It took longer to get fuel, it took longer to get a meal at a restaurant, it was more challenging to drive (especially in England), and the vehicles were all too small. It seems like everyone in Montana owns a pickup truck, but we didn't see any in Europe. How they survive without them is a mystery.

Our late departure from Caen and a nearly three-hour flight

meant that we arrived at Wiesbaden about ten p.m., just as it was getting dark. The approach into Wiesbaden at dusk was memorable, following the Rhine River as it meandered through a deep gorge before opening out onto the plain to Wiesbaden. We were all tired after a long day, but we expected to hang around a long time waiting for fuel, food, and transportation. We expected it to be a late night.

The difference between Wiesbaden, which is a U.S. Army air base, and our prior experiences in Europe was striking from the moment we parked. As soon as we shut down our engines on the ramp at Wiesbaden, a huge fuel trailer pulled up behind us and hands unreeled the hoses to give us fuel. Several shuttle buses ferried crew members from the ramp to a large hangar, where we efficiently cleared customs. We were presented with new credentials and sack meals prepared by the local Girl Scouts. It was very efficient and felt almost like being home. We were soon bused to a nice hotel that would be home for four days.

Stephen E. Ambrose interviewed thousands of soldiers after World War II and wrote many excellent books on the war. One of the things he mentions more than once is the affinity the American soldiers had for their enemies, the Germans. He says it best in *Band of Brothers*:

"The standard story of how the American GI reacted to the foreign people he met during the course of WWII runs like this: He felt the Arabs were despicable, liars, thieves, dirty, awful, without a redeeming feature. The Italians were liars, thieves, dirty, wonderful, with many redeeming features, but never to be trusted. The rural French were sullen, slow, and ungrateful while the Parisians were rapacious, cunning, indifferent to whether they were cheating Germans or Americans. The British were brave, resourceful, quaint, reserved, dull. The Dutch were regarded as simply wonderful in every way (but the average GI never was in Holland, only the airborne).

The story ends up thus: wonder of wonders, the average GI found that the people he liked best, identified most closely with, enjoyed being with, were the Germans. Clean, hardworking, disciplined, educated, middle-class in their tastes and lifestyles (many GIs noted that so far as they could tell the only people in the world who regarded a flush toilet and soft white toilet paper as a necessity were the Germans and the Americans), the Germans seemed to many American soldiers as "just like us."

GIs noted, with approval, that the Germans began picking up the rubble the morning after the battle had passed by, contrasted with the French, where no one had yet bothered to clean up the mess."[24]

One of the famous Band of Brothers, Private David Webster Kenyon (an English Literature major at Harvard University before he enlisted in 1942), wrote to his parents:

"The Germans I have seen so far have impressed me as clean, efficient, law-abiding people. They were churchgoers. In Germany everybody goes out and works and, unlike the French, who do not seem inclined to lift a finger to help themselves, the Germans fill up the trenches soldiers have left in their fields. They are cleaner, more progressive, and more ambitious than either the English or the French."[24]

According to Ambrose, this was nearly a universal reaction by Americans who fought in the war. They were surprised because our government propaganda said otherwise. As we began our time in Germany, it was ironic that most of us unknowingly echoed the same sentiment about Germans as being "like us." Lest this sentiment go to Nico's head, the beer in Germany still has far to go in terms of variety, if not quality and volume.

There was only one mishap the evening we arrived in Wiesbaden. In the rush to take care of our planes and crews in the dark, one of the base golf carts ran into and damaged the left elevator on *D-Day Doll*. She was parked right next to us, so we heard about it right away. The base personnel were embarrassed, and the *D-Day Doll* crew were none too pleased, but they were able to get it suitably repaired over the next few days.

This was the first experience for all of our crew being on an American military base in a foreign country. We learned that many of the workers on the base are Germans, and we met many of them. They were all polite, helpful, and seemed genuinely happy that we were there. There were some single-engine warbirds that showed up for the next two days, but the stars of the show were the C-47s. The schedule for the next two days was to have a public open house and airshow to which everyone was invited, and various events were planned.

German and American efficiency were on display again when we arrived at the base the next morning about eight thirty a.m. Dozens of concession stands had already been erected, picnic tables and benches put out, and people were scurrying around everywhere. We knew that we would not be flying for the next two days, so we resolved to enjoy ourselves. Tia, her girls, and Skip were still with us, and Mark Bretz joined us in Wiesbaden, so we had a big bunch of *Miss Montana* folks to attend the plane. Unlike in France and England, the crowds could come right up to the airplanes, which was great, but it also presented a bit of a dilemma.

For some reason, a few people tend to lose their common sense and manners when they are around airplanes at airshows. We saw some examples firsthand while tending *Miss Montana* in Germany. One day, I was standing outside the cargo door talking to somebody and saw a young boy running across the horizontal part of *Miss Montana's* tail right behind me. He was on the aluminum part, thankfully not the beautiful, fabric-covered left elevator that Wendy Pemberton had re-covered for us. The boy's father was standing there watching him. I don't know if they were American or German, but "Please get off the airplane!" apparently translates well in either language.

In Germany, we always opened up our plane and offered tours, sometimes charging a few euros. We quickly figured out that we needed to cordon off the cockpit because, without fail, someone would climb in the front seat and start moving levers or pushing buttons, which could cause real problems. As a precaution, we began to lower the jump seat and strap it down, which should have been a clear sign that getting into the cockpit itself was verboten. Of course, we made exceptions when young children came on board. We would always offer to put them in the cockpit to get a memorable picture—supervised, of course.

Nevertheless, several times we caught adults climbing over the jump seat and either sitting in the pilot seats or looking out the side windows for a picture. We eventually put a sign on the back of the jump seat to make it crystal clear, but even that didn't work for everyone. We had several thousand people come on the airplane and get a quick tour throughout our time in Germany. Most of them were polite, considerate, and we had great fun doing it. We never got tired of talking about it, and it surprised us how many had been following our story and our journey from the U.S.

Before we left Missoula, our visionary Eric had the idea of making a small cornhole game to take with us so people could play at the various airshows. Cornhole is a cross between a beanbag toss and horseshoes. You take turns tossing bean bags (usually filled with corn, hence the name) a short distance to land on a small wooden table that is on the ground slightly raised at one end with a hole in the middle. You score by getting your beanbags to land on the table, or better yet go in the hole.

We hadn't been able to use it in England or France because the public couldn't get close to our plane. In Germany we put it out, and it was busy all day. One of the cornhole tables was labeled "Allies" with an American flag and the other was labeled "Axis" with a black iron cross. The kids didn't understand the symbolism, but many grown-ups did. The game was a hit, and we even got it out and played it on the airplane during long flights.

We were amazed at the interest in our plane, and others. Once we opened her up for tours, we had a line at least a hundred feet long all day long. The other airplanes that were giving tours did also.

At Wiesbaden, there was a group of four fine-looking women wandering about who had dressed up for the event in period attire, complete with high heels, form-fitting 1940s U.S. Army uniforms, and period hairstyles. Early in the day, they stopped in front of our plane, and, never one to miss an opportunity to snuggle up with attractive women, several of our crew got pictures with them under the nose of *Miss Montana*. They were having great fun. That spot proved to be so popular that they stayed there quite a while, getting pictures with anyone who wanted—and many did.

Those were relaxing days. We weren't scheduled to fly and there were enough of us to give tours and keep an eye out for vandals, so we could take shifts. We wandered about the show, got tours of other planes, and met crews we had not yet met. We also drank some German beer, which Nico swears is the best in the world, but he clearly needs to get out more. Missoula, Montana, has about 70,000 people and at least thirteen craft breweries that produce amazing beers, so we know something about the topic.

Attendance at the first day of the airshow was impressive, roughly 50,000 people. Base staff told us it was the best turnout for a public event that they had seen in over twenty-five years. They were thrilled and said it would be a great boost to relationships with the local Germans and government. There were several flying events including a DC-3 flyby, some freefall jumpers, and perhaps most significant, a candy drop.

During preparation for the Normandy trip, plans were made to reenact the candy drop in Germany, hopefully at Tempelhof. One of the D-Day Squadron supporters is affiliated with the Jelly Belly company, and was kind enough to donate several pallets of small, custom-made Jelly Belly packages, each with a white cloth parachute attached. Before we left Caen, several cases of this candy were distributed to each plane.

As part of the June 10 events at Wiesbaden, four of our planes conducted a reenactment of the candy drop over the infield of the base. The entire area was cordoned off (couldn't risk anyone getting hurt by falling candy), and the planes made a low formation pass while dropping thousands of these candy packages over the infield. After they had all floated to the ground, someone blew a whistle and thousands of waiting children (and probably more than a few enthusiastic adults) rushed out to pick up the candy. That candy drop was fun, but we were still hoping to do it over Tempelhof.

We first met Colonel Gail Halvorsen at Wiesbaden. There were several events to honor him that we were privileged to attend. We were amazed at how incredibly spry he seemed for a ninety-eight-year-old war hero. He never seemed to get tired of meeting people, shaking hands, signing autographs, and generally being honored everywhere he went.

Colonel Halvorsen is a fine gentleman, always smiling, always eager to chat, and always kind, upbeat, and positive. It must have been the honor of a lifetime for him and his family, especially because he served in the Air Force at Wiesbaden for three years in the 1960s. He flew on *Placid Lassie* for the Wiesbaden candy drop, and a reliable source told us that he even landed her afterward in fine fashion.

We received sad news on June 9 at Wiesbaden. Our friend and D-Day veteran John Nelson had told his family he only wanted to live to see the 75th anniversary of D-Day, which was on the previous Thursday. The next day, John's health began failing, and he passed away peacefully Saturday evening, June 8. Kim Briggeman called us and told us the news when we were at Wiesbaden. It was afternoon in Wiesbaden, so Eric, Randy, Crystal, and I raised a toast to our good friend John Nelson under the nose of *Miss Montana* and sent a photograph of it to his daughter.

That evening we retired to the hotel, and Nico, being a native son and fount of energy, suggested we go to a local microbrewery and restaurant. Two of Nico's German friends had come to see him, so we made our way to the lovely old town of Idstein. Idstein has many very old buildings, including a tower where they allegedly burned witches in ancient times. By the time we got there, it was quite late and dark, so it was eerie walking around the ancient town at night, especially beneath the witch-burning tower. We had a great dinner at the Idstein Brauhaus. Beer, schnitzel, schnapps, and ice cream were had by all. It was very late when we made it back to the hotel, but it was a memorable evening.

Nico was usually the life of the party, so we couldn't resist ribbing him on a regular basis. We would give him a hard time about the monotony of German beer, the ubiquitous presence of schnitzel (is that all they eat here?), and occasionally needed to remind him who won the war. He took it all in stride and gave as good as he got. Not only was Nico a blast to have along, his German language skills were surprisingly good, which often came in handy.

The next day at Wiesbaden was another open house at the base, but only for U.S. personnel and their families. The turnout was smaller but no less enthusiastic. We gave tours to everyone who patiently waited in line. We got out of the base earlier that evening, and word had spread about the Idstein Brauhaus, so more of us, including some of the *Placid Lassie* crew, headed there again. This time we arrived before dark, so we took a longer stroll around town before tucking in for more refreshments.

One of the nicest guys on any of the crews was Garrett Fleischmann, a copilot for *Placid Lassie*. He was twenty years old during the time in Europe and a junior at ERAU in Daytona Beach, Florida. That means he's probably fairly bright, but he's also an accomplished aviator for his age. Garrett soloed on his sixteenth birthday and has earned commercial, multi-engine, and instrument ratings. He has flown several different airplanes and earned his SIC type rating in the DC-3. Besides all that, he's a nice young man. We first met him at Oxford when we stopped there on the trip over, and he was very helpful to us there. We saw him again in England when he met up with the squadron in Europe.

Eric Zipkin gave a press conference in New York City before the squadron left for Europe. One of the reporters, noting the demographic of the typical DC-3 crew, asked Eric what the prognosis was for keeping these old airplanes flying, since the crews were all so old. Eric laughed and responded that he didn't see the problem; in fact, his copilot (Garrett) wasn't even old enough to drink. Well, Garrett was old enough to drink in Germany, so we bought him a round or two (or three) at Idstein.

Garrett was getting pretty boisterous by the end of the night, so we were fairly sure he hadn't been doing much drinking at college. He confessed the next morning that he felt a tad rough. He was a good sport about it, and we always enjoyed having him along. Garrett truly does represent the next generation of DC-3 pilots and, if he is any indication, DC-3s will be in capable hands.

The plan for the next day was for the entire squadron to relocate to Fassberg, with two stops on the way. We arose very early, got on buses to the base, and then waited around for the weather to improve. Rain was falling steadily from low ceilings, and it was cold. *D-Day Doll* and *"That's All, Brother"* elected to take off for Nordholz. *Miss Virginia* launched and carried Colonel Halvorsen and his family to Fassberg. The rest of us decided to wait for another day and better weather.

By this time, the crews were starting to get a little grumpy. When the word went out that we would have a briefing the next morning at six a.m. at the base, a mutiny arose, so the briefing time was changed to seven thirty a.m. Crisis averted.

Tia, Taylor, Avian, Skip, and Art all left us at Wiesbaden to fly home on commercial flights. The remaining crew included the core four plus Nico and Mark Bretz.

Toast to John Nelson, Wiesbaden: (L-R) Crystal,
Randy, Eric, Bryan (author photo)

Pinup girls with (L-R) Nico, Bryan, and Art at Wiesbaden (photo by Eric Komberec)

55

Wiesbaden to Fassberg

THERE IS AN adage in aviation that weather-related accident investigations all start in beautiful weather. In other words, the day after a weather-related accident is often fine weather, meaning that the accident could have been avoided had the pilot only waited one day to fly. While not universally true, it must be true often enough to make it an adage.

Sure enough, weather on June 13 was excellent and we all arrived at the base rested, a little less grumpy, and ready for the next leg of our journey. We knew that all this excitement would soon be coming to an end. However, this day would be a busy one indeed, with DC-3s flying all over northern Germany,

The D-Day Squadron took off en masse from Wiesbaden at about 10:15 a.m., twelve DC-3s divided into five flights. All five flights, along with four T-6 Texans providing combat air support, flew north from Wiesbaden to Hanover at low altitude. We orbited Hanover before splitting into two formations that would each make interim stops before arriving in the evening at Fassberg. Eight DC-3s, including *Miss Montana*, headed for Jagel, where we would join *Miss Virginia*. The other four planes flew to Nordholz where they would join *D-Day Doll* and *"That's All, Brother."* Nordholz is the only remaining German naval aviation base, and the purpose of the stop there was to display a portion of the D-Day Squadron in honor of the Berlin Airlift.

Jagel is about twenty-five miles from the Danish border, and as Nico and Mark Bretz brought us in to land, we could see the Black Sea a short distance to the east. With the addition of *Miss Virginia*, there were nine DC-3s at Jagel, and we were warmly welcomed by the German military and a crowd assembled around the airfield. This was to be a short stop, so we didn't have time to visit with the locals, give tours of our airplanes, or even refuel.

The purpose for the stop at Jagel was to attend a solemn and formal memorial service in honor of Allied crew members who perished during the *Luftbrucke*. Jagel was one of the primary bases from which supplies, mostly coal, were airlifted to Tempelhof. During the airlift, seventy-one British and American crew members were killed. Just outside the gate to the base at Jagel is a small memorial to those who were lost.

We were bused from the ramp over to the memorial, where a tent was set up and we were ushered inside. The entire ceremony was in German; we didn't understand it, but the tone was somber and obviously respectful. Two members of the clergy made comments, as did the commander of the base. There was a German military honor guard and all the German military attending were in dress uniforms. Even though we couldn't understand the words, there was no mistaking the sentiment, and we felt honored to be there.

When the ceremony was over, we were taken to a large hangar for refreshments and some mingling with base personnel before heading back to our planes for departure. After two hours on the ground at Jagel, we made another mass formation takeoff and formed up for the flight to Fassberg.

On these cross-country flights, our formations would often pass over interesting or historically significant locations. On this day, our formation had flown over Hanover on our way from Wiesbaden to Jagel. Then we made low passes over airports at Hamburg and Finkerwerder en route from Jagel to Fassberg. Hanover was significant because it was a major transportation and manufacturing hub during the war that was the target of significant Allied bombing. A large portion of the city was destroyed.

The flights over Hamburg and adjacent Finkerwerder were significant because they are home to major Airbus facilities. Since the Douglas line of aircraft is now owned by Boeing, we couldn't resist showing off for the European competition. It's a safe bet that no eighty-year-old Airbus aircraft will ever fly over Boeing Field in Seattle.

As we approached Fassberg, the other formation was arriving from Nordholz, and we all got in line for a mass formation landing of fifteen DC-3s. After the one-and-a-half-hour flight to Fassberg, with Nico and Mark flying, it was getting late in the afternoon. After landing, we were instructed to get in a line for the fueling trucks so we would be fueled and ready to go in three days when we departed for Berlin.

It took two hours to get all the planes fueled, so in the meantime many of us wandered over to a barbecue put on by the Luftwaffe, the German air force. There was much food and drink to be had, and we enjoyed visiting with the Luftwaffe. Life was good.

After relocating the fueled planes to the main ramp, we made our way to a massive hangar with more food and drink. The Germans sure know how to throw a party. The hour was late, and the party was about done by the time most of us got there, but we were ready to head for the barn by that time.

Before departing from Wiesbaden, we had been told that our accommodations at Fassberg would be Luftwaffe barracks on the base. None of us knew what to expect, but we had been spoiled thus far, being housed primarily in nice hotels. There was a little complaining by text message about the news, but two people put a stop to it right away.

Nico, who heard the complaining, got as serious as we ever saw him and commented to our crew that we should be mindful of the people we were there to honor and remember that soldiers were sleeping in ditches and hedgerows during the days after the D-Day invasion. Soon after, Doug Rozendaal, chief pilot for *"That's All, Brother,"* sent out a similar message, bluntly castigating us for the same reasons.

They were both right, and the complaining stopped. Besides, once we got to the barracks, they were much nicer than my college dorm. We ate meals in a nice *kantine* nearby and…the barracks came with an unlimited supply of free beer, which was replenished like magic every day. A few of the crews and their supporters quietly found better accommodations in town, but they missed out on some memorable times in the barracks.

We got settled in the barracks, started sampling the free beer, and hung out in the hallway until the wee hours. Rumor has it that some of the old hands were up until four a.m. Once again, you couldn't help but look at that group of (mostly) old codgers and marvel at the assembled DC-3 experience sitting on the floor in that hallway, swapping stories.

The next day, June 14, there wasn't much happening, except the base was busy getting ready for the airshow on June 15. We performed a minor engine inspection, a few of us got to spend time on a high-tech Luftwaffe helicopter simulator, and then we went to a concert in the park in the evening.

The concert was by the excellent Bundeswehr (German Armed Forces) Big Band, and they played and sang many American tunes from the 1940s that were fitting for the occasion. There was a large stage, hundreds of people, and plenty of good music, drink, and food. Colonel Halvorsen was there enjoying the fun and was later invited on stage to be honored once again. He is a hero in Germany, and he couldn't go anywhere without being welcomed and honored. We got to meet him for the first time, and he and Nico had a lively conversation.

We retired to the barracks after the concert, and once again many of us assembled in the hall to enjoy beer and company. The end of our tour was approaching, and we wanted to savor our remaining time together.

The airshow at Fassberg was a huge event, with 60,000 people attending. Nico's father, Andreas, drove several hours from his home to join us, and we spent all day enjoying the aerial demonstrations, seeing other planes (including German aircraft), and giving tours of *Miss Montana*. We didn't open for tours until about three p.m., and we charged five euros per person, but we still had a line a hundred feet long until we closed around six p.m. when the show ended. The airshow was terrific. There was plenty of flying, music, food of all kinds, German beer, and a great crowd.

At the end of the day, we headed back to the barracks for our last night and prepared for our last day as a squadron. Mark Bretz left us early the next morning to fly home on a commercial flight.

Nico Von Pronay (L) and Mark Bretz (R) over Germany (author photo)

D-Day Squadron Lined up for fuel at Fassberg
(photo by Carsten Koenig, Airbase Fassberg)

Nico and Colonel Halvorsen, Fassberg (author photo)

56

Fassberg to Berlin! Or not

AFTER BREAKFAST AT the *kantine*, a briefing and a group picture of the entire D-Day Squadron, we all loaded up for the flight toward Berlin. By then we knew we would not be landing at or near Berlin or attending any events related to the *Luftbrucke*, but we were determined not to leave Germany without an appropriate aerial display.

Launching from Fassberg about ten thirty a.m. with Eric as PIC and Nico in the right seat, we made a low pass on our way to Berlin at Stendal, then made a circle around the City of Berlin passing over Tempelhof. We continued around Berlin and made low passes at Tegel, Gatow, Schoenfeld, Schoenhagen, and Leipzig. Tegel is the major international airport for Berlin, so we got quite a bit of exposure there, but there were crowds at all the places we passed. Many videos and pictures that surfaced the next day had captured the historic flight.

The events made the front page of every major newspaper in Germany. None of us read German except Nico, but we were told that the coverage unanimously criticized the Berlin politicians for not welcoming us and missing a huge opportunity to honor and remember those who had served so tirelessly during the *Luftbrucke*.

Colonel Halvorsen was asked by the German press about the brush-off we had been given by the Berlin politicians. Making a sharp point in a classy way, he said, "I wish they could have dropped candy so today's children could get an idea of what it was like in the past. *Back then they didn't mind us landing here.*" His remarks were published throughout Germany, and even back in the United States. Photographs of Colonel Halvorsen saluting the squadron as we passed over Tempelhof were on the front pages of newspapers across Germany the next day.

We had known for several days that we would be denied the honor of reenacting the candy drop over Tempelhof and still had several cases of parachute-rigged Jelly Belly candy on board. As we approached Tempelhof, we decided we would make a token statement to those in Berlin who didn't want us there.

As we passed over Tempelhof, we opened a side window and threw out a handful of the candy packages. We had written "2019 American Candy Bombers" on each parachute. We guessed that we weren't the only plane to have the same idea. We found out later that *Betsy's Biscuit Bomber* had also "lost" some candy over Tempelhof. Great minds think alike.

It was a symbolic act. We never heard if anyone on the ground found the candy or even saw it fall, but we felt a little better about representing our squadron and the United States of America. Hopefully, the statute of limitations in Germany has passed for dropping objects from aircraft.

Sherman Smoot, the famous and outspoken captain of *Betsy's Biscuit Bomber*, was quoted as saying he was very angry about the whole thing and, "If the politicians wanted, we would have had approval to land within minutes. We will never come again, even on the 75th anniversary." He added, "The Socialists tried to starve Berlin back then, and now they are governing again, and this is the decision they make."

Sherman's comments captured all our feelings, but we had done the best we could. After passing Leipzig, some of the squadron broke off for other destinations, and seven of our planes headed for the town of Erfurt for the night. The D-Day Squadron and Berlin Airlift missions were over, but we would have one more evening and morning with our friends.

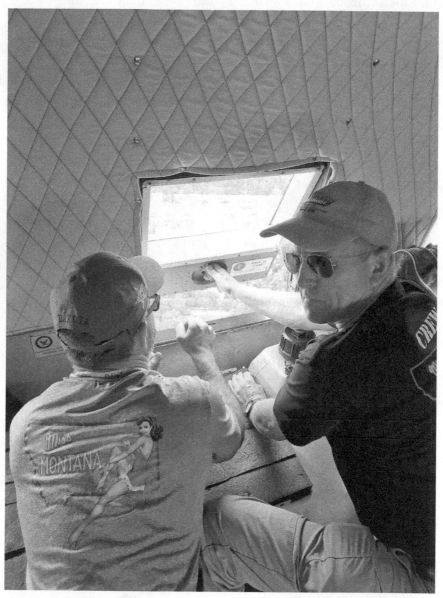

Randy and Bryan Losing candy over Tempelhof (author photo)

57

Erfurt Welcome

WE HAD NEVER heard of Erfurt, a small city about 150 miles southwest of Berlin. Several airplanes in the squadron decided to land there after being unable to land near Berlin. It was far enough from Berlin that we hoped we wouldn't be detained for dropping the candy or the low passes. We landed there along with *Spirit of Benovia*, *Placid Lassie*, *Pan Am*, *Virginia Ann*, *ChalAir*, and *Betsy's Biscuit Bomber*. Since the official events were over, we were all on our own again for expenses.

Our crew found a lovely hotel near the city center and walked through the old town to get something to eat. After supper we heard some music and made our way to the town center. There was a band playing in the open square and there we saw the crews from *Pan Am* and *Placid Lassie*. Someone told the organizers of the small concert about us, and at the end of the concert they asked that all D-Day Squadron crews stand up in front of the crowd to be recognized. Somebody made a speech about all that we had done in England, France, and Germany, and the crowd cheered. The speech was in German, but Nico assured us it was very good. It was a nice welcome.

Dancing and socializing in that ancient square, we enjoyed our last evening together with a remnant of the squadron. The next morning, we got word that the vice mayor of Erfurt had invited us to an evening reception at city hall in our honor. We had been planning an early departure that day, so we instead arranged a morning reception at city hall before we left.

Erfurt has a fascinating history. Like most cities in Germany, it is very old. However, many ancient towns in Germany were bombed to rubble during the Allied march to Berlin. Erfurt escaped major destruction by bombing, thanks to timely intervention by General George Patton. Patton's Third Army had been held back from the invasion on D-Day to convince the Germans that the invasion would come at Calais instead of Normandy. On July 31, 1944, Patton and his tanks finally went ashore at Avranches and began his historic march across France and Germany. As he approached Erfurt from the southwest in early 1945, several significant events occurred.

About sixty miles west of Erfurt, Patton's Army discovered secure vaults in a 2,000-foot-deep former salt mine. Patton ordered the doors blown open, and they found the entire stash of German gold bullion along with priceless artwork and other treasures. Eisenhower, General Omar Bradley, and Patton toured the mine on April 12, 1945. Then the three generals toured a recently liberated concentration camp about thirty miles west of Erfurt. As Patton was preparing for bed that night, he got word that President Roosevelt had died.

On April 15, Patton toured the Buchenwald concentration camp ten miles east of Erfurt, near the famous town of Weimar. Patton was sickened by the sights and convinced that the residents of Weimar could not have been ignorant of the atrocities. He ordered every citizen of Weimar to tour the camp and see firsthand the results of Nazi brutality.

The vice mayor of Erfurt told us that as Patton's Third Army approached Erfurt, the British Royal Air Force began bombing the historic town. Knowing that their fate was sealed and their historic town would be demolished, the city leaders petitioned Patton to spare their town further bombing. Patton agreed to halt the bombing if they surrendered, which they did. The vice mayor told us that the town credits Patton to this day with saving it from complete destruction.

After Germany was split into East and West after the war, the town of Erfurt was in East Germany. We were surprised not to see more evidence of the East German socialist era. The town today is clean, lively, and beautiful. Erfurt is another place worth visiting again.

When we went to city hall for the morning reception, we found it to be an old building on the same square where we had been celebrating the night before. We were ushered into a spectacular hall with a high ceiling, chandeliers, and paintings all around the walls depicting the rich and ancient history of Erfurt. We felt a little underdressed for the occasion. They brought out some refreshments for all of us. Soon the vice mayor arrived and welcomed us in English, telling us that Erfurt has a sister city in Shawnee, Kansas, and that he had visited the U.S. on several occasions.

He thanked us for what we had done, gave us a little history of Erfurt, then asked us all to sign the official city book. As the native son, Nico was the star of the day. The next day his picture was on the front page of many newspapers in Germany, holding the city book…and with his trademark grin, of course.

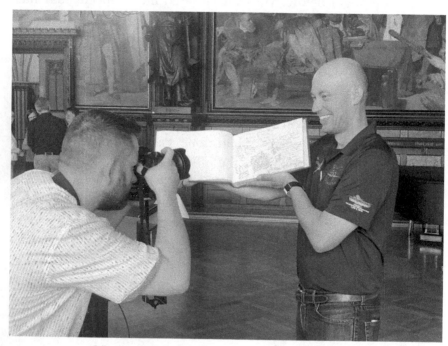

Nico at Erfurt City Hall Reception (author photo)

58

D-Day Squadron...Dismissed!

This is so freakin' awesome!
— Nico Von Pronay

JUNE 17 WAS a day to remember and to regret. We said goodbye to the other airplanes as they scattered to the four winds. Several of our squadron would go on to Tannheim, Germany; Switzerland; and Venice. Some even remained in Europe for the commemoration of Operation Market Garden in September. We had to head for home. The previous four weeks would be forever etched in our memories.

We knew Nico had to leave us on June 20 to get back to work, so we hoped to say our goodbyes in Iceland after enjoying a day off with him there. After our morning reception at city hall, we went to the airport, preflighted the plane, and took off for Duxford. During the last few days, Randy had noted that one of our oil coolers was starting to leak. Of course, about the only item we *didn't* have in our flyaway kit was a spare oil cooler. Such leaks are a common problem, and all oil coolers seem to leak a bit, but it was getting worse and was in a bad spot to make a repair.

The oil cooler probably would have been fine until we got home, but it isn't something you want to lose over the North Atlantic. You can't see the oil cooler from the cockpit, and there is no immediate warning that oil is leaking. The first indication of a big oil leak would probably be rising oil temperatures and dropping pressure, followed soon thereafter by engine failure. We decided that when we were in Duxford picking up a drum of oil we had left there, we would see if we could get our oil cooler repaired or replaced.

The flight from Erfurt to Duxford was about three and a half hours but very memorable. Nico was flying and I was copilot, so this would be Nico's last chance to fly over his native Germany in *Miss Montana*. As it happened, two significant places were along our route from Erfurt to Duxford. The first was a small roadside memorial to an American C-54 that crashed during the *Luftbrucke*.

A friend of Nico's, Florian Meyer, had asked if we would make a low pass over the site on our way home. Since it worked out and was on our route, we planned it. Nico had the coordinates of the location, and we headed that way. We came up on the memorial about fifty miles from Erfurt. We could see a few people on the ground and some flags suspended in the trees. Florian had tried to arrange a formation flyover with Colonel Halvorsen on board one of the planes, but the weather prevented it from happening. A solo pass by *Miss Montana* would have to do.

We didn't know the details at the time, but the C-54 crashed on March 4, 1949, during the airlift. Florian's grandfather, Kurt Siegmund, was a young boy in Heroldishausen, the village closest to the crash site. Herr Siegmund remembers seeing the C-54 flying low over the village, its number three engine on fire. The pilot, First Lieutenant Royce C. Stephens, maneuvered the plane to avoid crashing into the village. Two crew members and two passengers parachuted to safety near Heroldishausen, but Lieutenant Stephens went down with the plane and perished. Florian and his grandfather erected a memorial to the crash in 1999, by the side of the road where it happened. The surviving copilot, Donald Keating, was present at the dedication.

With an appropriate flair for the dramatic, Nico dropped down to a few hundred feet above the ground and we made a *very low* high-speed pass over the site. Then he cranked us into a forty-five-degree left bank and made a sharp turn for another pass. We were even lower the second time. We happened to have on board for that leg Tony Harmsworth, a journalist with *Aeroplane Monthly* in England. He told us he had never been so steeply banked at such a low altitude in a C-47 and that of all the many flights he's had in warbirds, that was the most memorable. Florian told us that ever since witnessing our flyover, his eighty-six-year-old grandfather has been a young man again. We later saw video footage from the ground and felt that we had done a proper job of it.

The next stop on Nico's farewell flight was his hometown of Bochum. This was another sentimental moment for him as we made several turns at low altitude around the place where he grew up. He showed us his father's house, his brother's house, and other important spots in town. The people of Bochum were probably puzzled about a lone C-47 making turns overhead. After that, we were off to cross the channel one more time en route to Duxford. Of course, Nico didn't fail to mention several times how "freakin' awesome" it was to fly over his hometown in a DC-3.

We crossed the channel south of Rotterdam, with Amsterdam in the distance. It occurred to me then that we had flown within sight of Washington, D.C., New York City, London, Paris, Berlin, and Amsterdam. Not a bad sampling of some major world cities.

On this day, it was hard not to be a little sad because we knew that this marvelous journey was nearing its end. We still had many miles to go to bring *Miss Montana* safely home, but by now, we were confident of her abilities, and ours. Events seemed to happen faster as we made our way home, like being on the last hill of a roller coaster shortly before it comes to an end.

We arrived at Duxford about one and half hours before the tower closed and determined we could not do anything on the oil cooler that day, so we called it a day.

59

Homeward Bound

RANDY IMMEDIATELY STARTED looking for a replacement oil cooler in England. The Duxford aerodrome has a shop that regularly works on warbirds, and they told us that there might be some folks who would sell us one and deliver it in the morning on June 18. Randy connected with Ben Perkins at Aerolegends in Kent, England, which owns and operates several warbirds, including the *Drag 'em Oot*. Ben graciously sold us a brand-new oil cooler and even delivered it by mid-morning. Randy and Crystal had it installed by two p.m., and we checked it with an engine test run.

After the oil cooler tested good, we loaded up and said goodbye to jolly old England, launching for Prestwick about three p.m. We checked the weather between Prestwick and Reykjavik, and it looked promising. With any luck, we could make a quick turn at Prestwick, pick up our survival gear, refuel, and head for Iceland.

We arrived at Prestwick right at five p.m. after about two hours of flying by Eric and Randy. The fuel truck was waiting, and we retrieved our survival suits and raft from a nearby hangar. The people at Prestwick airport were top notch except for their abuse of the English language. We knew we had to hurry to get to Reykjavik before the airport closed for the day, so we said goodbye to Prestwick and launched for Iceland. This would be our last flight with Nico, so I wanted to enjoy as much as possible of the entire five-hour flight

("This is so freakin' awesome!). I lasted for four hours then handed the seat over to Randy. As we approached Reykjavik, the fading light over Iceland was one of the more beautiful sights out of many from the last four weeks.

We were flying IFR most of the way and even had to climb to our highest altitude yet of 14,000 feet to get above the clouds and out of some moderate ice. The windshield was completely iced over and we could see ice forming on the props and the leading edges of the wings. This was the most substantial icing we encountered, but the plane didn't seem to notice. As we began our descent into Reykjavik, we were treated for the first and only time on our journey to the *bang, bang, bang* of ice coming off the props and hitting the fuselage just behind the cockpit. We arrived about half an hour before the airport closed on June 18, cleared customs, put the plane to bed, and headed to our hotel.

Icing up between Scotland and Iceland (author photo)

60

Iceland Again

JUNE 19 WAS to be Nico's last day with us, and we were all ready for a break. We wanted to go to the airport first thing to fuel and preflight the plane so it would ready for us the next morning. Even though avgas is much more common in Iceland, it still apparently takes a special person with a special key to be able to drive the fuel truck. We waited for two hours and then were told it might be two more. We decided to taxi over to the self-serve fuel pump and fill her up the old-fashioned way. That small pump was not accustomed to dispensing hundreds of gallons in a hurry. Still, we were fueled and ready to go sooner than if we had waited on the fuel truck.

We had enjoyed Iceland during our stop on the first crossing, and decided we would layover a day to see more of the area and enjoy time with Nico. Mark Bretz had recommended that we visit the Blue Lagoon, a famous hot spring not far from Reykjavik. Iceland has many natural hot springs, some of which are commercial. Blue Lagoon may be the most famous and, from appearances, the most commercial.

That day off was a much-needed break. June 19 marked one month since leaving Missoula, and we had been busy with something, usually many things, nearly every day since. We had not had a single complete day off with nothing to do. Most of us didn't realize how much we needed a break.

At the Blue Lagoon you pay too much money to sit in cloudy, blue, hot water, but the entry fee included one beverage and a mud mask. We spent several hours in the hot spring and we each got our free mud mask. This was one time when Eric fortunately didn't have his phone with him. All of us looked incredibly silly with the mud mask on, especially Nico, who applied the mud to his entire face and bald head. He looked terrifying.

We hit the same sushi restaurant as before and walked around a bit more before turning in. The next day, we were planning to make for Narsarsuaq, the mysterious and treacherous Greenland airport that had defied us on the first crossing.

61

Then There Were Four

ON THE MORNING of June 20, we prepared to start the return crossing in earnest. Although the flight from Prestwick to Reykjavik is over very inhospitable waters, at least Reykjavik and Iceland are fairly civilized with most things we might need readily available—and commercial air service. The miles ahead of us were some of the most remote territory on earth, and most things we might need are much harder to come by—such as a rescue.

The first thing we did was say goodbye to Nico. I drove him to the commercial airport at Keflavik and sent him on his way. Upon return to the Reykjavik airport, Eric and Randy already had the engines running and they were waiting for me to climb aboard.

Clipper Tabitha May, one of the Mighty Fifteen, had left us on June 9 to tour Europe on their own. They arrived at Reykjavik shortly after we did, on their way home. When we got to the airport on the morning of June 20, they were getting ready to take off for Narsarsuaq as well.

Our crew was down to Eric, Randy, Crystal, and me. We were now a small crew compared to every flight before, but by this time we had a rhythm, with everyone doing what needed to be done. The four of us would get to take *Miss Montana* the rest of the way home. In many ways it was simpler and more pleasant to fly with fewer people, and we all especially enjoyed the last few days as we rumbled toward home.

Jeff had hoped to catch up with us in Iceland, but, due to the premature end to the events at Berlin, we had departed for home three days early and, as usual, we made good time. He was just getting off his cruise about then, so his next chance to catch up with us would be in Canada.

62

Narsarsuaq

BACK IN DECEMBER 2018, we prepaid over seven thousand dollars for avgas in drums to be barged to Narsarsuaq, at the southern tip of Greenland, so it would be waiting for us when we crossed over in May. The airport at Narsarsuaq didn't have enough storage capacity for the avgas needed by all the DC-3s that planned to refuel there, and they understandably did not want to stock enough fuel on their dime for all of us in case we were unable to stop. The occasional small planes making the crossing would have taken many years to use up all that fuel.

Weather had prevented us from landing there on the first crossing, so we hoped to stop there on our return. Not only did we want to collect the gas we had bought, but we wanted to see famous Narsarsuaq. The weather looked promising that morning, with only morning fog that was forecast to burn off by late morning when we would arrive. The weather at Sonderstrom also looked good; we would have a decent alternate if the weather at Narsarsuaq did not clear as forecasted.

The direct route from Reykjavik to Narsarsuaq is close to the longest leg on the Blue Spruce route. However, being the prudent pilots that we were, we plotted a direct course for the east coast of Greenland, then planned to follow the southeast Greenland coast down to Narsarsuaq. We were treated to unmatched views of spectacular scenes all the way down the coast. *Clipper Tabitha May* departed Reykjavik about an hour after we did, but they flew direct to Narsarsuaq. Our theory was that if problems occurred, the closer we were to land—even if it's cold, frozen, rocky uninhabited land—the better our chances for survival would be. Fortunately, our theory wasn't tested.

By the time we left Reykjavik at 11:40 a.m., the weather at Narsarsuaq was looking great, so we were confident that our planned route would result with us safely on the ground there. The long flight over water was comfortable by this time, and we once again looked in vain for ships in the Atlantic below us.

As the coast of Greenland came into view, we were treated to magnificent views of glaciers coming all the way down to the water, thousands of icebergs large and small, and hundreds of rocky islands. Once again, our sense of wonder was stirred. We followed the coast for many miles before edging inland to make our approach to Narsarsuaq from the north.

After nearly five hours of flight, we started our descent down a deep valley north of Narsarsuaq. On the way in, we heard *Clipper Tabitha May* on the radio. They had nearly caught up with us, having flown directly from to Narsarsuaq.

We had to circle over Narsarsuaq to lose altitude before landing from the north. As we were setting our chocks, we got a front row seat to watch *Clipper Tabitha May* come in and land from the south. The crew of *Clipper Tabitha May* was one of the crews we had not had a chance to meet during the previous weeks in Europe. Once the plane was on the ground, we met owner Robert Randazzo and his crew and walked to the tower to see if it would be possible to fuel up so we could continue to Iqaluit.

Thus began another saga of dealing with Greenland airports. We were informed that their fuel truck was broken, but, not to worry, they could easily and quickly fill us up out of the drums of fuel we had purchased in advance. Sure enough, the line crew was efficient and got to work. Meanwhile, Eric went to the tower to arrange payment of landing fees and gas.

Clipper Tabitha May had experienced the same mess with Greenland airports on their first crossing. They had stopped in Narsarsuaq on a Sunday and had to pay the extra fee to land. For the return trip, Robert had called ahead to Narsarsuaq to make *sure* that there would be no surprises when he landed on Wednesday and departed either the same day or the next. He was assured there would be no special fees or problems.

Having gotten a bit of a late start from Reykjavik, after the five-hour flight and the three-hour time change, we arrived at Narsarsuaq at about two p.m. local time. By the time we got fuel, checked weather, and paid the landing fees, it was about 4:15 p.m. We talked about trying to take off and make it to our next stop. That was when one of the fuel guys mentioned that the airport closed in forty-five minutes. We all simultaneously looked at our watches and knew we couldn't get our paperwork finished, start engines, and take off in forty-five minutes.

Oh well, we thought, it's not the worst thing to spend another night in mystical Greenland. We might not ever get another chance. That was when one of the fuel guys casually mentioned that the next day, Thursday, was a national holiday and the airport would be closed (sort of). We would have to pay the fee again to take off.

When Robert Randazzo heard this, he hit the roof. He had called ahead to verify there would be no extra fees, but nobody thought to mention that June 21, the summer solstice and the longest day of the year, was a national holiday in Greenland. Are. You. Kidding. Me?

After some wrangling, the tower said that if we both departed on Thursday, we could split the $1,200 fee because we were sort of with the same "company." Since it was the best we could do, we put the plane to bed, grabbed our gear, and headed to Hotel Narsarsuaq, which was the best—and only—hotel in Narsarsuaq.

Arriving at the hotel, which was similar to the one in Sonderstrom and had the same utilitarian vibe, we checked in. There was a small bar in the lobby with a sign for Qajaq Brewery. We hadn't been able to find decent beer for several days, so an inquiry was in order. They offered my favorite style of beer, and the brewery itself was in the nearby town of Narsaq. When I asked how far away Narsaq was, the lady replied without emotion, "It's about a one-hour boat ride… or a three-day walk." The beer was forgettable, but the experience was not.

After our great experience with dinner at Sonderstrom, we were hopeful we could again find some great chow. The restaurant was again in the hotel and the food was good but not nearly as good as at Sonderstrom. As you might imagine, Narsarsuaq is not a busy place, and there were only a few other souls eating dinner in the restaurant. There was one other group, professionally dressed.

Since it was the day before the longest day of the year, I went for a walk after dinner, strolling down to the shore and looking around the small town of Narsarsuaq, population 145. I wasn't likely to return there anytime soon.

63

Longest Day

FRIDAY MORNING BEGAN like every other day on this journey—looking for coffee and breakfast. It was the longest day of the year, and our latitude was a little over sixty-one degrees north, so it never got very dark the night before and it was hard to sleep. The three-hour time change from Iceland meant I got to the cafeteria early. It was empty except for one of the professionally dressed gentlemen I'd noticed at dinner the night before. We sat at adjacent tables, and I asked what brought him to Narsarsuaq. He introduced himself as Niels Grosen and said that he was head of all the airports in Greenland. What a coincidence.

I told him who we were and, after exchanging pleasantries, I brought up our frustration with the airport "closures" and associated fees we had experienced at both Sondrestrom and now Narsarsuaq. I told him that several of our Mighty Fifteen in the D-Day Squadron had installed ferry tanks so they could bypass Greenland—and the consensus among the rest of us was that we would do the same if we ever made the crossing again. He listened and sympathized but didn't offer any solutions.

As I left the cafeteria, I ran into Robert Randazzo and told him with a grin that there was someone he needed to meet. I felt a little guilty introducing Robert to Niels, but Robert had cooled off since the afternoon before and was very polite with Niels. Nevertheless, he told him in no uncertain terms that our treatment felt like a "shakedown" and he would bypass Greenland if he ever had an option to do so.

Our plans for the day were to make it to Canada, hopefully Goose Bay, but two obstacles hindered us from that goal. The weather at Goose Bay was forecast to be windy, rainy, and cold with low ceilings—definitely IFR with a good chance for ice. Furthermore, we learned that the lone truck that delivered avgas had broken down and the estimated date to get another one to Goose Bay was seven or eight days. Our only other option, if we wanted to keep moving, was to go back to Iqaluit. A quick call to Iqaluit verified that they still had avgas and that they would reserve it for us. Consequently, on the longest day of the year, we took off from Narsarsuaq about eleven a.m. and headed toward Iqaluit.

After Eric and I took off from Narsarsuaq, we climbed out to the south over the infamous fjords that had terrified so many airmen and killed more than a few. However, on this day, the weather was stunningly beautiful and the views were once again spectacular to behold. We saw icebergs, glaciers, and artic lakes perched on hills above the bays—but still no trees. We passed Narsaq, home of the famous microbrewery, and after reaching land's end, turned east toward Iqaluit.

The flight from Narsarsuaq to Iqaluit was about five hours. Iqaluit is located at a latitude of almost sixty-four degrees north, but it was our best option for continuing our way home. We found out later that Robert and *Clipper Tabitha May* had made it to Goose Bay after flying a harrowing approach through lousy weather. They somehow found enough fuel to get them to the next fuel stop and then pressed on to their home in Virginia.

As we went feet dry east of Iqaluit, we celebrated our second successful Atlantic crossing. The most difficult and risky portions of the journey were over. Once again, the airplane had performed flawlessly. Ernest Gann said in *Fate is the Hunter* that pilots making the North Atlantic crossing during World War II "put their faith in God and Pratt & Whitney."[17] So had we.

When we landed in Iqaluit, we once again fueled up from drums, but it took longer this time to get everything done. We ordered some food to go, and this time the customs folks showed up and looked through the plane. They told us their biggest concern now was marijuana coming into the country. Apparently, it was legal to grow but not legal to import. Growing anything in Iqaluit looked like a challenge to me.

When we landed in Iqaluit, we resolved to keep going and not to spend another night in this remote outpost. Eric did some planning and decided that we could make it to Val d'Or, Quebec, south and a little west of Iqaluit...almost 870 miles away.

Val d'Or was at the outside of our range, but tailwinds were forecasted, which made it possible for us to make it. Still, it looked like it would be a six-hour flight and would put us in Val d'Or right at dark. There were not very many options between Iqaluit and Val d'Or for landing or fuel, so we took an extra drum of fuel from Iqaluit with us just in case. We launched from Iqaluit about 3:45 p.m. local time and headed for Val d'Or, with Eric and Randy driving.

The flight was indeed long but uneventful. The route took us one last time over incredibly remote and unpopulated country. We saw settlements, mines, and a few remote airports but fortunately did not need to stop. We landed in Val d'Or about 9:45 p.m. We had covered 1,435 miles in eleven hours of flight time, the longest day in both miles and hours since leaving Missoula over a month before. Our longest day was also the longest day of the year.

Typical view over southern Greenland (author photo)

64

Back in the USA

WE HAD HEARD that people in Quebec proudly speak predominantly French. Other than Scotland, Val d'Or was the only place we had any language issues, but we got by with the customary handwaving and help from a few bilingual people at the airport and hotel. *Val d'Or* is French for *Valley of Gold* and the area is still a busy mining district. Like many of the places we had stopped, none of us had ever heard of it. Val d'Or looked prosperous and clean, and we were treated very well during our short stay.

On June 22, we launched from Val d'Or at about 12:40 p.m. local time and headed for the Twin Cities in Minnesota. On his way home from Europe, Brandon Jewett had stopped at the old St. Paul airport in *Liberty* and reported good service there. St. Paul was in the right direction and within our range so off we went.

St. Paul was almost due west from Val d'Or and the distance was 575 miles. We had favorable winds and weather as Eric and I flew the four-and-a-half-hour flight. We crossed into U.S. airspace about twenty-five miles northwest of Sault Ste. Marie, Michigan. This day marked one month, approximately 14,000 miles, and 100 flight hours since leaving U.S. airspace north of Presque Isle on May 23. It felt very good to be back in the USA.

We landed at the St. Paul airport about four p.m. local time and were instructed to taxi over to the old tower/terminal building and wait for customs. After the customs officer finally showed up and inspected the plane, we opened *Miss Montana* for the crowd of assembled people. People were still tracking our progress on our satellite trackers and anxious to see *Miss Montana* in person. Then we taxied over to the Signature FBO, where they generously put us in a hangar for the night. At that point, the weather for the next day or two in the Twin Cities looked bad, with a cold front headed in from the west. Never knowing what the morrow would bring, we headed to the hotel and dinner, half expecting to be stuck for a day or two in the Twin Cities.

When we arose the next morning and checked the weather, we decided that we could file an IFR flight plan and make it out despite the bad weather. The incoming front was narrow, so we expected to be in clear skies after a short distance—and we were. Eric and Randy manned the front office as we took off about 11:20 a.m., climbed into the clouds, and headed for Baker, Montana about two and a half hours away. We had only been in the air about fifteen minutes, when Jeff texted me that he was about an hour out from landing in Minneapolis on his way home. He wondered if we were still at St. Paul so he could ride with us for the final legs home. We had missed him again.

65

The Last Best Place

"THE LAST BEST Place," coined by University of Montana professor William Kittredge in 1988, has been adopted as the unofficial motto of the State of Montana. On our journey it took on special meaning. We had been to some great places in the last month, all of them new and interesting. We enjoyed our times there and will never forget the experiences we shared with each other and with the crews from other planes. Still, it felt great when we finally crossed the border into Montana and landed at the small airport in Baker, Montana. Not only were we back in "The Last Best Place," but we had nearly completed our mission.

Word had gotten out that we would be stopping in Baker, a small town in far southeast Montana with a population of about 1,900 people. It seemed like most of them came to see us. We stayed there for an hour or two and gave tours to everybody who wanted one. After saying goodbye, we loaded up and took off about 3:45 p.m. for Billings. Eric and I flew this leg, and we did it as low as we could fly, 500 to 1,000 feet above the ground. It was reminiscent of the low flights we had made over Europe in formation. Our route took us almost directly over Interstate 90, and I couldn't help wondering how many of the people on the road knew who we were and where we had been. Hopefully we didn't cause any accidents. We landed at Billings about five thirty p.m. and were warmly welcomed by a crowd. We were scheduled for a static display the next morning, so we called it a night and headed for the hotel.

66

Homecoming

THE NEXT DAY, June 24, marked the end of our trip. We arrived at the Billings airport by nine a.m. and opened the plane for tours. Even before the appointed time, people started arriving, and they continued coming until after lunch. We enjoyed talking about the trip and our participation in the historic events. Many of them told us they had been following us the entire way and were amazed that we had made it all the way there and back. Late in the morning Art Dykstra, Mark Bretz, and Mike Anderson arrived from Missoula in Mark's jet. Mark wanted to fly one more leg in *Miss Montana*, and Mike wanted to ride from Billings to Missoula.

After several hours of tours, we loaded up one last time, and took off for Missoula. This was a bittersweet moment, knowing that this was the last leg of our trip and it would soon be over. We were happy that we had nearly completed the mission and would soon see our families again. The short two-hour flight from Billings to Missoula, with Eric and Mark flying, was also at low altitude, and included a low pass at the Bozeman airport. Art followed us in formation for part of it in Mark's jet. We finally landed at Missoula around five p.m. As was our custom, we made a big circle over Missoula and a low pass by the Museum of Mountain Flying before coming around to land. Fire trucks at the airport gave us a traditional water salute as we taxied into the museum. After so many months of work and worry, it was great to be home.

Dozens of people welcomed us, including many volunteers, donors, jumpers, and well-wishers. The media was there in numbers, and we did several interviews, relishing in the moment of our return. My first goal after coming down the steps was to find my wife, who was in the crowd on the other side of the plane. The *Missoulian* photographer captured us smooching under the nose of the plane for the next day's front page.

We greeted our friends and volunteers who had helped to make this story happen. We were glad to see them all again, and they felt a sense of accomplishment for their part in the successful mission. We couldn't help wondering, after such an epic journey, what we could do next that would surpass what we had just accomplished.

The story of this airplane has four beginnings, lots of middle, and two near endings. There is not yet a real end to its story. That's probably bad for a book, but it's good for the airplane. If there was to be an ending to this story for now, that was probably it. All's well that ends well. Mission accomplished. Triumph of wills. Grand achievement. Yet all that rings a bit hollow. For those of us who have been forever linked with this old airplane, the suspense lies in what happens next, what new history can she make, and will we be there to share it with her?

The next two chapters describe what we hope her future will be like: teaching the next generation about the past and serving when duty calls.

The author kissing his wife, Dawn, upon returning to Missoula
(photo by Tom Bauer, Missoulian)

67

Bonus – Mann Gulch Anniversary

EVEN THOUGH THE *"Miss Montana* to Normandy" story officially ended upon our return from Europe, it seems fitting and proper to extend the story to include the events commemorating the 70th
anniversary of the Mann Gulch tragedy. After all, it was the Mann
Gulch tragedy that gave N24320 much of her identity and certainly
her cachet as the most historic plane in Montana—not to mention
the primary reason she was brought home in 2001.

August 5, 2019 was the 70th anniversary of that tragedy, and
we spent most of the time after returning from Europe trying to put
together an event that would do it justice. Our first idea was to drop
jumpers in real smokejumper gear from *Miss Montana*—either over
Mann Gulch itself, or over the airport in Helena. Al Charters, who
would be in charge of any jump, soon vetoed the idea of jumping
into Mann Gulch. The original drop zone is very rugged and the actual memorial site is a tiny picnic area right on the river so very few
people could see it. Also, trying to steer round chutes into that small
opening without landing in the water would be challenging. So, for
the safety of the jumpers, plan B was to drop the jumpers over the
Helena Airport.

However, three government bureaucracies blocked our attempts to perform this modest reenactment. When Eric Komberec requested approval from the FAA for the airport drops as part of the commemoration, the local tower denied his request. The reasons they gave were confounding, because the Army Golden Knights received approval to jump on the same day at the same location. It was eerily reminiscent of one of the reasons for being denied a chance to land at or near Berlin: our request wasn't submitted in enough time. The other agency that waylaid our efforts was the United States Forest Service.

Smokejumper gear is unique, not something available from some online smokejumper supply store. By tradition and necessity, smokejumpers fabricate their own equipment using needles and thread and sewing machines. This means actual smokejumper gear is the property of the U.S. Forest Service smokejumper bases around the country. And so are the parachutes we wanted to use—round ones.

Despite repeated attempts to get approval from the USFS to use their gear, we were denied at every turn. They wouldn't even let active duty smokejumpers make the jump in their gear on their own time. We were very disappointed with the response from the USFS. We had just completed an epic journey and were bringing important attention to the USFS, smokejumping, and the Mann Gulch victims, and all they were concerned about was covering their own butts. The USFS and FAA missed a huge opportunity to recognize the thirteen men who died in the Mann Gulch tragedy and to bring their story to a new generation.

Ironically, the third reason we couldn't drop jumpers over the Helena Airport was because there was an active wildfire nearby that required aerial support. The helicopters dropping water on the fire were operating out of the Helena Airport, and the airport manager did not want any airspace interference. Still, it would have been completely doable from our perspective.

After being rejected by our own government bureaucracies in the planning of something that needed to be done, we came up with an alternative that was almost as good. We would drop thirteen ceremonial wreaths from *Miss Montana* over Mann Gulch on August 5. Leah Rediske, one of our volunteers, made each wreath by hand from local pine boughs; each one was inscribed with the name of one of the victims. No bureaucracy could stop us from doing that.

We flew from Missoula to Helena on the morning of Sunday, August 4. We parked on the ramp at the Helena Airport and opened the plane and a display of smokejumper gear to the public. The turnout was outstanding. People had come from all over the state and as far away as Spokane. Without a doubt, there was still some enthusiasm from our trip to Europe, but that only added to the significance of *Miss Montana* being involved in this commemoration. We sold more hats, T-shirts, and other gear than we had at any other event, raising nearly $10,000 in a little over twenty-four hours.

Not long after arriving at the Helena Airport, we met Scott Diettert and Carol Kneiper, niece and nephew of Eldon Diettert, the Mann Gulch victim who died on his nineteenth birthday. Neither Scott nor Carol ever knew their uncle, but his death was part of their family lore. A few weeks before the 70th anniversary, Carol donated a box of memorabilia about her uncle to the Museum of Mountain Flying. The collection included some heartbreaking mementos, including Eldon's death certificate and letters he had written home during his brief smokejumping career.

Sunday afternoon we made a practice flight over Mann Gulch, with Art in the left seat and Randy as SIC. This was mainly a practice flight so Art could figure out the best flight path for the next day, but also an opportunity to take some of our supporters, as well as Carol Kneiper and her husband, on a flight over the place where her uncle had perished. The flight was emotional for Carol, flying in the same airplane her uncle had jumped from, over the place where he died. Art did a great job navigating the crags and canyons that surround the area. He flew so low that it was possible to see the thirteen white crosses on the ground marking the location where each victim fell.

That afternoon, we also met a remarkable young man, eleven-year-old Colt Barnard from Fromberg, Montana, who had established a special connection to the Mann Gulch disaster. Colt's mother, Audrey, had been a firefighter, and she and Colt had visited Mann Gulch earlier in the year. As they placed flowers at each of the white cement crosses, Colt noticed how deteriorated the crosses had become since they were placed soon after the tragedy. As part of a 4-H project, Colt decided to raise money to replace the crosses as a tribute to the victims. We introduced Colt to the crowd and encouraged donations to his cause.

As the sun started to dip toward the horizon, Art Dykstra had the idea to put thirteen chairs in front of the jump door on *Miss Montana* and display the thirteen beautiful wreaths that we would be dropping the next day. Scott Diettert wrote the name of a victim on each wreath, and we placed them on the chairs. The ramp got quiet as the setting sun and lowering light illuminated the scene. Many photos were made of the wreaths in front of the same door the victims had jumped out seven decades before. One particularly good image that was posted on social media went viral, attracting thousands of shares and likes.

That evening we held a dinner at the Helena Airport and were entertained by Dave Turner, a retired Forest Service official and historian on the Mann Gulch event. He told a brief but concise story of the tragedy from another, less-known perspective.

On the morning of August 5, we taxied *Miss Montana* across the airport to the Army National Guard ramp, where we would remain for the day. The ANG held an open house on that same day, so we shared the ramp with a C-130, ANG helicopters, and many other aircraft. The public was invited, and the turnout was once again outstanding. Even the governor made an appearance, and we gave him a tour of *Miss Montana*.

At about ten thirty a.m., Art and Randy took off with Al Charters and several of our jumpers on board, along with Scott Diettert, Leah Rediske, and the thirteen wreaths. Local pilot Kevin Danz offered to fly his Long EZ airplane as a chase plane to record the event. Art made several very low passes over Mann Gulch, so low that he was below the surrounding ridge tops.

Many ambitious fans had made the challenging hike into Mann Gulch early that morning—and many of their photos from the ridges above Mann Gulch are looking *down* on *Miss Montana* as she made her passes. Over 200 others had taken boats down the river to the memorial site, where a commemoration was taking place. Art made six passes over the memorial site, and Al and the smokejumpers threw out two wreaths each pass, like the smokejumpers who had jumped seventy years before. In between each pass, Art flew over the exact spot where the jumpers had landed, and they threw out a smaller laurel each time. In a remarkable coincidence, Brian Sallee, cousin of Robert Sallee, one of the three Mann Gulch survivors, was on the ground at the commemoration and found one of the wreaths we dropped that day.

For the smokejumpers in *Miss Montana*, it was a perfect trifecta. They were in the same smokejumping plane that had dropped the jumpers in 1949, flown by a smokejumper pilot, and dropping wreaths to honor their fallen brothers seventy years later. Smokejumpers, like elite soldiers, are a tightknit and loyal bunch. They stick together and take care of their own.

After returning to Helena and saying our goodbyes, the *Miss Montana* crew and supporters loaded up and made the short flight back to Missoula. Our final homage to the Mann Gulch victims that day was a low pass over the smokejumper base at Missoula, where we dropped thirteen streamers. All the streamers landed on the practice jump spot at the Missoula smokejumper base, affectionately known as the "Field of Shame." All in all, we felt we had done a good job of remembering those men who had gone to their deaths so many years before. Earl Cooley and Wag Dodge may not have been lying on either side of the door when those wreaths went out that day, but they were there in spirit.

Memorial Wreaths for Mann Gulch Commemoration (author photo)

Miss Montana dropping wreaths over Mann Gulch on 70th Anniversary
(photo by IFlyBigSky and Chris McGowan)

68

Bonus – Bahamas Hurricane Relief

ON SEPTEMBER 1, 2019, Hurricane Dorian made landfall on the Bahamas as a Category 5 hurricane, the strongest ever to hit the islands. The damage to parts of the Bahamas was catastrophic as the hurricane inexplicably lingered in one spot for two days. Winds exceeded 185 mph and virtually wiped parts of Abaco Island clean. Parts of the Bahamas were ravaged by extreme storm surges of twenty feet. The storm dropped an estimated three feet of rain in the three days it battered the islands.

Not long after Dorian hit, organizations contacted us, asking if *Miss Montana* could help transport supplies to the Bahamas. After much discussion, planning, and preparation, the decision was made to fly *Miss Montana* to Fort Lauderdale and ferry supplies to the Bahamas for as long as we were needed. Eric mustered enough crew (Eric, Mark Bretz, Dave Hoerner, Randy, and me) to make the trip. We also brought along volunteers Natalie Abrams, Guyle Guderian, and John Haines to help on the ground.

Once we began advertising this new mission, the response in Montana was again terrific. We raised money, we collected supplies to take with us, and got a lot of press supporting the mission. On September 14, we took off for Florida, stopping in Billings to pick up more supplies donated by Montanans before landing at Rapid City for the night. On September 15 we flew from Rapid City to Kansas City, landing at Wheeler Downtown Airport for fuel.

Kansas City was my hometown, and this was the same airport where I had first encountered a DC-3 as a child. The original terminal building and viewing lounge are still there. After treating ourselves to some local barbecue provided by my mother and sister, and some interviews with local television stations, we took off for Florida. I mentioned my long-ago history with the airport to our crew, and when he heard it, Dave Hoerner kindly offered to let me be copilot for the takeoff. That takeoff brought my DC-3 history full circle and was incredibly meaningful. By the time we stopped at Meridian, Mississippi, for gas, the weather in Florida had turned worse, so we stopped for the night in Tallahassee.

We got an early start the next morning before daylight, flying from Tallahassee to Fort Lauderdale Executive Airport, where we would be based for the next two weeks. At the time, we didn't know much about the duration or specifics of our mission. Well-meaning individuals or groups commonly send supplies, manpower, or other resources to disaster areas, only for them to end up wasted. Worse yet, well-intentioned efforts sometimes get in the way of professional relief efforts. We certainly didn't want to be like that, but needn't have worried. Shortly after landing we met up with the wonderful folks from Operation BBQ Relief.

OBR is a nonprofit that started after a tornado destroyed much of Joplin, Missouri, in 2011. Professional barbecue chefs and hobbyists decided to mobilize their equipment to Joplin to provide hot, quality meals to survivors and responders. Since that humble beginning, OBR has expanded into an incredible service organization and provides barbecue meals to millions of people at many different disaster sites—tornadoes, floods, wildfires, hurricanes, even a train derailment and fertilizer-plant explosion. They have now been joined by hundreds of volunteers and served disaster victims across the country. However, Hurricane Dorian was their first international deployment and the first time they could not mobilize to the disaster site and provide the food directly. Reminiscent of the Berlin Airlift, *Miss Montana* went to work.

Shortly after arriving at Fort Lauderdale on September 16, we got a glimpse of the efficiency of the OBR team. We had a short meeting with them in which they told us they needed us to fly to the airport at Freeport, Grand Bahamas. We did some research on local flight procedures and clearing customs. Soon, OBR drove up with a truck full of supplies that would be needed in advance of the hot food. We had given them specific instructions on how much we could carry (6,000 pounds) and how many pallets we could fit. Each plastic-wrapped pallet was weighed and the weight was written on the plastic. We quickly figured out how to load six pallets of bread, utensils, Styrofoam containers, and other supplies, and Eric and I took off for Freeport.

Most of us had never seen a disaster area so soon after the event. We didn't know what to expect on the ground in Freeport, but local intel advised that the airport was operational, and OBR had people on the ground ready to unload and distribute the cargo. The flight from Fort Lauderdale Executive Airport to Freeport is only about ninety miles, usually a bit less than one hour each way.

As we approached Freeport from the west, we could begin to see the effects of the hurricane. The vegetation on the island was brown from the saltwater flooding, many trees and buildings were damaged, and it looked like a flood had hit the island from the effects of the storm surge. Upon landing at the airport, we saw many other planes, including another DC-3, but also some light single-engine and twin-engine planes that were coming and going. Most of the hangars and other metal-sided buildings on the airport had been severely damaged. As soon as we parked, OBR arrived with a truck and a forklift, and we quickly unloaded and returned to Fort Lauderdale. The plan was to make an afternoon flight with hot barbecue meat and side dishes that OBR had prepared.

Upon returning to Fort Lauderdale, we had to go through

customs, which was at the opposite end of the airport from our parking spot at the marvelous Banyan FBO. This was one of the biggest
hassles of the mission: we had to go through customs at Freeport and
at Fort Lauderdale every flight, taking valuable time and having (at
Fort Lauderdale) to restart our hot engines just for a short taxi back
to our parking place. On the third day, Banyan kindly offered to tow
us from customs back to our parking place each time.

As soon as we arrived back at Banyan, OBR was waiting with
a truckload of hot beans and pulled pork. Once again, it was all on
individually weighed pallets exactly meeting our requirements. All
the meat and side dishes were in heavy-duty, thermally insulated
Cambro boxes that were neatly stacked on each pallet and plastic
wrapped. It was incredibly efficient. We soon had the hot food loaded and strapped down, and at about five thirty p.m. we started the
engines for a return flight to the hungry people of the Bahamas.

Eric and Dave were flying this leg, and Randy was riding in the
jump seat. Startup was normal, but five minutes later the engines
shut down. That wasn't normal. Randy informed us that an aluminum tube at the hydraulic accumulator, right behind the copilot, had
cracked and was leaking hydraulic fluid. Once again, as with the oil
cooler in Germany, the only spare parts we had neglected to bring
along were spare hoses. All things considered, this wasn't a disaster,
because it happened on the ground in Florida and Randy caught it
before takeoff. However, it put OBR in a big bind.

They had 6,000 pounds of hot meat and side dishes that had a
shelf life of a few hours before it had to be thrown out. OBR is so
precise about their business that they know and monitor the actual
temperature in each container and, from experience, know how long
it is safe to eat. They made a few quick calls and later told us that
there were some very happy people at a local homeless shelter. They
had been able to find a home for it within the critical time window,
and it went to a good cause.

Still, we felt bad. Not only because we had failed to deliver on
our first real mission, but because the poor people in Freeport would

end up eating cold Ramen noodles for dinner that night. The folks at OBR were very gracious about it, assuring us, "things happen" and not to worry about the hot food because it still went to hungry people. Meanwhile we had a hydraulic hose to fix.

After a few calls to some local contacts, Randy got a lead on a source for a hose. Randy, John Haines, and I jumped into the crew van and drove a short distance to a very sketchy looking group of industrial buildings—they looked a bit like large storage units. Our instructions were to find the right unit and the key to the shop would be in a wrecked Volkswagen Beetle parked outside. Sure enough, we found the unit, the Beetle, and the key, and opened the shop.

The place was stacked from floor to ceiling, front to back, with airplanes and airplane parts...and no lights. There were at least two wrecked Cessnas in there in various states of disrepair and disassembly. The place was a mess, no organization or hint of where we might find hoses. We searched where the owner had told us to look but found nothing. A few minutes later, Randy was crawling through the cabin of a wrecked Cessna in the dark, when he put his hand down to steady himself—right on top of the exact size and length of hydraulic hose that we needed. It looked brand-new and was all by itself.

Back at the airplane, Randy had it installed in about fifteen minutes, and we pressure tested it to make sure it worked. Thus, the day ended with a small victory after a discouraging mechanical problem. However, it was only our second mechanical issue since our first flight in May. Moreover, we had arrived safely in Florida, figured out how to get to the Bahamas, made one flight with supplies, and we were ready to finally take some hot food to the Bahamas the next day. Randy and Mark Bretz had to go home the next morning, which left Eric, Dave, and me for flying duties.

On September 17, we arrived at the airport ready to make as many flights as needed. OBR advised us they wanted us to make only an afternoon flight with hot food, so we relaxed for the first time and got a tour of the impressive OBR operation across the airport.

In the afternoon, we loaded up with a new load of hot meat and side dishes, and took off for Freeport.

Once again, OBR showed up with a truck, a forklift, and many helpers, and the plane was quickly unloaded. On this trip, we brought along some of the people who were in charge of getting OBR there and operational—and they wanted to watch and help with the first distribution. We were invited to stick around on the island and see the people being fed.

After unloading the plane, Dave, Eric and I crammed into two beat-up old cars and drove a few minutes away to a large black church on the outskirts of Freeport. Actually, the church building was bright white, but the parishioners were all black. We parked under a large shelter near the front of the church and waited for the work to begin. The OBR crew set up tables, spread out the serving supplies, opened the food, and started serving meals.

Apparently, we had carried 10,200 hot meals on the afternoon flight. As we watched them work, it was obvious that there was no way all that food could be served quickly enough in one location. Sure enough, as we watched over the next hour, at least a dozen cars pulled up to the church, and someone would load a box of meat, a box of sides, plus the other supplies, and drive off with 200 complete meals to be served at another church somewhere on the island. Their organization was impressive.

Our first day, we had taken a pastor named Kelvin from Florida to the Bahamas to help, the plan being for him to come back with us on the afternoon flight—which was canceled due to our hydraulic leak. So, Kelvin had to spend the night on the island. There was no power and therefore no air conditioning (it was incredibly hot and humid the entire time we were there), little or no running water, and little food. The next afternoon when we arrived with hot food, this very nice pastor helped with the distribution and returned to Fort Lauderdale in the evening with us.

When we parked at customs at Fort Lauderdale and got out of *Miss Montana* to walk over to the customs office, Kelvin put his hands up in the air and shouted, "Jesus! Thank you, Jesus, I'm home!" We all got a good laugh out of it but certainly didn't envy the man for having to spend the night, probably on a church pew, in steamy Freeport.

Our work continued until September 27, when OBR ended operations; the conditions in Freeport and the Bahamas had improved such that their work was no longer needed. Shortly after arriving in Florida, we were privileged to deliver OBR's 3 millionth meal served. Miss Montana flew to Punta Gorda, Florida, for a few days to get Dave Hoerner trained for his PIC type rating with Frank Moss, then remained there for a few weeks due to bad weather in Montana. Our old friend Frank Moss flew *Miss Montana* home, leaving Florida on October 13 and arriving in Missoula the next day, another successful mission in the books.

Epilogue

PEOPLE STILL TELL us, "You made Montana proud." It's the highest praise we get because it is, ultimately, what we set out to do. Shortly after returning from Europe, I was in the barber chair chatting with the barber about our adventures of the past few weeks. The only other man in the shop listened silently. After a few minutes, he asked if I had been on the *Miss Montana* crew. When I said I had, he stood up, walked over to me, extended his hand, and said only "Thank you," with moist eyes. This still happens to all of us periodically, and it makes all the effort worthwhile.

On June 2, 2019, the *Vintage Aviation Echo*, an online publication dedicated to historic aviation[25] wrote: "The transatlantic journeys of the 'mighty fifteen' American C-47s and DC-3s of the D-Day Squadron alone ranks as one of the greatest feats in historic aviation to date, let alone their upcoming return to Normandy alongside the European contingent." That was a bit unexpected, but when you consider all that had occurred, it made sense. It is unlikely to ever be repeated.

N18121 was one of the Mighty Fifteen and was a DC-3 built in 1937. It was the oldest plane in the squadron. When it landed in Scotland in May 2019, it is believed to have been the oldest airplane ever to cross the Atlantic. The rest of the squadron were only a few years younger.

The Museum of Mountain Flying and her board (including Dick Komberec and Kathy Ogren) made all this possible by originally acquiring N24320 and taking care of her for eighteen years until this opportunity arose. There is no other museum like it. If you are ever in Missoula, Montana, stop by the museum and see *Miss Montana* for yourself. It is officially open between Memorial Day and Labor Day, and you can spend as much time as you like. Even if it is closed, it's likely one of us will be there and let you in. You might be welcomed by one of The Crew or volunteers that helped restore *Miss Montana*, and you might get a personal tour.

The D-Day Squadron has formed an operating group that will plan future events and share information, parts, and other resources. Other planes beyond the Mighty Fifteen have joined us. Hopefully, you will see these planes together again soon.

There are parts of this story that have only touched on other, much bigger stories that would require several books to tell. Fortunately, those have already been written.

To read more about the Mann Gulch disaster, read *Young Men and Fire* by Norman Maclean. To learn more about the early days of mountain flying, Johnson Flying Service, and Bob Johnson, there are several excellent choices: *Fly the Biggest Piece Back* by Steve Smith, *Tall Timber Pilots* by Dale White and Larry Florek, and *Tall Trees, Tough Pilots* by Kathy Ogren and Dick Komberec. An excellent book about smokejumpers, by a pioneering smokejumper, is *Trimotor and Trail* by Earl Cooley.

The Berlin Airlift has been the subject of many good books. Two that I found helpful and thorough are *Daring Young Men* by Richard Reeves and *The Candy Bombers* by Andrei Cherny. Last, if you want to know anything about World War II history (not to mention the transcontinental railroad in America and the Lewis and Clark Expedition), read everything that Stephen Ambrose ever wrote. You won't be disappointed.

There are also many books written about the DC-3. For starters, I recommend *Grand Old Lady, Story of the DC-3* by Glines and Moseley.

Throughout the project, and especially during and after the trip to Europe, we found ourselves grasping for new words to describe the whole experience. Superlatives like awesome, epic, remarkable, incredible, inspiring, aspirational, amazing, and even "freakin' awesome," started to get worn out. Many times, I sat in the cockpit looking out over vistas that few will ever see and could only shake my head—words were inadequate. Some started using "miracle" to describe what had happened. I resisted the use of that word because it implied that divine intervention was involved, or the story was so implausible that human explanations are insufficient. On second thought—maybe miracle is a good word, after all. We truly did have every reason to fail.

APPENDICES

Special Volunteers

Bob Sneberger

Bob is a dynamo. He is a crop duster who spends the spraying season in Indiana and winters in Missoula. He started work on the plane in December 2018 and worked for a good part of the winter, especially when we had no heat in the hangar, then had to leave in late March for work. We really felt his absence after he left. Bob knows a lot about engines, including radial engines. He worked long days and accomplished much while he was with us. He says he didn't have much to do during the winter, so he would work five or six days a week, helping with a variety of jobs from painting and helping to install the elevator, helping Jeff Whitesell with the firewall-forward work, helping with the fuel tanks, and cleaning and cleaning and cleaning. Coincidentally, Bob had worked on N24320 when she arrived in Missoula in 2001.

Tall Adam

Tall Adam is Adam Hubel. We call him Tall Adam to distinguish him from another Adam because he is—taller. His long arms came in very handy during the inspection of the tail and reaching remote spots. Tall Adam was one of the quiet ones. He didn't say much, but he was there all the time, even in the cold hangar before we got heat.

It turns out that Adam has an extensive history working on—and flying—airplanes. He earned his private and commercial pilot certificates as well as his airplane mechanic certificate. He spent time in Alaska and Idaho flying and working on airplanes until he tired of the life and the locations and moved to Missoula in 2000, just before N24320 did. He worked some odd jobs for a few years before hiring on at the city cemetery. His official title is maintenance technician, but he'll tell you he's a grave digger.

Adam started working with us in August 2018 and did all kinds of dirty jobs, like cleaning gunk from under the floors, in the tail, and on the belly, as well as technical jobs like removing the left elevator and checking torques. He helped with the fuel-tank removal, overhaul, and reinstallation, and he was helpful in the installation of the engines and associated hoses and wiring.

Adam says he joined the project because he had known about N24320 from the time she returned to Missoula. He came to the Aircraft Owners and Pilots Association event and saw the unveiling of the nose art, then met us under her wing. He said to himself, "I should be part of this. I could honor my love of aviation and my uncle who flew these planes in World War II. Plus, how many people get to crawl around inside a DC-3?"

Larry Depute

Larry was a family practice physician's assistant in Alaska for over thirty years, has built and flown three kit airplanes, and is also an airplane mechanic. He still flies the RV-4 kit airplane that he built. He retired to Missoula several years ago and was one our earliest volunteers, showing up in August 2018 with Tall Adam, Perry Francis, Randy Schonemann, and Crystal Schonemann. He showed up early and often, and helped with some of the more technical tasks like removing and reinstalling the left elevator. He also did some of the more unsavory jobs, like cleaning the gunk out of the belly, cleaning and repairing the fuel tanks, opening and closing inspection hatches, working on the heating system, and many "other duties as assigned." Larry donated tools and compressors. He is always happy and contributed significantly with his extensive knowledge about airplanes. He was another of the quiet ones.

Jim Gillan

Jim was a tireless volunteer. He heard about the project and started coming out in mid-September 2018. Jim was not one of the quiet ones. He loved to talk to anyone within earshot with his big, booming voice. Earshot was the entire hangar. There were many times when we had to politely ask Jim to pipe down so the rest of us could converse—but he took it in stride and never lost his good humor. For a while it didn't seem that he could work if he couldn't talk to someone, but it turned out there were plenty of times when he would just slave away by himself for hours at a time.

The most memorable task that Jim took over was the cleaning of the "dishpans," also known as the venturis. These are large stainless-steel pans that fit between the engine and the engine mount. They protect the area behind dishpans from the heat of the engine, and they also direct hot air from the engine out through the cowl flaps.

Radial engines are known for being extremely untidy, constantly dripping oil, and regularly belching smoke and fire. The dishpans take the brunt of the dripping oil and smoke during flight. They become caked with baked-on oil and grime. Jeff Whitesell required that the dishpans be thoroughly cleaned and inspected for cracks and that various gaskets be replaced. Jim was the man for the job. We tried different solvents and degreasers to remove the grime, but none of them worked.

Jim figured out that Carb-Off, a commercial product for cleaning commercial stove tops, worked splendidly. He found a local source for it, and we bought it for him by the gallon. He would don a respirator, brush on the nasty and odorous Carb-Off, wait for it to do its magic, and then patiently remove it with abrasive pads, towels, and perseverance. When Jim finished, the dishpans were sparkling clean. We found a few cracks that required repair, but one of the most difficult and unpleasant jobs was done because Jim took it on and accomplished it with good humor. Pretty remarkable, considering he's a retired Boeing engineer.

Bill Schonemann

Bill is Randy's dad and a talented mechanic, fabricator, and all-around good guy. He lives in Arizona with his wife, Kathy, and neither of them like the cold. He helped on the restoration during the summer and early fall of 2018 and then returned as soon as warm weather returned in 2019. Bill did much of the metal work, helping to install the paratrooper seats and other technical tasks.

Bill built a custom motor home for them to travel in after Kathy became ill a few years ago. When he was working in Missoula, he would park the motor home outside the museum. Kathy would typically remain in the motor home, due to limited mobility and the cool temperatures in the hangar. She would honk the horn whenever she needed something, and Bill would dutifully go see what she needed. He was a great example of a devoted husband for everyone who witnessed this day after day.

Bill is also a private pilot. He learned to fly shortly after Randy got his license so they could share the fun. He also served as a Seabee for two tours in Vietnam and one in Cuba.

During the last month before we departed, Bill worked for four weeks without taking a single day off. Bill was also our unofficial chaplain, praying for our safety before our first flights and before we departed for Europe. He probably didn't stop until we returned home, for which we are grateful.

Natalie Abrams

Natalie is another of our "Rosies" who made such important contributions to the restoration. She also had a previous connection to DC-3s. Natalie was born in Missoula but grew up in Nome, Alaska, moving back to Missoula in 1999 to attend college. In Alaska in her twenties, she worked for a now-defunct bush airline that happened to operate a DC-3 hauling cargo to remote villages. She loaded and unloaded that DC-3 and even scored a memorable ride in the jump seat at low altitude up the Bering Sea coast north of Nome.

With no other connection to aviation or the museum, Natalie first met *Miss Montana* at the AOPA fly-in but promptly forgot about her. Until December, that is, when she ran across a social-media post about the restoration project. She contacted Eric Komberec and was soon at the museum several days a week, getting dirty. Natalie helped with the fuel tanks, cleaning and degreasing everything imaginable, stripping paint, cutting and fitting the new cabin insulation, and lots of other miscellaneous tasks. She also helped with the send-off gala in May.

Natalie joined us in Europe for several days, captured the memorable "Merci" image on Sword Beach on June 6, and accompanied *Miss Montana* to Florida for hurricane relief in September. Like many other volunteers, she is grateful for the opportunity, having met lots of new people, had incredible experiences, and learned new things. She says seeing *Miss Montana* flying over the beaches on June 5 and 6 was an incredible reward, the culmination of many months of work. Natalie's sharp and irreverent humor and great attitude and work ethic are refreshing to have around. We hope she will be part of the *Miss Montana* ground crew forever.

Cindy Fulks

Cindy was a particularly fun and engaging volunteer. She showed up for the first time at the Rosie the Riveter party on January 18. She heard about it on social media but had no other connection to the museum or the airplane. She was just looking for something to do, and she kept coming back.

I remember the first day she came—one of those days when all my time was spent trying to keep volunteers busy and getting no work done myself. The paratrooper seats had arrived, but we hadn't done anything with them yet.

Cindy assured me she would do anything, so she got the job of cleaning the paratrooper seats. She jumped right in, and soon they were all done. Her next job was applying oil to the leather tabs on the old seat belts, which had become dry and stiff. Done. Cindy kept coming and doing anything we asked: cleaning gunk from the fuel tank flanges, learning to use a band saw, cleaning and replacing plexiglass windows, and helping to seal the fuel tanks.

Mike Anderson decided to make up Ground Crew T-shirts to give to our most dedicated volunteers to express our appreciation. We presented each one personally to make sure they knew that their work was important—and appreciated. The day I presented Cindy with hers, she had brought a friend to the museum to show him the project. She squealed with delight when she saw the shirt. Then her friend asked me, "How much would it cost me to get one of those?" I told him that he could buy any other shirt on the rack in the gift shop, but he would have to *earn* a Ground Crew shirt.

John Haines

John was one of our most enthusiastic and regular volunteers. Born and raised in Montana, he started working on the project in January 2019 about ten or twenty hours per week; by May, like many others, he was working over thirty hours per week. John had no background in aviation, but he did whatever needed to be done. He helped rebuild floors, install windows, clean (and clean and clean), helped with removal and reinstallation of oil tanks, painted inside the cockpit, ran for parts, cleaned the museum toilets, cooked meals for volunteers, and arranged for the practice jump site over his hometown of Plains, Montana, before our departure. After we left for Europe, John took over as the coordinator of volunteers for the museum.

John accompanied us to Florida and sweated like the rest of us to help the people in the Bahamas.

Perry Francis

Perry Francis has been a volunteer/docent at the museum for many years, sitting for long hours at the front desk and giving tours to visitors. When the restoration started, he jumped right in, one of the earliest volunteers to touch the airplane. Perry worked almost single-handedly on the cowl flaps from the beginning. He is another of the quiet heroes who worked long days on very important and detailed tasks but needed almost no supervision or help.

Perry was the definition of low maintenance. He would ask me or someone else from time to time what we thought about how to fix this or that, then he would quietly press on. He would usually find his own parts or mention to us that he needed this or that bolt or nut. Perry was a distinct pleasure to have around and made a huge contribution to the project. He seemed to have fun doing it.

Guyle Guderian

Like several other volunteers, Guyle met *Miss Montana* at the AOPA fly-in in June 2018. He thought that if he helped maybe he would get a ride in her. If he only knew. He forgot about her until January 2019, when he read an article in the *Missoulian* about the Rosie-the-Riveter workday. A few trips to the museum later and he was enlisted to work on odds and ends. Jeff Whitesell then enlisted him to read some wiring diagrams and rewire the landing-gear position sensors, which are in the wheel wells. This job led to others in the wheel wells, until Guyle spent so much time standing on the tires with his head up in the wheel wells that we saw only his lower half for days at a time.

Guyle followed us to Europe with the tour and got his wish to ride in *Miss Montana* on our June 9 scenic flight over the invasion beaches. Upon returning home, Guyle accompanied us to the Mann Gulch events and to Florida in September for the hurricane relief, and continues to volunteer at the museum. Being retired, Guyle is available to help with lots of jobs and his assistance is needed and appreciated.

Dan McCaffery

Dan is a retired environmental engineer and was an auto mechanic in a previous life. He had never worked on airplanes, but his mechanical and engineering skills were a big help. Dan had also been volunteering at the museum for some time before the *Miss Montana* project. Dan and I worked for several years at the same company in the early 1990s, and he was always a contrarian. He would ask the question that everyone was thinking but nobody wanted to ask. He was good to have around because of that. He is a smart, hardworking guy who isn't afraid to point out the obvious but inconvenient truth, so he kept us on our toes.

Dan started working on the plane in January 2019, pulling a lot of wires, cleaning the "dishpans" with Jim Gillan, installing the exhaust system after the engines were installed, installing wiring in the wheel wells, and supporting Jeff Whitesell wherever needed. Three-hour days, five days a week quickly turned into eight hours or more, seven days a week near the end.

Dan says he was drawn to the project because he grew up an Army brat and spent some of that time in England, where his dad was stationed in the early 1950s. Mostly it was the camaraderie and being part of the ambitious undertaking. He just couldn't stay away, which seems to be a pretty common sentiment.

Chad Elliott

Chad Elliott is an aircraft mechanic at Neptune Aviation and one of the many people that Eric Komberec "conscripted" into service, otherwise known as being "voluntold." Chad says he couldn't resist and started in January 2019. Nearly from the start he would bring his son, Dane, a young man who started out cleaning "just about everything" and then graduated to more complicated and technical tasks.

Like many volunteers, both Chad and Dane showed up early and often and did whatever they could or was needed at the time. Chad did a lot of metal work, helped install the paratrooper seats, worked on the landing gear and rear strut, resealed and reinstalled the oil tanks, and replaced and resealed the landing lights.

Dane has become a regular helper to the mechanics and now

knows quite a bit about DC-3s and their engines. It's been said that without mechanics, a pilot is just another pretty boy with fancy sunglasses *walking* down the street. This is true in general but truer about mechanics who are knowledgeable about DC-3s. While it's difficult to find type-rated and current DC-3 pilots, if anything spells the end of the DC-3 it will be the lack of qualified mechanics. Hopefully, Dane and Chad represent the next generation that can work on these planes. As a result of his involvement in the project, Dane has joined the Civil Air Patrol and aspires to a career in aviation.

Bob Kovac

Bob Kovac (aka "Buffalo") was a big asset, standing head and shoulders above everybody else on the crew except Tall Adam. Bob is a big man and a retired infantry officer, having served all over the world, including some time in Korea with Al Charters. Al Charters jokes that when Bob jumped out of airplanes, it wasn't falling from the sky, it was a "reentry event," and he would be on the ground long before anyone else.

Bob started working on the restoration in October 2018 and endured the months in the cold-soaked museum. Bob didn't say much, but he didn't miss much, either, and he did whatever was necessary. He worked on cleaning just about everything: engine nacelles, oil coolers, carburetors, fuel tanks, and the lovely gunk beneath the cargo floor. He worked with Jeff Whitesell, cleaning and installing spark plugs, mounted starters, generators, and feathering pumps. He helped clean, repair, and reinstall the troublesome fuel tanks, run wiring, and install the engine cowlings. Bob is another example of a volunteer with no prior mechanical experience, unless you count field stripping weapons or performing preventive maintenance on Army vehicles.

Addison & Wendy Pemberton

Addison and Wendy Pemberton are some of the most accomplished and experienced people in the world who restore and operate historic airplanes. More than that, they are really nice people. I had met Addison several years earlier and had kept in touch with him. Addison and his family business, Pemberton & Sons Aviation in Spokane, Washington, have restored many historic aircraft, including multiple Stearman, a Boeing 40 (the only one in the world), and most recently a gorgeous Grumman Goose. Most of these vintage airplanes have major parts of the structure covered in fabric.

During the summer of 2018, Addison stopped at Missoula with his Grumman Goose on the way to a nearby fly-in. As a fan of all old airplanes, especially with radial engines and tailwheels, he was immediately enamored with our project. I gave him a tour of *Miss Montana* and thought to ask him how much he would charge us to recover the left elevator, which had failed a test of its fabric. I knew that his shop was world class. Addison said he would talk to Wendy and get back to me. Wendy is the fabric wizard.

A few days later Addison called and told me that they would recover the elevator for no charge. We gratefully accepted and soon took the elevator to Spokane. The recovered elevator was ready in early 2019, and we returned it to Missoula, applied the necessary coatings, and reinstalled it on the airplane a few weeks before our first engine start. It is a thing of beauty.

Addison told me that he would never attempt the North Atlantic crossing in a DC-3 because the margin of safety was so thin. He said if you lose an engine at the wrong spot you can't make it to dry land. I'm sure he was right.

Miss Montana Volunteers

Natalie Abrams
Tiana Albery
Andrea Albery
Mike Anderson
Kathryn Anderson
Michela Anderson
Howie Anderson
Sharon Anschutz
Bob Anschutz
Ron Bauer
Andy Boas
Mark Bretz
Kim Briggeman
Dave Bright
Kelly Brown
Janine Brown
Chris Brown
Bob Bungarz
Al Charters
Marc Childress
Steven Clough
Pat Collins

Jesse Cooney
Torrie Cooney
Steve Cooper
Fred Cooper
Chris D'Ardenne
Matt Dauenhauer
Adam Davis
John Paul Delucca
Larry Depute
Sergio Desiati
Bryan Douglass
Dawn Douglass
Daniel Douglass
Annette Dusseau
Art Dykstra
Ryan Dykstra
Lauren Dykstra
Michelle Dykstra
Chad Elliott
Dane Elliott
Desiree Evans
Charity Ewald

Dustin Fanning
Joe Fitzgerald
Perry Francis
Cynthia Fulks
Rob Gibson
Jim Gillan
Jeff Gordon
Sharon Gordon
Guyle Guderian
John Haines
Kay Hale
Jay Hanchett
Sharon Herbert
Amanda Holt
Adam Hubel
Dick Hulla
Radd Ice Noggle
Cory Johnson
Barbara Komberec
Eric Komberec
Dick Komberec
Avian Komberec

Taylor Komberec

Tia Komberec

Tim Komberec

Kraig Kosena

Megan Kosena

Bob Kovac

Karen Laberna

Katie Lammons

Paul Lanz

Leisa Lanz

John Lazarowicz

Greg Lee

Rachael Lockwood

Dan LoParco

Clifford Lynn

Nic Lynn

Dave Maurer

Kim Maynard

Dan McCaffery

Michelle McCue

Don Micknak

Shawn Modula

Bryan M

Sarah M

Rusty Nicol

Kathy Ogren

Shannon O'Keefe

Hayes Otupalik

Maurice Owen

Skip Owings

Sharon Palmer

Bill Paullin

Lisa Paullin

Ron Peeples

Pat Peeples

Addison Pemberton

Wendy Pemberton

Greg Postell

Shawn Powers

Vida R.Z.

Joe Rediske

Leah Rediske

Suzanne Reneau

Jack Reneau

Eric Ristau

Misty Rockwood

Bryce Rowe

Spencer Rowe-Lynn

Marina Ruediger

Bill Ruediger

Matt Russell

Bill Schonemann

Randy Schonemann

Crystal Schonemann

Terry Sharp

Jeff Sholty

Brennan Simmerman

Erica Simmerman

Caeilin Simmerman

Hans Skovlin

Jay Skovlin

Chris Smith

Steve Smith

Bob Sneberger

Jerrel Storrud

Greg Tabish

Leah Talalutu

Lloyd Thorsrud

Skip Tomb

Bill Tubbs

John Tubbs

Steve Tubbs

Mark Vance

Major Donors (2018-2019)

Phillips 66
Anonymous
Bretz RV & Marine
Neptune Aviation
Big Sky Brewing Company
Family Dental Group
KLS Hydraulics
Minuteman Aviation
Aviation Partners, Inc.
Bank of Montana
Metalworks of Montana

Jeff & Cody Gordon
Standard Capital Real Estate &
   Development
City Service Valcom
First Security Bank
Pacific Steel & Recycling
Vemco
Aeroleds
Dynon Avionics
Warren Wilcox
Doc Lammers

Original Donors (2001)

Dick Komberec
Kathy Ogren
Dirk & Kim Visser
First Security Bank
Tom Gummer
Rick Nash
Steele-Reese FD

Seat Honorees

Wilbur Komberec, 1ˢᵗ Class, U.S. Army Aleutian Campaign

Norman Allen, Corporal, U.S. Army, 517 Parachute Infantry, 17ᵗʰ Airborne, European Theater

Joseph Kratville, 1ˢᵗ Lt., U.S.M.C. Air Group, Pacific Theater

Frank Bretz, founded Bretz RV 1967

Mike Albert, MOMM, U.S. Navy, Pacific Theater

Tubbs Family

Eli Albert, served on a Destroyer in Guadalcanal, U.S. Navy, Pacific Theater

Jack Dersam, Capt.,, U.S. Air Force, WWII Retired, Master Navigator, Berlin Airlift

Hollister A. Larson, 1ˢᵗ Lt., U.S. Army Air Corps, Capt. DC-3/C-47, Pacific Theater

Paul D. Lanz, Sp. 4, 198ᵗʰ Infantry, U.S. Army, Vietnam, Purple Heart

Arthur Good, Chief Petty Officer (AA), U.S. Navy, Seabees, Pacific Theater

R. Preston Nash, Private First Class, U.S. Army

Fallen Comrades, Smokejumpers & Paratrooperss, To Their Legacy

Kenneth Roth, Gunners Mate 1ˢᵗ Class, U.S. Navy, Pacific Theater

Malcolm Enman, Capt., U.S. Army Air Corps, Pacific Theater

Robert D. Clark, 1ˢᵗ Lt., U.S.M.C., VMTB 134, Pacific Theater

Ivan Carl Odom, Lt. Col., U.S. Army Air Corps, Pacific Theater

John Podawiltz, 2nd Lt., U.S. Army Air Corps, 7th Bomb Group, Pacific Theater

Annette Dusseau, Lt. Col., U.S. Army

Shawn Modula, Major, U.S. Army

Jonathan A. Holloway, Flight Surgeon, U.S. Air Force

Christopher K. Ives, U.S. Army Special Forces, Master Parachutist

Charles G. Copping, SFC, Master Parachutist, 505th Regiment of 82nd Division, Airborne

Sarah M, U.S. Army 82nd Airborne

Bryan M, U.S. Army Special Forces, Master Parachutist

Robert S. Kovac, U.S. Army Parachute Infantry

Kimberly A. Maynard, Smokejumper, MSO-82, Spotter/Squad Leader

Alan S. Charters, U.S. Army Special Forces, Master Parachutist

Endnotes

1   *Fly the Biggest Piece Back*, Steve Smith
2   *Young Men and Fire*, Norman Maclean
3   www.nfpa.org
4   *Pittsburgh Press*, December 23, 1954
5   http://www.aerialvisuals.ca/AirframeDossier.
    php?Serial=47467
6   Interviews with Dick Komberec, September 2019
7   Ian Twombly, AOPA *Pilot Magazine*, "The Seven Percent," April
    1, 2019
8   https://airandspace.si.edu/stories/editorial/women-wings-75-
    year-legacy-wasp
9   Mireille Goyer, *Women of Aviation Week*, "Five Decades of
    American Female Pilot Statistics, How Did We Do?" March 2,
    2020
10 Ken Raymond, *The Oklahoman*, "A Real-Life 'Rosie the Riveter'
    from southwest Oklahoma City," May 14, 2017
11 *Missoulian*, "Flying Museum Prepares to Take Historic Mann
    Gulch Plane to Normandy in 2019," Kim Briggeman, June 3,
    2018.
12 *Missoulian*, "CBS Films Miss Montana to Normandy Story,"
    Kim Briggeman, April 10, 2019.

13 *Idaho State Journal*, "Local D-Day Veteran Heading Back to France for 75th Anniversary of Invasion," Jerry Painter, June 1, 2019

14 *Missoulian*, "From Polson to War and Back: WWII Paratrooper Remembers D-Day," Kim Briggeman, April 19, 2019

15 *Missoulian* obituary for John Nelson, June 16, 2019

16 *Tall Trees, Tough Pilots*, Kathy Ogren and Dick Komberec

17 *Fate is the Hunter*, Ernest Gann

18 General Eisenhower, Order of the Day, June 6, 1944

19 Margalit Fox, *New York Times*, "Robert S. Buck Dies at 93; Was Record-Setting Aviator," May 20, 2007

20 *UK Airshow Review*, "Top 10 Airshow Moments of 2019," December 6, 2019

21 https://www.abmc.gov/cemeteries-memorials/europe/netherlands-american-cemetery

22 *Daring Young Men*, Richard Reeves

23 Department of the Air Force, "Report on the Airlift Berlin Mission," June 27, 1975

24 *Band of Brothers*, Stephen Ambrose

25 *Vintage Aviation Echo*, online magazine, June 2, 2019

CPSIA information can be obtained
at www.ICGtesting.com
Printed in the USA
FSHW010418200520
70417FS

9 781977 225740